Studies in
LITERATURE AND BELIEF

Martin Jarrett-Kerr, C.R.

Studies in

LITERATURE

and

BELIEF

Essay Index Reprint Series

 BOOKS FOR LIBRARIES PRESS
FREEPORT, NEW YORK

INTERNATIONAL STANDARD BOOK NUMBER:
0-8369-1978-5

LIBRARY OF CONGRESS CATALOG CARD NUMBER:
74-134101

PRINTED IN THE UNITED STATES OF AMERICA

FOR GORDON LEWIS PHILLIPS
(WHO—TO PARAPHRASE KANT—
FIRST INTERRUPTED MY UNDOGMATIC SLUMBER)

AUTHOR'S PREFACE

TO DEAL adequately with the subjects within the wide range of this book would require a polymath and a multilinguist. There are such, though their critical judgments do not always inspire confidence. The present writer, in any case, is not one of them. One excuse may, however, be made to condone the lack of such qualifications. In so far as the literature of Europe is a family affair, it is due, more profoundly than is often realized, to the unobtrusive hack-work of the translator. Mr. W. H. Auden has even hazarded the paradox that " It does not particularly matter if the translators have understood their originals correctly; often, indeed, misunderstanding is, from the point of view of the native writer, more profitable".[1] There is certainly a sense in which (say) Florio, Constance Garnett, Scott-Moncrieff, Lowe-Porter, Edwin and Willa Muir, or Gerard Hopkins are more important to the unity of European culture than Montaigne, Dostoevsky, Proust, Thomas Mann, Kafka, or François Mauriac. This book is but a minor symptom of what would have been impossible without them.

Some parts of the individual studies contained here have appeared already in periodical form. But in spite of the fact that some are quite recent and some were written up to fifteen years ago there has seemed to me a unity—due no doubt partly to the writer's particular interests in approaching them—which has not been imposed upon their diversity but runs subtly through it.

It may, of course, be said that the writer's interests have read this unity into them. And we must agree that a theological concern may indeed interfere with the objectivity of the literary critic's judgment; what Dr. Leavis has termed,[2] referring specifically to the present author, a ' deflection ' may certainly occur. Whether it has done so in the present book is not for the writer to judge. But the matter receives general attention in the following pages; and perhaps to be aware of the danger is already to have half averted it.

For Notes 1 and 2, see " Notes " in pp. 188-199.

The first chapter, being necessarily an abstract introduction to the problem, will probably be found the most difficult. The rest of the book will, it is hoped, provide concrete clarification.

My most direct debt is to Mrs. Margaret Rawlings Cross, who read the whole manuscript and provided the most stimulating comment and criticism.

I am also indebted to Prof. Henri Talon, of the University of Dijon, for checking references in Chapter 6; and to Father Mark Tweedy of my Community, whose knowledge of Russian has been of considerable assistance to me in Chapter 5; to Mr. R. Pring-Mill who has given such generous and valuable help in Chapter 3; Mr. Graham Clarke, of the Anglo-French Literary Services, has constantly been of assistance in the obtaining of, or of information about, French books; and the assistant librarians of the City Library of Johannesburg and of the University of the Witwatersrand have been courteous and punctilious in their service.

My thanks are also due for their painstaking compilation of the Index to Mr. L. P. Day and Mr. K. K. Ward.

Thanks are due to the editors of the following periodicals for permission to use material which appeared in their pages:

Messrs. Constable & Co., *The Twentieth Century* (*The Nineteenth Century* as it was then called).

Messrs. Burns, Oates & Co., *The Dublin Review*.

The S.P.C.K., *Theology*, and the S.C.M. Press, *The Student Movement*.

Messrs. A. R. Mowbray & Co., *The New Outlook*.

New English Weekly, for a passage from an article by N. Read.

The University of Nebraska for a passage from an article by L. C. Wimberly: " Death and Burial Lore in English and Scottish Ballads " in *Studies in Language, Literature and Criticism.*

Figaro for a passage appearing in *Le Figaro Littéraire.*

The Criterion for passages by D. A. Traversi.

Dr. Leavis for passages from *Scrutiny.*

M. Charles Gimbault and *France Soir* for passages from that Journal.

Also to the following publishers, authors and translators for permissions to quote:

Messrs. William Heinemann, for passages from Constance Garnett's translation of the novels of Dostoevsky, also from R. Curle's *The Characters of Dostoevsky*.

Messrs. Pearn, Pollinger & Higham Ltd. and the author for passages from Graham Greene's *The Heart of the Matter* (published in England by Messrs. William Heinemann).

Messrs. Eyre & Spottiswoode (Publishers) Ltd. for passages from *When the Mountain Fell* (English translation of Ramuz's *Derborence*).

Editions Bernard Grasset for passages from the novels of C. F. Ramuz, and from H. Bazin's *Lève-toi et Marchè*.

Imago Publishing Co., New York, for passages from Erik Erikson's *Childhood and Society*.

The Hogarth Press Ltd. for a passage from Edwin Muir's *Essays on Literature and Society*.

Librairie Gallimard for a passage from Claudel's *Morceaux Choisis*.

Messrs. Faber & Faber Ltd.and Messrs. Harcourt Brace Inc. for passages from T. S. Eliot's *Selected Essays*.

Messrs. Eyre & Spottiswoode (Publishers) Ltd. and the Viking Press Inc., and the authors for passages from Auden and Pearson's *Poets of the English Language*.

Messrs. Pantheon Books Inc. and the author for passages from Joseph Campbell's *The Hero with a Thousand Faces*.

Messrs. The Macmillan Co. (New York) and the author for passages from F. B. Gummere's *The Beginnings of Poetry* (Macmillan. 1908).

Messrs. Jonathan Cape Ltd. and the authors for passages from Dr. Elias Canetti's *Auto-da-Fé*, translated by V. Wedgwood, also for a passage from H. Myers' *The Root and the Flower*.

Messrs. Derek Verschoyle Ltd. and the author for passages rom Gustav Janouch's *Conversations with Kafka*.

The Clarendon Press, Oxford and the author for passages from Gerould's *The Ballad of Tradition*.

The Oxford University Press and the authors for passages from M. Bodkin's *Archetypal Patterns in Poetry* and E. M. Simpson's *Prose Works of Donne*.

Messrs. Routledge & Kegan Paul Ltd. and the authors for passages from C. F. Ramuz's *The Triumph of Death*, Charles

Neider's *Kafka: His Mind and His Art*, and Adler's *The Practice and Theory of Individual Psychology.*

The Syndics of the Cambridge University Press and the authors for passages from H. M. and N. K. Chadwick's *The Growth of Literature* and from Gerald Brenan's *Literature of the Spanish People.*

Messrs. Sands & Co. (Publishers) Ltd. and the author for passages from M. Turnell's *Poetry and Crisis.*

Messrs. J. M. Dent & Sons Ltd. and the translator for passages from C. J. Hogarth's translation of *Letters from the Underworld.*

Messrs. John Lane the Bodley Head Ltd. and the translator for passages from Louise Varese's translation of *Joy*, by Georges Bernanos.

The Harvard University Press and the author for passages from George Santayana's *Three Philosophical Poets* (Harvard University Press. 1910, 1938).

The S.P.C.K. for passages from the works of *St. Tikhon Zadonsky* (1951).

Messrs. Charles Scribner's Sons, and the translators and authors for passages from John Garrett Underhill's translations of *Four Plays by Lope de Vega*; from George Santayana's *Poetry and Religion (Tragic Philosophy)*; and from Boris Brasol's translation of *The Diary of a Writer*, by Feodor Dostoevsky.

The University Press of Liverpool and the author for passages from Ramón Silva's *Spanish Golden Age Poetry and Drama.*

Messrs. Bohme & Co. for passages from Goethe's *Conversations with Eckermann.*

The Harvill Press Ltd. for passages from V. Ivanov's *Freedom and the Tragic Life.*

The Committee for Ezra Pound for passages from *Guide to Kultur.*

Messrs. Hutchinson for a passage from Hodgart's *The Ballads*, also for a passage from Ramuz's *Vie de Samuel Belet.*

Librairie Plon for a passage from C. Virgil Gheorghiu's *La Vingt-Cinquième Heure.*

Messrs. Macmillan & Co. Ltd. and Messrs. A. D. Peters for passages from Rebecca West's *Black Lamb and Grey Falcon.*

CONTENTS

REFERENCES

References indicated by superior figures will be
found in the " Notes " printed on pp. 188-199.

THE LITERARY MARGINS OF BELIEF

I

" IF MEN with impartiality, and not asquint, look towards the offices and functions of a poet, they will easily conclude to themselves the impossibility of any man's being the good poet, without first being a good man."

Since the day when Ben Jonson thought it necessary to use these words in dedicating *Volpone* to 'the sister Universities', the relations between literature and belief have undergone many changes. Perhaps the clearest example of the exact contradictory of Jonson's sentiments may be found in some remarks of Lord Russell on the subject of Wordsworth: " In his youth he [Wordsworth] sympathized with the French Revolution, went to France, wrote good poetry, and had a natural daughter. At this period he was a ' bad ' man. Then he became 'good', abandoned his daughter, adopted correct principles, and wrote bad poetry. . . . It is difficult to think of any instance of a poet who was ' good ' at the time when he was writing good poetry."[1]

Miss Edith Batho, who quotes this charmingly naïve generalization, asks whether Mr. Bertrand Russell really prefers *An Evening Walk* or *Descriptive Sketches* (written before 1797) to most of the rest of Wordsworth's poetry (the greatest of which was written between 1797 and 1815). Admittedly Lord Russell's remarks were made in an occasional, journalistic context, and need not be taken seriously; but they are worth quoting because they represent a widely held attitude. It is interesting, however, to note how the wheel comes full circle with, for instance, Mr. Ezra Pound. (He is referring to belief rather than behaviour here; but the two, ' goodness ' and 'faith', cannot be separated.) Talking to W. B. Yeats he once observed that all men of culture might find it necessary sooner

or later to make an alliance with the Catholic Church, because
with its traditionalism it might help them to oppose the mass
philistinism of our day, typified by Mr. Sinclair Lewis' *Babbitt*.
And Yeats had to remonstrate, " But CONfound it! In my
country the Church IS Babbitt."[2]

★

In our time this problem of the relation between literature
and belief has obsessed critics, especially during the last thirty
years or so. I do not propose to offer a new solution to the
problem, grubby and thumbed as it is. But the reasons for its
prominence are worth examining and will be found instructive.
The first and perhaps the deepest reason may be found, I think,
in the particular complication of our age. The absence of
cultural unification leads paradoxically to an artificial overlap-
ping of its constituents; the loss of a single religious tradition
has meant, it seems, that the metaphysical and religious implications of literature, of history, or of natural science, become
more, not less, marked than in an age when the metaphysic or
religion could be taken for granted and so leave the writer to
get on with his job.

But there is a further reason for this obsession, and that is
simply that these years have seen Western man advancing into
a post-sceptical period. The late George Santayana believed,
it is true, that " If any similar adequacy [to Dante's] is attained
again by any poet, it will not be, presumably, by a poet of the
supernatural. Henceforth, for any wide and honest imagination, the supernatural must figure as an idea in the human
mind—a part of the natural. To conceive otherwise would be
to fall short of the insight of this age, not to express or to
complete it."[3] But this does not contradict the above statement. For when man's attention is forcibly directed, whether
by physical disaster, by social change, by moral hesitation, or
by disquieting historical prediction, to the competition between
scepticism and belief, then the recovery, or in most cases even
the retention, of a belief becomes a self-conscious operation;
and what is less obvious, the resistance to a belief, or the
retention of a particular scepticism, becomes no less self-
conscious. The critic is then inevitably tempted to attribute to

poets of the past a self-consciousness in *their* belief—or in their scepticism—which was probably quite lacking to them.

It is well known that Mr. T. S. Eliot has been much concerned (in theory and in practice, as poet and as critic) with this problem; and also that he has shifted his ground to some extent in this matter. In his essay on Dante he firmly declared that " you cannot afford to *ignore* Dante's philosophical and theological beliefs, or to skip the passages which express them most clearly; but that on the other hand you are not called upon to believe them yourself. It is wrong to think that there are parts of the *Divine Comedy* which are of interest only to Catholics or to mediævalists. For there is a difference (which here I hardly do more than assert) between philosophic *belief* and poetic *assent*. . . ."[4]

Some years later he makes a remark which seems to imply an even more extreme adherence to this view. Commenting on Mr. I. A. Richards' statement that *The Waste Land* effects " a complete severance between poetry. and *all* beliefs ", he says that one meaning of Mr. Richards' remark might be that that poem was " the first poetry to do what all poetry in the past would have been the better for doing ".[5] But earlier than this, in an appendix to the second section of the essay on Dante, Mr. Eliot, discussing the same passage of Mr. Richards', makes important qualifications which are, I believe, in the right direction, but which almost completely reverse the position adopted above. Referring to a line of Dante, he says that he (Mr. Eliot) believes it to be *literally true*; and then adds:

> And I confess that it has more beauty for me now, when my own experience has deepened its meaning, than it did when I first read it. So I can only conclude that I cannot, in practice, wholly separate my poetic appreciation from my personal beliefs. . . . The theory of Mr. Richards is, I believe, incomplete until he defines the species of religious, philosophical, scientific, and other beliefs, as well as that of ' everyday ' belief.
>
> I have tried to make clear some of the difficulties inhering in my theory. Actually, one probably has more pleasure in the poetry when one shares the beliefs of the poet. On the other hand there is a distinct pleasure in

enjoying poetry as poetry when one does *not* share the
beliefs, analogous to the pleasure of ' mastering' other
men's philosophical systems. It would appear that
' literary appreciation ' is an abstraction, and pure poetry
a phantom; and that both in creation and enjoyment much
always enters which is, from the point of view of ' Art ',
irrelevant.[6]

This seems to me so patently true that I do not know how
Mr. Eliot ever came to make the other, unqualified, statements.
But I think the reason may be found in some other remarks of
his, this time about Shakespeare; and it is a reason which also
illuminates the topic we are discussing—viz. how this problem
of ' literature and belief' has become such a prominent one in
our time. In his famous essay on *Shakespeare and the Stoicism of
Seneca* Mr. Eliot says that the poet does not ' think ' but makes
poetry out of thought, and therefore cannot *qua* poet be said
to ' believe ' in the system that lies behind his poetry. And he
adds, " What I have said could be expressed more exactly, but
at much greater length, in philosophical language: it would
enter into the department of philosophy which might be called
the Theory of Belief (which is not psychology but philosophy,
or phenomenology proper)—the department in which Meinong
and Husserl have made some pioneer investigation; the
different meanings which belief has in different minds according to the activity for which they are oriented."[7]

Mr. Eliot never followed up this hint about phenomenology;
and I think he was right not to do so. For though it is true that
Husserl was always anxious to avoid ' psychologism '—in his
' phenomenological reduction ' his aim was to abstract from the
concrete objects of belief (as of volition, knowledge, etc.), to
put them in a ' bracket ' and to examine these phenomena as
' essences '—and therefore Mr. Eliot is formally correct in
saying that ' Theory of Belief ' would not belong to the domain
of psychology; yet Husserl's critics, including some of his
former disciples, became increasingly afraid that his system led
inevitably to a subjectivism and ultimately therefore to the
very psychologism which he was so anxious to escape. But
this is precisely what is so characteristic of our time. As Santayana said, in the quotation above, that the ' supernatural '

must now merely figure as ' an idea in the human mind ', so belief, and scepticism too, becomes one of the specimens that is fixed to a slide to be examined by the psychologist's microscope. And the danger of this, as even of Mr. Eliot's distinction between ' philosophic belief and poetic assent ', is that of a relativistic psychologism: the suggestion, that is, that ' belief ' is one way of employing the stuff called ' thought ' which is stored up in the mental basement (and this is the way— according to this view—that the poet does *not* normally employ it), whereas ' emotional expression ' or some such activity is another way of employing it (and this is the way that the poet usually does). As if, almost, there were one crop, barley, which the philosopher makes into bread, the poet into whisky.

It is clear, I think, that the basic inadequacy of Mr. Eliot's account here can be traced to a too narrow conception of ' thought '. Shakespeare, we are to understand, did not ' think '; he took the muddled and mutually inconsistent thought of Seneca, Machiavelli, Montaigne, and played poetry on them. Dante did not ' think ' either; he took the superb intellectualizations of St. Thomas and used them as the foundation of his *Divine Comedy*. But the contrasts here seem to me to be in the wrong place. If, as I am sure we must, we start from the initial conviction that one of the first marks of the major poet or novelist is the possession of a *fine mind*, we must refuse to concede that Shakespeare or Dante did not think but had their thinking done for them. Surely to accept a cogent system of thought (which includes some appreciation of its cogency) is to think: thus Dante. And surely to select certain philosophical generalizations (even inconsistent ones) and to see them exemplified in human experience is, when performed with the acuity and eye for relevance of a great poet, to think very hard indeed: thus Shakespeare.

In all this I am accepting, for the sake of the argument, Mr. Eliot's view which in fact I do not accept, that Shakespeare's is a ' rag-bag ' of ideas, that the Senecan or Montaignean aphorisms put in the mouths of certain characters represent his ' thought ', and that therefore the only unity in Shakespeare's total work is, as Mr. Eliot says, Shakespeare himself. The concentration of many recent critics[8] upon Shakespeare's ' evolution ', his passage to a point in the last plays when the tumultuous ideas and activities of the variegated creature man can be given a total framework in which each may have its meaning —this concentration seems to me wholly justified. And what goes for ' thought ' goes also for ' belief '. Belief is rarely if ever the ' propositional ' thing that some like to make out, though it may and must sometimes express itself in propositional forms. It is related so closely to thought on one side and to feeling and consequent action on the other that it is, I am sure, absurd to say that the poet ' *qua* poet ' does not ' believe ' in his thought-system. There is an old tag, " How do I know what I think till I see what I say? " This suggests sheer irrationalism—' let us rely on our intuitions '. But in fact it is an ordinary psychological process : normally our beliefs govern our actions, but sometimes, when our minds are bemused with much thinking, it is our actions that reveal even to ourselves our beliefs. This process is analogous to that of poetic composition. We can, for the poet, make a distinction between ' believing that ' and ' believing in ' (believing that twice two is four, that a snark is a boojum, that hops go to make beer; believing in the Ineffable, in progress, in the strength of human pity . . .); but the distinction is only relative—the one shades into the other. There is a parallel formula popular in modern analytic philosophy which is relevant: the distinction between ' knowing that ' and ' knowing how '. (For instance, to give Professor Gilbert Ryle's examples, ' knowing how to make good jokes, conduct battles or behave at funerals ', contrasted with ' knowing that certain rules obtain ', etc.)[9] But here again these two operations shade into each other—' knowing how ' may be on occasions simply the extension into action of ' knowing that ', on other occasions it may be precisely the way from factual ignorance to factual knowledge. It may well be true that the poets ' know how ' better than they ' know that '; and similarly they may ' believe in ' more continuously, because more unselfconsciously, than they ' believe that '. But these contrasted operations are not absolute contrasts; they represent a contrast of vocations rather than a contrast of being.

   There is a further qualification that needs to be made, though it is often overlooked. In considering the relations between ' art ' and ' belief ' we are bound, as people with the particular history we inhabit, to have in mind, among others, the Christian system as one relevant type of belief. But those who operate with the concept ' the Christian system ' frequently imply, whether they are Christians or not (and perhaps especially if not—the Christians can afford to be more generous), something much tighter and neater than that which history in fact reveals. (Mr. Eliot admits as much in his essay on Dante, when he says that Dante's Catholicism is not our Catholicism.) If St. Thomas supplied Dante with his supernatural logic, Virgil supplied him with much of his picture-language. Indeed, I think we underestimate the extent to which even the official Catholic formulæ, concerning Purgatory for example, have as a propulsive background the imaginative visions of Acheron or Phlegethon. So that within what we call a poet's ' belief ' we may have to distinguish several varied intellectual and mythological pedigrees. It is interesting, for instance, that at the time that Senecan stoicism was exercising a powerful influence on Elizabethan drama—an influence which is generally taken as positively pagan—in Spain Seneca had been thoroughly baptized. In one of Calderón's plays he is called *el Seneca español* (Spanish Seneca)[10], and Sr. Ramón Silva, among others, has shown how deeply Seneca had influenced all Spanish thought in the Spanish ' Golden Age ', how his fatalism and his emphasis upon the transitoriness of life had been worked into and modified by Catholic theology.[11]

No doubt it is by the final and total direction of a writer's work that his ' beliefs ' are to be assessed; but we must expect to find great local variety of colouring and imagery within the larger whole. What makes the task of the critic so delicate is that—as we are increasingly learning in many fields—two opposites have constantly to be combined. First, form and content cannot be separated, the wearer cannot be judged apart from the clothes he selects. It is interesting that in the realm of Biblical studies the attempts at ' demythologizing ' the Holy Scriptures (stripping the primitive imagery from the basic concepts) are now regarded by many experts as chimerical; so we find it in the critical study of poets. And second: it is often precisely by a poet's imagery—where he is employing it unselfconsciously—that his real beliefs can be most certainly gauged.[12] This second reason has tempted many into the desert of psychological theories of art (the relation of the Unconscious to poetic creativity, etc.)—a Sahara we propose to skirt. But it remains true that the poet, especially when writing in full spate, cannot afford to interrupt the circuit. The current must flow (to use for a moment the romantic terminology employed by the late Abbé Bremond in his *Prayer and Poetry*) directly from his basic convictions out into his language and imagery, without reflection back upon the process itself; and therefore it is examination of the latter that will be the most revealing, since here there will be the least possibility of deception.

II

It is clear, then, that a discussion of the topic with which this book is concerned must avoid exaggeration in two directions.

(i) We cannot say that the beliefs of the poet (or novelist—to treat these two very different modes, for the moment, as one) are irrelevant to his poetry ' *qua* poetry '. We have quoted one of Mr. Eliot's essays as an example of this error. We might also have quoted his longer and better essay on *Seneca in Elizabethan Translation*. After discussing again the different philosophical backgrounds of the two poets, he says: " Shakespeare and Dante were both merely poets (and Shakespeare a dramatist as well); our estimate of the intellectual material they absorbed does not affect our estimate of their poetry, either absolutely or relatively to each other. But it must affect our vision of them and the use we make of them. . . ." And he adds, somewhat inconsistently (for why should this be singled out for praise unless there is in fact an *inverse* necessary connection between poetry and belief?) that " Perhaps it is part of [Shakespeare's] special eminence to have expressed an inferior philosophy in the greatest poetry ".[13]

Santayana discusses this passage, and explains why

Shakespeare, although Christianity was at hand, and Seneca, although a Platonic philosophy was at hand, based like Christianity on moral inspiration, nevertheless stuck fast in a disillusioned philosophy which Mr. Eliot thinks inferior. They stuck fast in life. They had to do so, whatever may have been their private religious convictions, because they were dramatists addressing the secular mind and concerned with the earthly career of passionate individuals, of inspired individuals, whose inspiration contradicted the truth, and were shattered by it. . . . Shakespeare was not expressing, like Seneca, a settled doctrine of his own or of his times. Like an honest miscellaneous dramatist, he was putting into the mouths of his different characters the sentiments that, for the moment, were suggested to him by their predicaments. . . .

This, with qualifications, will perhaps just stand. But he goes on,

Possibly if he had been pressed by some tiresome friend to propound a personal philosophy, he might have found in his irritation nothing else to fall back on than the animal despair of Macbeth. Fortunately we may presume that burgherly comfort and official orthodoxy saved him from being unreasonably pressed.[14]

This sort of speculation seems to me somewhat profitless. It might even be better to say, with Mr. W. H. Auden, that " the emergence of a purely secular English drama with little overt reference to religious beliefs was perhaps encouraged by an unwillingness to look too closely at the reasons for the nation's having become Protestant. The new nobility, who patronized the players, was discharging one of the duties of the Church whose money it had stolen; a religious drama would have reminded men of events which were better forgotten ".[15] But this statement itself is too specific about motives which were no doubt much more complex. Taken together, all these quotations add up to a view of the independence of poetry or drama from theological belief which seems to me untrue to human nature, since it fails to distinguish between what a writer does deliberately and what his work in fact, and in spite perhaps of his conscious purpose, conveys. In a lesser-known essay Mr. Eliot himself states the position more guardedly. Writing on " Poetry and Propaganda " in 1930, he is taking Professor Whitehead to task for saying that certain poets ' bear witness ' to certain philosophies of nature, or that a philosophical doctrine is to be ' gained ' from (e.g.) Shelley or Wordsworth.

On the contrary, says Mr. Eliot. " Poetry cannot prove that anything is *true*; it can only create a variety of wholes composed of intellectual and emotional constituents, justifying the emotion by the thought and the thought by the emotion: it proves successively, or fails to prove, that certain worlds of thought and feeling *are possible*. It provides intellectual sanction for feeling, and æsthetic sanction for thought."[16] This is interesting, for it concedes an element of ' thought ' to the poet (' intellectual sanction ' . . .) contradicting Mr. Eliot's earlier view; and even if it leaves the impression that, because poetry cannot prove anything is true, therefore even the intellectual sanctions for feeling can only be judged ' æsthetically ', it seems the nearest approach to a balanced view that we have had.[17]

(ii) The other exaggeration is more obvious: that which leads to the opposite conclusion—that ' good belief ' makes ' good poetry '. Mr. Turnell, himself a Catholic critic, made the point well long ago: " Theory perverts sensibility. As an example, we have the Marxist critic's enthusiasm for Shelley on account of his alleged ' revolutionary ' outlook, and the admiration of Catholics for a poet like Francis Thompson. . . . Francis Thompson's *Hound of Heaven* may, as a distinguished preacher once argued, be an excellent ' retreat book ', but the soundness of its theology or the ' majesty ' of its central idea does not concern the critic. What does concern him is that the language of the poem is tired, stale, effete."[18]

This is the type of warning so often issued to Christians (also to Marxists and other ' believers ') by Dr. F. R. Leavis and his colleagues in the pages of *Scrutiny*. Q. D. Leavis, for instance, in a vigorous cautionary article on " Charlotte Yonge and ' Christian Discrimination ' " says that " There is no reason to suppose that those trained in theology, or philosophy for that matter, are likely to possess, what is essential to the practice of literary criticism, that ' sensitiveness of the intelligence ' described by Matthew Arnold as equivalent to conscience in moral matters. A theological training seems to have a disabling effect and has subsequently to be struggled against when literary criticism is the concern."[19]

What is true of literary criticism is true also of literary practice. The possession of the correct devotional sentiments does not qualify a man to write good poetry, even good devotional poetry.   From this point of view the seventeenth-century Anglican revival was perhaps not an unmixed blessing, as Henry Vaughan himself realized:

> After him [George Herbert] followed diverse—*sed non passibus æquis*; they had more of *fashion* than of *force*.   And the reason of their so vast difference from him, besides differing spirits and qualifications (for his *measure* was eminent), I suspect to be, because they aimed more at *verse* than *perfection*, as may be easily gathered by their frequent *impressions* and numerous *pages*.   Hence sprang those wide, those weak, and lean conceptions which in the most inclinable reader will scarce give any nourishment or help to *devotion*; for, not flowing from a true practick piety, it was impossible they should effect those things abroad which they never had acquaintance with at home: being only the productions of a common spirit, and the obvious ebullitions of that light humour, which takes the pen in hand out of no other consideration than to be seen in print.[20]

In the realm of criticism it would be invidious to mention contemporary examples of this danger; but we can readily think of good, sound, Anglican scholars of the last century— Richard Chevenix Trench, Dean Church, even (*pace* Hopkins) R. W. Dixon—of impeccable classical training and of very good sense, whose taste was yet spoilt in some particulars by a too directly moralistic or theological bias.   Nor must we altogether blame them.   Dr. Leavis himself, the protagonist of a purist literary criticism, also describes himself as a moralist; and much of his adverse criticism of writers past and present includes an ethical judgment upon their response to life as a whole.   It is sometimes difficult in Dr. Leavis' criticism (e.g. of writers such as Swift—and *a fortiori* of the Lawrence Durrells, Wyndham Lewises, Stephen Spenders or Henry Millers of our time) to decide how much of it is an æsthetic objection to the writers' *mœurs*, how much a moralistic objection to their language.   This is as it should be—an inter-relationship without which he could not have achieved his distinguished literary criticism; but it inevitably raises the question why Dr. Leavis should stop at morals and *mœurs*.   I have had occasion

elsewhere to suggest that Dr. Leavis could without loss extend
his critical net more widely; allowing a moral element, there
is no reason why he should not admit also a metaphysical, and
finally a theological element too. Indeed, unawares I think
he already does so. At any rate I believe it would be possible
for others, if not for Dr. Leavis himself, to construct what I
have called " a scale of philosophies on which the relative
proximity of one or another to Dr. Leavis' type of criticism
could be plotted". And I also added, tentatively, that one
weakness of his criticism is its rather too conscious proximity
to that utilitarian, realist-empiricist tradition in philosophy,
with its somewhat stern, humourless moralism, represented, for
example, by Leslie Stephen, rather than to the 'personalist',
even 'existentialist' tradition which would seem more appropriate to a critic of literature.[21] I cannot think that Dr. Leavis'
hesitation, his unwillingness to pass on further and include
more, is due to convictions similar to those of Sir Herbert
Read.

> To me [said Sir Herbert, in 1938] the superstitions and
> the dreams are more real and have more meaning than the
> ideas. I believe that this is true of the vast majority of
> people—they prefer the concrete imagery of dreams to the
> abstract entity of ideas: they are more influenced by sym-
> bols than by signs.
> I write as one who has often been tempted into meta-
> physical paths, but who has renounced them. I have
> learned, not only to prefer æsthetics to ethics, but to believe
> that æsthetics is an adequate substitute for metaphysics.
> Metaphysics must, of course, be distinguished from
> natural philosophy. I have no desire to inhibit the activity
> of induction, the process of scientific classification. But,
> to use Saurat's words, I stop at the Actual. . . . To live in
> the Actual, to contemplate the Actual, to describe the
> Actual, to create the Actual (as works of art)—these now
> seem to me to be the only necessary activities. The rest
> is a waste of time.[22]

In any case, the kind of literary criticism which results from
Sir Herbert Read's 'existentialist æsthetic' is not that with
which Dr. Leavis would particularly wish to be associated.

To remove the discussion from the narrowing context of one particular school of literary criticism, the *Scrutiny* group, let us say that since man is a whole, his basic attitudes to life, his 'ultimate presuppositions', and therefore his beliefs, run into his behaviour (public and private) at one point, into his imagination and his dreams at another, and so at yet another into his language, imagery and (if he is a poet) versification. The difficult task of literary criticism is (1) to avoid making an artificial cut between any of these three processes which would destroy the unity of the act; (2) because they so inter-penetrate, to avoid interpreting all in terms of one of them, which would distort them all; and yet (3) not to interpret the whole without regard to the specificity of each, which would end in a vagueness and a fruitless generality characteristic (alas!) of philosophers who develop barren æsthetic theories.

III

There is one very general and indirect way in which theological criteria could be employed in literary criticism. It is a way which starts from the so-called 'comparative study of literature', and which would end in a contrast between Western literature ' as a whole ' and the literature of the East, especially of India. It is generally agreed by the experts that, in the words of Max Müller, " history, in the ordinary sense of the word, is almost unknown in Indian literature ".[23] The concrete evidence for that is given by H. M. and N. K. Chadwick, who when they set out to write their monumental comparative study of some dozen early literatures have to admit that " One of the greatest difficulties in early Indian literature is the absence of historical records. In Hebrew, on the other hand, historical study, together with a keen sense for chronology, was cultivated from a very early period."[24] And it is even more interesting that when they come to discuss early Indian literature they have to confine their attention to the period which in other literatures they have called the ' Heroic Age ': " The only literary genres which we have not been able to trace in ancient India are those which [in the earlier volume of their work] we included under the term ' Post-Heroic poetry

and saga '. We do not know of any personal poetry or poetry
of national interest except, to a limited extent, in the earliest
period. We cannot point with confidence even to narratives
relating to times later than the Heroic Age. Consequently this
Part contains no ' Post-Heroic ' chapter."[25]

These two facts are surely connected. We can disentangle
from the two great Indian epics, the *Mahabharata* and the
Ramayana, something like the original epic material from the
Brahmanic accretions. And this early fragmentary material—
though it may have been much altered from the original tales—
does have a personal and human quality which is quite un-
characteristic of the literature that supervened. Literature, in
fact, was captured by the Brahmans, and from then on never
really escapes from the narrow shafts between which they steer
it. There are moments of vivid writing in the *Gita*, but almost
at once they are swallowed up into the Upanishadic philosophy
which the poem, as we have it, is designed to convey. And this
increasing lack of interest in persons is consonant with the lack
of concern about history.

To examine these themes, and the contrast with the West,
would require a knowledge and a sympathetic understanding
of Eastern literature to which I do not pretend. But it is safe
to conclude that for the Eastern writer history is only important
as that *from* which man needs and strives to be redeemed. In
the West, history is that *in which* man's decisions are, once for
all, made. The ordinary man, whether or not he knows the
theological foundation for the belief, holds that events matter
and that history is irreversible—that, as St. Thomas stated,
even God cannot make that which has happened to ' unhap-
pen '. This is not necessarily true of Eastern man's beliefs; and
the consequence is that real drama—especially tragedy—seems
to be rendered impossible in the East. (It is certainly con-
spicuous by its absence.) And perhaps we can only fully appreciate the homogeneity of our own unquestioning belief by a
comparison with another culture where that belief does not
obtain.

The relevance of this to our theme should be clear. However
much we may desire a literary criticism purged of all theological or moral considerations, there is that in the history of the
West which makes it impossible. Even a writer like Henry

James, who has often been described as the most totally lacking in any vestige of supernatural or even merely religious sense, cannot escape the Western heritage. It is true that some critics have pointed to his *Altar of the Dead* as an exception—as giving a feeling for the sacred; but this late and rather maudlin work is not a happy example: more characteristic of James is the death of Miss Birdseye in *The Bostonians*—a quiet, superbly tactful close to the life of a gentle, selfless character, but a close which has not the least suggestion of a ' beyond ' to it. Yet it remains that we cannot conceive James' handling of persons in his great novels—for instance, in Chapters 51 and 55 of *The Portrait of a Lady*, which are among the finest pieces of dramatic writing in English literature—apart from the history of Western thought; thought about man and about history which has been profoundly affected by its roots in Christian doctrine. This means that when we use words like ' maturity ', ' health ', ' seriousness ' or ' responsibility ', as applied to works of art, we are using criteria which have at least a distant theological resonance. The fact that, for example, Henry James was remote even from his father's Swedenborgianism, let alone from orthodox Christianity, is irrelevant here; what matters is the place of his, or any great writer's, novels within the total Western outlook, an outlook largely shaped by Christian theology.

And since the relationship between that theology and that outlook has differed at different times—now more, now less direct—we can see that it is impossible to discuss, simply and univocally, ' the relationship of belief to literature '. Since there have been so many such relationships the only way of discussing them is historical. And that may easily suggest relativism; but at least it will be a safer way than that of taking one phenomenon and making it the criterion of the poetic act.

If, therefore, eschewing any unilinear theory, we simply say that the relationship between belief and artistic practice differs at different times, appears with more or with less obtrusiveness, etc., we may be evading the task of making a final and universal formulation of the relationship, but we shall do more justice to historical and artistic reality. Certainly without such a prior examination of what in fact have been the varied relationships in the past, we shall never be able to draw conclusions either about the whole of the past, or about the confusing present, still less about the tentative future. And perhaps the widest, as well as the deepest generalization about the creative writer's total relation to life, society and ' belief' that we shall be able to make is that which was made forty years ago by a writer whom we have dared to criticize in this chapter but who is nevertheless capable of the acutest and profoundest judgments of any in our time. Writing in 1913 Mr. Eliot said that " The artist, I believe, is more primitive, as well as more civilized, than his contemporaries; his experience is deeper than civilization, and he only uses the phenomena of civilization in expressing it."[26]

THE BALLAD AND SOCIETY, OR THE ASSIMILATION OF BELIEF

I

THERE are two ways in which the coming of a new Belief may affect the literary and artistic products of the society to which it comes. There may be an immediate welcome of the new Belief and an assimilation of it to existing forms. This—whatever view we hold of the Gandhara sculptures (and experts are divided as to the extent to which the Greek influence there evidenced was something genuinely new)—is probably true in general of Indian culture, so hospitable to all comers. Or there may be an initial antagonism, and such later assimilation as there is may be assimilation by the visitor rather than the visitant. This seems to be partly true of the spreading of Christianity around the Mediterranean littoral. An interesting book was written recently by an expert in these matters, showing that before a new, developed Christian art was possible there had to be (at any rate, there was) a prior movement of asceticism, of sculptural puritanism.[1] The art of the Catacombs, he says, eschews the graces of contemporary humanist expertise: the pictures are crude, badly drawn, but vigorous. Only after this period of austerity could classical modes and conceptions be safely incorporated into the now securely held Christian world-view. And he calls this period of austerity " The Baptism of Art " in the double sense, that baptism implies a descent into the purifying waters before the emergence into daylight; and also that the actual themes of ' Christian Art ' at this early period were almost limited to illustrations of the rites of Initiation. No doubt it is possible to dispute whether the process ' had to be ' of this kind.[2] The fact remains that thus it was; and this fact is significant.

Later stages of this assimilation are also instructive. In the

realm of ' educational theory ' it is clear, for instance, how
much longer the ' baptism ' of pagan culture took than of
pagan art. Professor M. L. W. Laistner has shown how slow the
Christians were to acknowledge any value in classical writings;
they were afraid of the religious implications of pagan literature,
and tended to scorn it as being mere training of the intellect,
apart from the moral virtues.[3] It is to these Christian writers,
for instance, that we owe the condemnatory sense of the word
' rhetoric '; and St. John Chrysostom thought it was better to
instruct the youth through stories of the Old Testament than
through legends like the voyages of the Argonauts. It was only
the Alexandrian school that saw any value, apart from direct
apologetics and catechitical instruction, in pagan lore. And if
we move on to a later period—though it might be described as
culturally a more primitive one—it is interesting to study the
attempt at assimilating Northern heroic poetry to the Christian
scheme of things. Mr. R. E. Woolf has persuasively argued[4] that
the devil is an exception to the rule that the heroic convention
was never satisfactorily adapted to Christian themes in Old
English poetry. " The apostles, for instance, even though they
are the apostles of the Apocryphal tradition, rather than of the
New Testament, are ill at ease in their disguise of Germanic
retainers, *Cristes thegnas*." But the devil had natural affinities
with characters in Northern mythology and literature: " There
was a counterpart to the devil, not only in Loki of Northern
mythology (' the evil companion and bench-mate of Odin and
the gods ', ' the enemy of the gods ') but also in certain characters native to Germanic literature." And Mr. Woolf concludes,
significantly, that one of the reasons why *Genesis B* is a remarkable exception to the usual mediocre standard of extant religious
poetry in Old English may be that it can make use of the
tragic theme of the devil's fall and condemnation: * " Germanic
inspiration is essentially tragic, whilst Christianity left little
room for tragedy." There is one exception, that is, to the rule
that Christianity allows no place for ' final sadness ': " the
devil could still be the greatest tragic figure . . . because (for
him) there is no remission of unhappiness "; we have for the

* This poem, however, was a translation (*c.* 900), having come from an Old
Saxon original, fragments of which were found in the Vatican library. (Old
Saxon being a North German dialect of the Germanic language.)

devil, as for Faust, Macbeth, etc., " a pity which is not theologically justified ". Mr. Woolf is here employing a thesis of Dr. Una Ellis-Fermor,[5] who argues for the incompatibility between Christianity and tragedy. As we shall have to consider this question briefly at the end of the next chapter, I shall postpone the matter till then. But meanwhile we must allow that there is undeniable truth in these generalizations about Old English poetry.

★

I propose, however, to take a slightly later stage (culturally as well as chronologically) in this relationship between culture and belief for my discussion, a stage which illustrates a somewhat different process from any of the above, though one no less significant. In taking what must be regarded as ' popular entertainment ' as provided by the Ballad for my sample (and popular, of course, includes the squires and gentlemen farmers who were so often the ballad-singers' patrons[6]), I shall seem to be either making things deliberately difficult for myself or introducing subtleties where none exists. I shall, that is, be told that the matter is simple : here in the ballads we find primitive pagan belief, with an occasional top-dressing of later Christian phraseology, usually as a polite concession to the clerics who frowned on this type of product in general. (Though we may note that clerics—and once even a bishop, compelled thereto by Robin Hood—are often to be found dancing at weddings, etc.[7]) This is certainly the usual view:

In its tragic moments English and Scottish balladry recalls inevitably such early Northern poetry as Beowulf, certain of the Eddic lays, and the Nibelungenlied. That is, in mood or spirit, at least, a song like *Earl Brand* or *Child Maurice* or, again, *The Cruel Brother* may be regarded as a *précis* of the Nibelungen Lay. With the exception that in the ballads we have little of the mythological, there is the same coming to grips with life, the same clash of man with destiny, the same sombre, fatalistic outlook, the same crushing imminence of death and disaster. And it is noteworthy that this grim mood or philosophy of the Teutonic ballad, its awareness of and insistence upon the darker side of human experience, is seldom brightened by Christian thought. Indeed, Christianity seldom enters the ballads legitimately. As a rule where it does enter, it is readily detected as a superimposition on the basically pagan character of folksong.[8]

This is perfectly true. When, for instance, we read in *The Fire of Frendraught* that the dying man is concerned for the future welfare of his soul—

> He's taen a purse o the gude red gowd,
>   And threw it oer the wa :
> " It's ye'll deal that among the poor,
>   Bid them pray for our souls a' "
>   —(No. 196, C.15)

or when in *The Cruel Brother* we read that

> This ladie fair in her grave was laid,
> And many a mass was oer her said . . .
>   —(Tytler Brown's version, No. 11, A.28)

we realize that the connection with Christian practice is still very tenuous; and in any case it is, as we have hinted in the previous chapter with regard to Dante and Virgil, in their attitude to the dead that pagan and Catholic rites and language have been most easily acclimatized to each other. Perhaps a clearer example of direct intrusion may be given, *Leesome Brand*:

> He put his hand at her bed head,
>   And there he found a gude grey horn,
> Wi three draps o' Saint Paul's ain blude,
>   That had been there sin he was born.
>
> Then he drapped twa on his ladye,
>   And ane o them on his young son,
> And now they do as lively be,
>   As the first day he brought them hame.

Dr. L. C. Wimberly[9] points out that in an Aberdeenshire text of this ballad Saint Paul is omitted:

> He's done him to his mother's bed-head,
>   An found a horn had hung lang,
> An' there he found three draps o bloed
>   That had hung there since one was born.[10]

Here, however, I suppose it is possible that this is not an original version to which ' St. Paul ' was obtrusively added, but more likely a later protestantized version. Wimberly also refers to *The Wife of Usher's Well* and *Tam Lin*, where holy water and the name of Jesus are brought in as part of a magical process.[11] Finally, we may mention the little group of ' ecclesiastical ' ballads with a heretical tinge. *The Bitter Withy* is a charming example, in which the child Jesus goes out to play at ball. He tries to persuade three young lords to play with Him, but they look down on Him as a child of low birth; as a result He pays them out:

> Our Saviour built a bridge with the beams of the sun,
>   And over it He gone, He gone He.
> And after followed the three jolly jerdins *
>   And drownded they were all three.

When the child Jesus returns,

> Mary mild, Mary mild, called home her Child,
>   And laid our Saviour across her knee,
> And with a whole handful of bitter withy
>   She gave Him slashes three.

> Then He says to His mother, " Oh! the withy, oh!
>   the withy,
> The bitter withy that causes me to smart, to smart
> Oh! the withy, it shall be the very first tree
>   That perishes at the heart ".[12]

As Mr. M. J. C. Hodgart (who quotes this ballad) says of this group, " For some reason these barbarous and fantastic legends seem to have been preferred by folksingers to the normal Gospel stories, perhaps because there may have been an undercurrent of heresy and paganism in the Christianity of the English peasantry."[13] Though, if this is true, we may for them invoke Mr. Eliot's famous reference to Marlowe—" the most thoughtful, the most blasphemous (and therefore, probably, the most Christian) of his contemporaries ".[14] Just as Marlowe's blasphemy reveals his belief, so the ballad-writers' ' heresy ' may indicate the strength of the tradition from which they are bold enough to diverge. Nevertheless in general we admit that

* ' Pitchers ', or, in other versions, ' rich young lords.'

in all these and many other instances such specifically Christian
references as do occur in the ballads are marginal after-
thoughts, or conventional formulæ, not profoundly altering the
basic pre-Christian or ' extra-Christian ' motifs of these
poems.

Indeed, it is only the imperialistically theological-minded*
who would wish to raise any objection to this being so. We
may put it, perhaps, that a healthily and solidly Christian
culture can contentedly allow a considerable infusion by or
survival of pre-Christian or non-Christian elements, especially
at the level of popular entertainment or innocent diversion.
Not that this was always allowed by the ecclesiastics, of course.
In 797 Alcuin wrote to Hygebald, Bishop of Lindisfarne,
declaiming against the clergy inviting harpists to entertain
them when they dined together: " When priests dine together,
let the word of God be read. It is fitting on such occasions to
listen to a reader, not to a harpist, to the discourses of the
Fathers, not to the poems of the heathen. What has Ingeld
to do with Christ? . . . The King of Heaven will have no part
with so-called kings who are heathen and damned; for the one
king reigns eternally in heaven, the other, the heathen, is
damned and groans in hell. . . . In your houses the voices of
those who read should be heard, not a rabble of those who make
merry in the streets."[15]

But this is special ruling for the clergy. It would be possible
to maintain that the Inquisition has only been strong where
Catholicism was beginning to weaken—that it marks the clerical
failure of nerve. And this will be true also of literary inquisi-
tions. Nevertheless, there is a more delicate and subtle question
that needs to be asked. Granted that there are and must be
these survivals, indeed often these undigested mouthfuls, of
pagan thought and inspiration within a formally Catholic
whole, has there really been no assimilation? Are the morsels
all totally undigested? Are they, that is, transferable without
alteration back into their original pagan setting? This is the
question that we shall have in mind—and not fully to answer,
though we shall hint at the reply that might be made—taking
the ballads as a case in point. But first, what is a ballad?

* For a discussion of them, see the following chapter.

One day in 1937 a young poet is reading his poems aloud to another Serbian poet in Ochrid. A Yugoslav priest overhears: " ' Verses, tut! tut! ' he exclaims. ' It's all right to make up a song in one's head, but to write it down, you can't tell me that's not a waste of time ' ".[16] This is strikingly similar to the famous remark of Margaret Laidlaw, mother of James Hogg, to Sir Walter Scott: " There was never ane o' my songs prentit till ye prentit them yourself, and ye hae spoilt them a'togither. They were made for singin' and no for readin', but ye hae broken the charm now, and they'll never be sung mair."[17]

The two together give us a sufficient approach to the ballad. There has, of course, been much fluctuation of opinion as to what constitutes a ballad, and whence ballads arose. Once it was thought to be simply a song composed and sung by a minstrel—travelling or at Court. That opens the door to the widest of classifications, and allows ' Q ', in his *Oxford Book of English Ballads*, to refuse an exact definition and to include many charming poems which cannot really be called ballads at all. In answer to the question ' What is a ballad? ' he can only reply that it is " About the dead hour o' the night / She heard the bridles ring," or " In somer when the shawes be sheyne, / and leves be large and long," etc. In other words, there is no definition—you must *feel* it. But the Romantics came along and gave us their account. The brothers Grimm are supposed to have said " das Volk dichtet ". (In fact, it is doubtful whether they ever used this phrase, but Jakob Grimm certainly said " every *epos* must compose itself, must make itself, and can be written by no poet ".[18]) Herder went farther: " Art came along, and extinguished nature. . . . Aforetime these songs rang out in a living circle sung to the harp and animated by the voice, the vigour and the courage of the singer or poet; now [with the appearance of printing] they stood fixed in black and white, prettily printed on—rags! . . . Nature made man free, joyous, singing; art and institutions make him self-contained, distrustful, dumb."[19]

Since then experts have modified this easy view. The Chadwicks, Professor E. K. Chambers, Professor Entwistle and other modern opinions have tended to restore the individual

author, and to allow him to have been a minstrel. Yet there
still remains some substance in the old view. Child said:
" Though they do not ' write themselves ' as William Grimm
has said, though a man and not a people composed them, still
the author counts for nothing, and it is not by mere accident,
but with the best reason, that they have come down to us
anonymous."[20] Kittredge went so far as to concede that most
ballads we have were not of ' communal composition ' at all;
he only claimed that such composition " is not improbable for
some of them. The actual facts with regard to any piece in this
collection are beyond our knowledge, and the matter need not
be insisted on. Even if none of our ballads were composed in
this way, still many of them conform to a type which was
established under the conditions of authorship referred to."[21]

It is not, I think, altogether just to say of this statement, as
Mr. Hodgart does, that this is as much as to say " that the
theory applies only to hypothetical and unknowable ballads
which may have existed in the irrecoverable past, applies as it
were to the Platonic Idea of a Ballad which lies behind all
phenomenal ballads ".[22] For what Kittredge is saying is something much less romantically extravagant. Another quotation
from him, not given by Mr. Hodgart, will make the matter
clearer. " He [the author] is not, like the artistic poet among
us, an exceptional figure with a message. . . . He takes no credit
to himself, for he deserves none. What he does, many of his
neighbours could do as well. Accordingly, he is impersonal
without self-consciousness. He utters what everybody feels—
he is a voice rather than a person."

As a clinching argument in favour of the old view it was
alleged, for example, by Professor Gummere, that the ballad
tradition is now ' a closed book '. Discoveries during the last
forty and more years, especially among the South Appalachians,
have modified this view, for not only have old ballad themes
been preserved, with the usual local accretions, but new topical
ballads have been composed in the old style. Yet a similar
decline in taste has been observed there to that which we shall
discover in England and Scotland. Curiously, the music
appears to have suffered less in transmission than the words; the
old vigour of phrase has gone, and sentimentality has crept in,
but the melodies, with all their variants, have remained. It

would seem that this is largely due to the lack of attention paid to the music, which, unconsciously preserved, is thus little tampered with. Cecil Sharp observed that, among Scottish and American singers of folk-songs, the singer usually could not sing the tune apart from the words, and when he made a variation on the melody in one verse could not repeat it, but made up another, in the next: " I gather that when singing a ballad, for instance, he is merely relating a story in a peculiarly effective way which he has learned from his elders, his conscious attention being wholly concentrated upon what he is singing." And finally, it has been remarked that even where no ' magic of phrase ' has been preserved, the variations on the old ballads have kept a good narrative structure—and this even in American ballads of comparatively recent origin.[23] So that not all variation, through process of time, has been deterioration.

It is necessary, of course, to distinguish the ballad proper from the ' broadside '. (In the seventeenth and early eighteenth centuries they were not always so distinguished.) Such ballads as have grown from broadsides are on the whole poor jingles; they have not, we can say, been submitted to the discipline of popular employment, that slow filtering process by which in the best times the true ballad comes out clear and sweet. In the towns these broadsides were often bad money driving out the good; but in the country, when they did circulate there, they seem not to have contaminated the real local article. It was only in the nineteenth century, with the gradual spread of primary education and the shift of emphasis from ear to eye, that the genuine ballad tradition was doomed. Perhaps the survival of the ballad in America—Maine and New Brunswick—may encourage us to believe that it is not altogether dead; but their decline in stylistic vigour, their weakness and sentimentality, in spite of the continuance of the mode, is significant of changes in public literary values. As Gerould says, " As long as there were homogeneous communities with relatively static populations, not easily affected by influences from outside, a tradition of good artistry had a chance to develop and to continue. As conditions changed—in England through the operations of the ballad-monger,[24] in America through a variety of causes—the effective power of taste declined."[25]

It is not only, however, in this way that the English ballad taste declined. Percy gives us a good start for our examination of actual examples in his *Reliques*. A favourite old ballad (twice quoted in *The Knight of the Burning Pestle*) was *Fair Margaret and Sweet William*. The oldest version we have is, as a matter of fact, from a stall copy of the seventeenth century, but it has something of the genuine ring about it. William has deserted Margaret and married another:

> Fair Margaret sat in her bower-window,
>   A combing of her hair,
> And there she spy'd Sweet William and his bride,
>   As they were riding near.
>
> Down she layd her ivory comb,
>   And up she bound her hair;
> She went her way forth of her bower,
>   But never more did come there.

Out of spite, her ghost appears to the married pair, and says:

> " God give you joy, you two true lovers,
>   In bride-bed fast asleep;
> Loe I am going to my green grass grave,
>   And am in my winding sheet."

When William wakes he tells his bride he has had a terrible dream:

> " I dreamed my bower was full of red swine,
>   And my bride-bed full of blood."

He goes to see her corpse, and Margaret's brothers try to drive him from the funeral. But though he protests he has done nothing wrong in marrying another, for he was never vowed to Margaret, yet he cannot escape the toils of her grief:

> " Pray tell me then how much you'll deal
>   Of your white bread and your wine;
> So much as is dealt at her funeral today
>   Tomorrow shall be dealt at mine."
>
> Fair Margaret dy'd today, today,
>   Sweet William he dy'd the morrow;
> Fair Margaret dy'd for pure true love
>   Sweet William he dy'd for sorrow.

Bishop Percy gives this ballad, but only to prepare us for what he calls " one of the most beautiful ballads in our own or any other language", a poem by David Mallet, based on the old one but published as his own in 1724 as ' Margaret's Ghost'. Here are some specimens.

'Twas at the silent solemn hour,
    When night and morning meet;
In glided Margaret's grimly ghost,
    And stood at William's feet.

Her face was like an April morn,
    Clad in a wintry cloud:
And clay-cold was her lily hand,
    That held her sable shroud.

So shall the fairest face appear,
    When youth and years are flown:
Such is the robe that kings must wear,
    When death has reft their crown.

. . . .

This is the dark and dreary hour
    When injur'd ghosts complain;
Now yawning graves give up their dead,
    To haunt the faithless swain. . . . (etc.)

The good Bishop is entitled to his opinion, but it is noticeable not only that the language is weaker but that Mallet has quite gratuitously added solemn generalizations of a trite nature. Moreover, with a significant insensitiveness, he has missed the graphic touch by which in the original William dies in spite of having broken no formal contract with Margaret:

(" If I do kiss my jolly brown bride,
    I do but what is right;
For I made no vow to your sister dear,
    By day or yet by night.")

In other words, the old theme of romantic love pitted against, and defeating, contractual love is hinted at in the original poem, but has been altogether lost in the eighteenth-century re-writing of it.

This leads us to a feature of the ballad which has been perhaps inadequately noted: its setting within a clearly understood social convention which provides the stresses and strains necessary for the life of the story. Let us take one of the best-known and finest of the English ballads, *Childe Waters*, and analyse it with this in view. A young woman, Ellen, comes to Child Waters and tells him she is expecting a child by him:

> " My girdle of gold, which was too longe,
>   Is now to short ffor mee.

> " And all is with one chyld of yours,
>   I ffeele sturre att my side;
>   My gowne of greene, it is to strayght;
>   Before it was to wide."

She longs to marry him, but he puts every difficulty in her way: she has to dress as his page, to follow him through rough country on foot (he on horseback), and finally to put up with the indignity of being ordered to join the footmen while he sits with the ladies, one of them being his paramour. She, with loving deference, does not complain:

> " I doe see the hall now, Child Waters,
>   That of redd gold shineth the tower;
>   God giue good then of your selfe,
>   And of your paramoure! "

Finally he orders her to give his steed corn and hay, and when she goes to do so she bears the child in the stable. He hears of this, and comes to find her, and now at last gives way to her love.

> Shee said, " Lullabye, my owne deere child!
>   Lullabye, deere child, deere!
>   I wold they father were a king,
>   Thy mother layd on a beere! "

> " Peace now," he said, " good Faire Ellen,
>   And be of good cheere, I thee pray,
>   And the bridall and the churching both,
>   They shall bee upon one day."

(' Q ' in his *Oxford Book* has made excisions in this as in other ballads, saying that he would rather bowdlerize them than

" withhold these beautiful things altogether from boy or maid".)
Apart from its virtue as a lively and well-told tale, the last
stanza is remarkable for the way in which it gathers up the
tensions hinted at throughout the song, and so comes upon its
hearers with an effective double assault. First, after the movement of pity accompanying poor Ellen on her trials (the
accepted superiority of the male would tend to exempt Child
Waters' brutality from criticism), there would be the normal
relaxation of anxiety, the smoothing of the taut, strained
expression of sympathy and fear as to how the tale will end for
her, by the happy solution. Even though such an end was no
doubt expected, the poem is so constructed as to carry its shock
of feigned surprise. But cutting across this would be the—
much slighter, subtler but still operative—movement of social
condemnation. The situation ' ought ', of course, never to have
arisen, according to the current social code; without that
' ought not ' there would have been no tale worth the telling.
This complication of an otherwise simple theme adds a different
dimension, as it were, to the poignancy of the story. Now it is
felt that Ellen's case is more serious than that of the ordinary
jilted lover. But left just like that it would have been an intol-
erable complication, if you like, a pull which ended in a rent;
had it not been for the element of modification which appears,
cumulatively throughout, but capitally in this last stanza. I
mean, the emotional modification of laughter. It is there
earlier:

> There were four and twenty faire ladyes
> Was playing att the chesse;
> And Ellen, shee was the ffairest ladye,
> Must bring his horsse to grasse.
>
> And then bespake Child Waters sister,
> And these were the words said shee:
> " You have the prettyest ffootpage, brother,
> That ever I saw with mine eye;
>
> " But that his belly it is soe bigg,
> His girdle goes wonderous hye . . ."

But it is in the last stanza that all is resolved. Passed off as a
jest, and a witty one—" The bridall and the churching both, /
They shall bee upon one day "—the harmony is restored. Put

into words, the contemporary comment might have been, unconsciously, something like this: " Of course, we know he should never have put her into that condition: but she loved him well enough—look what she went through for him—and in the end he does the right thing by her, so all is well. And after all, which of us doesn't go a bit wrong sometimes. . . ? " It is against the background of that sort of comment that we have, I think, to set the ballads; and to do so is to see them gain enormously in depth and effectiveness.

We can see the same if we compare the early heroic epic with the English and Scottish ballad tradition. It is true that there are elements of the ' heroic ' in many of the ballads—especially in the long, straightforward battle stories, from the earliest, *Chevy Chase*, to some of the late seventeenth-century Scottish songs of war. We have already seen, in our first section, that they are in many ways extraordinarily near to the old pagan, Germanic mood. But admitting as we have these origins and these survivals, it remains significant that the corpus of English and Scottish ballads that we possess achieved its formulation within a Christian culture. (They extend, apparently, from the exceptionally early ballad, like *Judas*, preserved in a thirteenth-century MS., to the seventeenth and even mid-eighteenth century.) And further, something of their literary effectiveness derives, at least in part, from their appropriation into that Christian medium. There is a difference in ' feel ' between the early heroic epic which has come down to us unaffected—uncontaminated, if you will—by the Christian culture which supervened, and those ballads in which ancient pagan elements have been built into and modified by the mediæval schema; and that difference in ' feel ' is something more than just a difference in chronology. The many ballads of Robin Hood present us with a theme which is no doubt as old as the Icelandic saga: the outlawed hero, honour among thieves, the stupidity of authority as represented by the Sheriff, etc. But what might have been a mere crude story of rivalry and alternating fortunes does seem to have attained a deeper significance and a greater dignity through the representation of such a rivalry as a relative affair compared with the obedience due from both sides to a higher moral authority. We must be careful not to prove too much. And so we must leave aside

those songs which have obviously been tampered with—
altered, or added to, or officially given the *nihil obstat* of a pious
conclusion ; such as the last verse of *Robin Hood and the Monk*,
which, with no sort of relevance to anything that has gone
before, suddenly observes:

> Thus endes the talkiying of the munke
> And Robin Hode i-wysse;
> God, that is ever a crowned kyng,
> Bryng us all to his blisse!

It yet remains true that the light-hearted, almost frivolous
handling of life-and-death oppositions and adventures seems
to be acceptable where else it might have been irritating or
even shocking, within the larger whole of supernatural loyalties.
And this wide framework has its foundations in the stratification
of society here below. We can sense the importance of this
factor behind Robin Hood's catalogue, when he is directing
his men whom to hunt and whom to spare:

> But loke ye do no husbonde harme,
> That tilleth with his ploughe.

> No more ye shall no gode yeman
> That walketh by grene-wode shawe;
> Ne no knyght ne no squyer
> That wol be a gode felawe.

> These bisshoppes and these archebishoppes,
> Ye shall them bete and bynde;
> The hye sherif of Notyingham,
> Hym holde ye in your mynde.

It is to be noted that this is no mere anti-clericalism *per se*, but
a criticism of abuses derived, like Chaucer's, precisely from a
respect of ' degree '; and beneath that respect is the assumption
that the degree, and the responsibility attaching to it, is of
divine ordinance. Something of a similar implication can
occasionally and more faintly be discerned in the battle tales
(on sea or land) where the victors give the impression of acting
not simply for themselves but as in some sense agents of
Providence, or of ' the right '—even if the definition of ' the
right ' is limited by loyalty to the family or tribal circle, or by
pre-Christian standards of the blood-feud, etc. The result is

that something of the mediæval code of chivalry has at least been inserted into, even if it was not originally in, these rough, vigorous ballads of fight; and the insertion has often had a deepening and not necessarily a weakening effect.

Let us take what might seem an intractable instance, a very good, and very early, ballad which has no obvious mediæval Christian colouring: the tragic *Babylon* (or *The Bonnie Banks of Fordie*).

> There were three ladies lived in a bower,
> Eh vow bonnie
> And they went out to pull a flower.
> On the bonnie banks o Fordie.
>
> They hadna pu'ed a flower but ane,
> (Eh vow, etc.)
> When up started to them a banisht man.
> (On the bonnie banks, etc.)
>
> He's taen the first sister by her hand,
> And he's turned her round and made her stand.
>
> " It's whether will ye be a rank robber's wife,
> Or will ye die by my wee pen-knife? "
>
> " It's I'll not be a rank robber's wife,
> But I'll rather die by your wee pen-knife."
>
> He's killed this may, and he's laid her by,
> For to bear the red rose company.
>
> He's taken the second ane by the hand,
> And he's turned her round and made her stand.
>
> " It's whether will ye be . . . ? " etc.
> (Answer and murder as before.)
>
> He's taken the youngest ane by the hand,
> And he's turned her round and made her stand.
>
> Says, " Will ye be a rank robber's wife,
> Or will ye die by my wee pen-knife ? "
>
> " I'll not be a rank robber's wife,
> Nor will I die by your wee pen-knife.
>
> " For I hae a brother in this wood,
> And gin ye kill me, it's he'll kill thee."
>
> " What's thy brother's name ? come tell to me."
> " My brother's name is Baby Lon."

" O sister, sister, what have I done!
O have I done this ill to thee!

" O since I've done this evil deed,
Good sall never be seen o me."

He's taken out his wee pen-knife,
And he's twyned himsel o his ain sweet life.

There is something quite elemental about this very simple and moving song. It is dramatic in structure, preserves evidently the choric participation (the refrain repeated between every line), and may even show signs, perhaps, of mimetic survival. (Professor Gummere, who was, however, the ardent champion of chorus, mime and dance in the ballad, suggested that the ' taking by the hand ' and the ' turning about ' look like the stage directions of a play or the actions of a dance.) The concealment of the robber's identity is superbly achieved and contributes much to the success of the melodrama. The three sisters can be paralleled, no doubt, in many other ballads: a threefold arrangement, three leagues, three ravens, three brothers, etc., is very frequent. But it provides a most natural method of building up the plot with its suspense. Finally the horrible suggestion that what the robber has been trying to intimidate the three sisters into is, unknown to himself, nothing less than incest—this suggestion does not occur till the robber's identity has been revealed and the danger is over. The effect of this is to cast a backward threat over the reminiscence of the plot (' see what might have been '), and thus combines the full horror of that particular breach of the social code with a ' distancing ' of it into the immediate past of unfulfilled possibility which makes the thought endurable. (Incest, or the threat of it, occurs in other ballads—*Lady Isabel, Brown Robyn's Confession, The Bonny Hind* and *The King's Dochter Lady Jean* —but however lightly it may at first sight appear to be treated there is always an element of seriousness which heightens the plot.) Finally the whole poem may be analysed into five stages: opening or *mise en scène*; two sisters threatened and killed; third sister threatened and resistant; revelation of the robber's identity; débâcle. Here are the normal five acts of tragedy, quite undeliberately reproduced. Does not this instinct for dramatic division and structure indicate an emotional maturity surprising for its times; and does not that in turn suggest that maturity of culture is not a question of chronology, but is attainable at various levels, analogically, according to the particular shape of the cultural graph?

'Analogically ', we say; and this will protect us against the usual censure of those who equate admiration for the ballads with morris dancers, wheelwright shops, home-weaving, and support of every lost cause. There is no point in making direct comparisons between popular and literary poetry; the two must be judged by different standards, and the fact that self-conscious literary elements entering into popular poetry generally tend to weaken and diffuse it is no necessary argument against explicitly literary writing. It is this conclusion of the romantic ' volkish ' school that spoils their case and renders suspect the whole tribe of ballad-admirers. For fruitful comparison we must rather seek out that stage in the formation and clarification of a literary tradition most closely analogous to the stage of popular tradition which gave us our best ballads. What will be common to both traditions will be a symmetry of appeal, a give-and-take of writer and public, a responsible and operative critical *milieu*. In the best ages of the ballad we find this—pitched in a lower key, no doubt, and less obvious or explicit than in the case of a literary tradition such as the early eighteenth-century prose, or the Elizabethan drama, yet none the less discernible. It works in the field of morals. Professor Gummere has said:

> The real ballad of tradition, while it never boggles at a plain name for things now understood rather than expressed, is at a vast remove from the obscene, and from those hulking indecencies which, along with the vapid and the sentimental, make up the bulk of modern unprinted and unmentioned song. . . . Communal poetry, sung in a representative throng, cannot well be obscene; made by the public and in public, it cannot conceivably run against the public standard of morality. . . . A song made by a really communal crowd will give no room to private vices and to those events and situations which get their main charm from a centrifugal tendency with regard to public morals. This hole-and-corner minstrelsy is no part of communal song.[26]

Perhaps we see something of this kind of censorship in the history of some ballad versions. In one version (Motherwell's) of *The Cruel Mother*, we find verses which may suggest burial alive (so Professor Child).

> She took the ribbons off her head,
> She tied the little babes hand and feet,
> She howkit a hole before the sun,
> She's laid these three bonnie babes in.

In other versions the mother clearly slays the babes before burying them. Of course even in this version it may merely be that the slaying has been omitted. However, we are told that a case of burying alive occurs in Norse analogues of *Leesome Brand*; and Child observes that " the horrible circumstance of the children being buried alive is much more likely to be slurred over or omitted at a later day than to be added ".[27] This, however, is only a surface indication of what we mean by the public discipline of taste. No doubt the popular filter tended to exclude sometimes the good with the bad. It is significant that the purely negative, cynical attitude to death of *The Twa Corbies* is comparatively rare: and the attitude of the ravens themselves is not necessarily that of the author of the ballad. One raven tells another where they can find their dinner today—off a dead knight, whose hound has gone off to the hunt, whose hawk has gone after wildfowl, and whose lady has ' ta'en another mate '; so that

> " Ye'll sit on his white hause-bane [neck]
> And I'll pike out his bonny blue een;
> Wi ae lock o his gowden hair
> We'll theek our nest when it grows bare.

> " Mony a one for him makes mane,
> But nane sall ken where he is gane;
> Oer his white banes, when they are bare,
> The wind sall blaw for evermair."[28]

And with the moral, even, we might say, the metaphysical, protection which a society with its own clear beliefs has given to the rather foreign and prickly paganism of the ballad inheritance, there has gone also a maturity which they would have lacked had they remained entirely in their original primitive setting. It looks as if the more or less choric—even, we could call it, the liturgical—origin of much ballad singing has forced many ballads into dialogue form, which may have resulted in the ironing out of a certain amount of individuality, and the reduction of drama, by this simplification, to melo-drama. But this is not all loss—as anyone who appreciates the brilliant end of *Edward* will agree; or, on a less tragic note, these lines from *The Lass of Roch Royal*, where Annie and her baby son have been parted from her mate, Love Gregor:

> " O wha will shoe my fu fair foot?
>   And wha will glove my han?
> An wha will lace my middle gimp
>   Wi the new made London ban?
>
> " Or wha will kemb my yallow hair,
>   Wi the new made silver kemb?
> Or wha'll be father to my young bairn,
>   Till Love Gregor come hame? "
>
> Her father shoed her fu fair foot,
>   Her mother gloved her han;
> Her sister lac'd her middle gimp
>   Wi the new made London ban.
>
> Her brother kembed her yallow hair,
>   Wi the new made silver kemb,
> But the king o heaven maun father her bairn,
>   Till Love Gregor come hame.

Even the obvious and happy endings avoid sentimentality by their abrupt simplicity. Take *The Queen of Scotland*, in which young Troy Muir is tempted by the Queen to sleep with her. He resists, and in anger she snares him into being bit by a serpent. He is saved by a passing maiden:

> But by there came a weelfaird may,
>   As Troy Muir did tauk,
> The serpent's furious rage to lay,
>   Cut off her fair whit pap.

This heals the poison, and in gratitude he marries her; and later

> A lovely son to him she bare,
>   When full nine months were gane.

As heaven was pleased, in a short time,
    To ease her first sad pain,
Sae was it pleased, when she'd a son,
    To hae a pap again.

This is by no means one of the best of the ballads, and shows signs of the weakening of age; yet it does escape banality where it might have been expected. Thus it is not necessary to claim an exaggerated greatness for the ballad to establish its place among other materials for a study of the history of taste. One would have to include, in such a study, the significant fact that many later ' literary ' poets are only bearable when they depend closely upon the ballad (Southey, Scott, Kipling), or else owe much of their effectiveness to the influence of ballad technique (some critics would claim that *The Ancient Mariner* is the only really great, because the only uncontaminated, poem Coleridge wrote). On the other hand it is significant that such poets have seldom been able exactly to imitate the ballad. True, it is said that Scott wrote *Kinmont Willie*, *Proud Maisie*, *From the Red God Keep thy Fingers*, and considerably re-wrote *The Twa Corbies*, *Clerk Saunders*, *Thomas the Rhymer*, *The Wife of Usher's Well*, and the *Douglas Tragedy*.[29] But it was a re-writing of, or an imitation of, what already existed as a given form; and in the case of *Thomas the Rhymer* the third part which he deliberately wrote as completion and imitation of the original ballad is easily distinguishable as his. So that at least we can say, without any false sentiment or nostalgia, that in a time like our own, when the evil results of cultural, and therefore of social, disintegration are so apparent, it is instructive to turn back, not wistfully but with disinterested appraisal, to the sort of achievements possible to an unlettered but homogeneous society. They are not the achievements that would perhaps have wholly satisfied Lawrence in his search for " the strangeness and rainbow-change of ever-renewed creative civilizations "[30]; but he would not have altogether despised even these more modest products. Ballads, says Gerould, are not the poetry of really primitive folk, and they are far from primitive in the art they show; but they do illustrate well the persistence—and, we might add, the trustworthiness—of racial memory.

CALDERÓN AND THE IMPERIALISM OF BELIEF

I

ONE would expect the problem of the relationship between belief and creative literature to be presented as starkly as it ever could be in the career of Pedro Calderón de la Barca. To put it in the crudest terms: Calderón was a priest who wrote plays. True, his predecessor, Lope de Vega, was the same. But Lope was rather a playwright who got ordained—and, as a matter of fact, lapsed into concubinage only two years later; and, in any case, Lope's plays, unlike his poems, are almost entirely 'secular', except for a number of *autos* which in any case are not typical of that *genre*. Racine, the other obvious example for this sort of examination, is largely disqualified, since his ' conversion ' was to a somewhat eccentric form of the Christian faith (Jansenism), and since he wrote only two plays after it on which we can judge of the effect of conversion upon art. In any case, Racine is, for reasons of style and of his place in French letters, a special case.

Calderón had led the normal life of the Spanish adventurer. The usual duels, interspersed between times of military service; but also an unpleasant episode when an actor, Pedro Villegas, stabbed Calderón's brother (actually half-brother, the son of Calderón's father's mistress) and took refuge among the discalced Trinitarian nuns—Calderón and his friends broke into the convent, and tore off the nuns' veils, " if not *injuriously*, at least *grossly*," as the memoir says. However, in 1650, after a series of personal disasters (among them the death of his mistress), Calderón, already in minor orders, decided to leave the King's service in which he was employed, and became a priest.

We must not expect the result to have been the birth of a conscience as scrupulous as that of a Hopkins. Calderón had written religious pieces before his ordination, and continued to write secular *comedias* after it. The only extant letter of Calderón's is one written to the Patriarch of the Indies, in which he defends his play-writing. He says he had excused himself from writing his regular annual *autos sacramentales**, because as a priest he now ' disdained ' this art; but had agreed to take up play-writing again on festivals dedicated to prayer for restoration of the Queen's health, and because the Queen herself had suggested that even the greatest of prelates should consider it an honour to possess a talent capable of distracting her. From this time he had devoted himself solely to religious plays, the *autos*. Even so his doubts returned; he was challenged and had to reply, not merely by distinguishing religious from secular plays and dissociating himself from the latter, but by discussing whether the writing of poetry at all could be permitted to a priest. His reply is:

> The honourableness of the subject and of the profession does not rule out the unworthiness of its exercise; and so long as you will not grant that the exercise of it is worthy, you will not get me to accept any use of it whatever as worthy. . . . Let it be declared whether it is worthy, or whether it is not. If it is good, then I am ready to serve the king, to obey him the rest of my life; but if it is not, neither His Majesty, nor your Lordship, could help finding it reprehensible that, knowing my error I should not work to correct myself—and the Holy Sacrament [in whose honour the Autos were written] itself will gain by it. For what is defined as unsuitable for one altar, cannot serve for the festivals of another. . . . Let me reduce this whole discourse to one sentence . . .: either this is good or it is bad. If it is good, do not obstruct me, and if it is evil let me not be commanded to do it.

It is clear what answer these rhetorical questions expect; and Calderón went on writing plays—though now mainly for royal festivals and feasts of the Holy Sacrament.[1] But the Church herself remained divided on the issue, and it appeared necessary for his editors to preface his published plays with clerical apologies. " There is none [of these *comedias*] which does not contain a great moral doctrine for the reform of life, many

* *Vide infra.*

good warnings against the dangers of this world, many useful examples for youth, many warnings for the imprudent, many ingenious satires to distract the mind . . . [In these plays] there is nothing to be found contrary to the catholic truth of our holy religion, nor dangerous for morals." And finally in the preface to the third volume a bishop is brought in as counsel for the defence—the great preacher, Fray Manuel Guerra y Ribera. It is worth quoting, as a contemporary contrast to the puritanical thunders of a Jeremy Collier or a Bossuet.

Plays are of three sorts: there are also three sorts of minds. For minds that are moderately open, they are indifferent; for the intelligent they are good, for the stupid they may be bad. This distinction is founded upon nature itself. Moderately open minds are, normally, those ' soft ' intelligences who do not get very deep down into things, and who only half taste the sugar of what they see and hear. They accept this light distraction [of a play] with their eyes and ears, without penetrating further into the hidden depth of the object. For these, then, plays are purely indifferent.

For sensitive minds they are good. If it is a saint whom the poet puts on the stage, as they are sensible to the grace of his poetry, the subject moves them and softens them. If it is a historical subject, it is an example which strikes them; if the subject is love, and if it is not presented with the purity which they would want to see, they will be offended. Each subject, then, has its usefulness for them; for them, no danger, and the reason is that their understanding being occupied in discerning the defects or the beauties, their intelligence has no leisure to let themselves go astray.

It is this same reason which can make plays bad for the stupid; for not having any intellectual faculties to occupy them, they apply all their sense in watching, and it can easily happen that, their understanding finding itself without a guide, this or that of their senses may take a wrong route. I would with all my heart desire that the door should be shut against them. For, although I know that the eventuality of evil is distanced, I believe that of the good will be less near still.[2]

Today we should of course consider this as giving an excessively didactic interpretation of the function of drama, and one that could be used to justify a rigorous, if discriminating, application of the *index expurgatorius*. But for the late seventeenth century, and for the country of the Inquisition (Lope de Vega had himself been an inquisitor), and further considering the public to which the apology is directed, we ought in fact to recognize it as the expression of a remarkably liberal attitude on the part of a Prince of the Church.

II

Of the four great periods of national drama, the Greek, the Elizabethan, the Spanish and the French, it is probably the Spanish that seems to us the most inaccessible. This is partly because Catholic Spain, and especially the Jesuit Spain of the seventeenth century, is far away, in every sense of the word. The good Anglican Archbishop, Richard Chevenix Trench, who did so much in the nineteenth century to introduce Calderón to English readers, had his frequent hesitations about Calderón's ' superstitious ' (i.e. in Trench's view only) religion, and especially about what he considered the antinomian implications of Catholic supernaturalism. And perhaps even we, who deem ourselves free from the more rigorous Protestant prejudices, find it a little startling that, for instance, Eusebio, the villain-hero of *La Devoción de la Cruz* (written 1620: printed 1634), should be able so continuously to prostrate himself before the Cross with so little alteration in his manners— manners which include plunder, attempted incest (though in ignorance that it is incest), and the rest. Yet perhaps it is not so much the theology as the baroque marvels that we find hard to swallow today. The apostrophe to the Cross by the dying Eusebio is, after all, a moving piece of rhetoric:

> Let me stop before the Cross, so that they [his pursuers] may deal me a sudden death, and it in turn may deal me life eternal. Tree whereon heaven willed that the true fruit should ripen, remedy for that first fruit whereby man was lost, flower of the new Eden, rainbow of light whose message over a deeper sea proclaimed the peace of the world, beautiful plant, fertile vine, harp of the new

David, tablet of the second Moses! [Behold me] a sinner,
begging your favour in all justice, since God suffered upon
you solely for sinners. . . . My innate devotion ever in-
treated you with such faith, oh Holy Cross, not to permit
that I should die without confession. . . .   (III, xi)

And he reminds the Cross that when he had killed his rival,
Lisardo, he had first carried his dying victim in his own arms
to a priest who could absolve him. We are, however, somewhat
nonplussed when Eusebio goes one better than Lisardo, and
rises up from his bier of leaves and branches after his own
death in order to be shriven, so that, dying a second time, he
may go straight to paradise.[3]

It is, then, these baroque extremes, together with the Spanish
code of honour, that we find hard to accept.[4] In Corneille we
can make the necessary allowance for the standards of *l'honneur*
and *la gloire* because Le Cid, and still more Polyeucte or Cinna,
are sufficiently formal, classical, stiff and non-naturalistic to
match the conventions. But so much of Calderón is ' good
theatre ' that we feel the discrepancy more sharply. The first
act, for instance, of one of his most famous comedias, *El Médico
de su Honra* (1635), is immediately gripping: the Infante, Don
Enrique, falls on the ground in a faint, having been thrown
from his horse, and his cry " Jesus—Jesus " (" *Jesus mil veces!* ")
as he falls is the striking opening speech of the play. But soon
after, when he comes to, and finds himself brought for safety
into the house of his former beloved, Doña Mencia, and indeed
in her very presence, his opening words as he comes out of his
faint consist of an involved and ingenious series of witty
paradoxes, based on his rapture at seeing her.

I wonder whether I am dreaming awake, or whether I
speak in my sleep, for I wake and sleep both at once. But
wherefore—since thereby I endanger the truth? Ah!
that I might never awake, if it is true that I am sleeping
at this moment, and may I never in my life sleep again, if it is
true that I am now awake!   (I, v)

It is elegant—but ill matches the realism of what precedes it.
It is, however, the end of this same play that presents us with
the greatest difficulties; indeed, it strikes us as an unbelievable

anti-climax. The development of the theme—Don Guttiere's gradual suspicions of his wife Doña Mencia's fidelity, and his resolve to kill her, since he cannot kill her suspected lover, the Infante Don Enrique, he being of royal blood—has often and with justice been compared to *Othello*. It is dramatically worked out—and here I cannot agree with Mr. Gerald Brenan's complaint that Don Guttiere " is unsympathetic. . . . What we cannot stomach is his prudence, his secretiveness and his mastery of himself. . . . His value as a tragic hero is weakened when we see him, in spite of his very real love for his wife, planning to kill her with such secrecy that his act will not be discovered: that he will be able to resume his normal life and even, as happens at the end of the play, to marry again."[5] For there is no hint, at this early stage in his plotting against her life, that he has any other motive than that of defending his honour as a husband in the correct contemporary way. Could he have defended it by killing his rival, that might have been done with less secretiveness; but as Don Enrique's royal blood (he is the King's brother) forbids that, there is no alternative but to kill his wife, and that must be done by a ruse. After all, the words Don Guttiere uses when he warns his wife that he is going to kill her summarize the position perfectly, and are true to the conventions; the note he leaves her to read runs:

> Love adores you; honour loathes you; that is why the one kills you, the other gives you fair warning. You have two hours left to live; you are a Christian, save your soul; to save your life is no longer possible.   (III, x)

Granted these conventions, which admittedly are hard to grant, we can go with him thus far. Remembering Webster or Tourneur, we can even go so far as to accept the ghoulish method of murder—a blood-letting which can later be explained away as an accident. What nothing will make us accept is what follows the murder. Don Guttiere comes out, after murdering Doña Mencia, and exculpates himself before the King. He had had, he says, to send for a doctor to bleed his wife who was unwell; in the morning he had himself gone into her room, and found that the bandages had come undone and that she had bled to death. The King, however, had discovered the truth, for he had met the physician that night and traced the marks left by the doctor's blood-stained hand upon the walls and doors leading to Don Guttiere's house. But instead of revealing what he knows, the King's reaction is as follows:

> KING (*aside*) Singular happening! Here we need prudence, and I must restrain myself. He has strangely revenged himself.—Cover up these sad remains which grip us with horror, this portent which terrifies us, this spectacle which amazes us, this symbol of sorrow. Guttiere, you have need of consolation, and in order that in so great a loss you may find an equal compensation, give your hand to Leonore.

Don Guttiere is somewhat taken aback—and well he might be! —at this so immediate suggestion of a new bride. He argues that he may find cause to suspect this new wife, Leonore, too one day, and what then?

> KING   There will be a remedy for all.
>
> DON GUTTIERE   Will there be one even for that?
>
> KING   Yes, Guttiere.
>
> DON GUTTIERE   What remedy, Seigneur?
>
> KING   Yours, Guttiere.
>
> DON GUTTIERE   That is to say . . . ?
>
> KING   A bleeding.
>
> DON GUTTIERE   What d' you say?
>
> KING   You had better have the doors of your house washed. The imprint of a blood-stained hand can be seen on them!   (III, xx)

Don Guttiere then, seeing that the secret is out, offers his hand obediently to Leonore and, with a warning that he has once had to be " the physician of his own honour " and may have to be so again (to which Leonore agrees with singular alacrity), the play ends with the usual plea to pardon the author's faults.

That so powerful a drama should start by seemingly moving towards tragedy and end by thus turning (almost) into farce reveals an extraordinary trait of weakness in so competent a dramatist as Calderón. We shall see later that this has theological implications. But meanwhile, to confirm the criticism, let us cite what is often described as his best play—it is certainly his most unusual—*El Alcalde de Zalamea* (printed 1651). What has struck all critics is its democratic emphasis—frequent in Lope's plays, unique in Calderón's—in the theme of the rise to favour of Pedro Crespo, the old peasant. Crespo rises to be Alcalde (roughly, Mayor) of Zalamea; and in that capacity passes sentence on the Captain, Don Alvaro, for having violated his own (Crespo's) daughter, Isabella. With admirable impartiality Crespo announces that he will try him like any accused. The Captain protests that he is under military law and that the Mayor is acting *ultra vires*, but Crespo brushes this aside. The King arrives and hears that the Captain has been arrested. He asks what it is all about.

CRESPO   . . . If a stranger came to make an accusation, ought I not to see that justice is done for him? Of course. Then why should I not do for my daughter what I would do for any other? . . . So, if the procedure is irregular, if I have not observed impartiality, if I have suborned any witnesses, then let me be put to death.

KING   The trial is regular; but you have not the authority to execute the sentence. That is the duty of another tribunal: it will do justice. So hand over the prisoner.

CRESPO   Sire, I should have difficulty in handing him over. Since here we have but one tribunal, whatever the sentence, it must execute it itself. And so the arrest has been carried out. . . .

(A door opens, the Captain is seen in a chair, garrotted. What will be the King's reaction to this summary piece of justice? After the first shock, he proclaims:)

KING   Don Lope, the matter is finished. Death has been justly dealt: what matters, then, if there has been a defect in the form, since at bottom justice has

been satisfied? . . . [*to Crespo*] You shall be
Alcalde of Zalamea all your life long. [*Departs*].

CRESPO (*as the King goes out*)　Sire, you are the only one who
knows how to honour justice.

And the play ends with Crespo's announcement that the
unhappy victim, his daughter Isabella, is going into a convent
—" She has chosen a husband who takes no note of rank."
All's well that ends well, no doubt—and with the conventional
polite bow to royalty.　But again, in an author otherwise so
skilful, it is curious that there should have been so little awareness of bathos. [6]

III

The skill is pre-eminently there in the plays that more nearly
concern the theme of this chapter.　There are three full-length
Comedias with directly ' religious ' themes.　Perhaps we could
also count *El Principe Constante*[7], one of his most successful
because most tightly constructed, less sprawling, plays.　But
here the religious motive is too mixed up with the political for
clarity.　The Portuguese Infante, Fernando, is captured by
the Turkish King.　His ransom is the town of Ceuta, which the
Turks covet.　He refuses to be ransomed, and dies in slavery
and great suffering—but his ghost ultimately leads the Portuguese to victory.　Fernando's refusal to cede Ceuta, however, in
return for his own freedom, is partly due to respect for Portu-
gal's honour, and partly to his reluctance that a Catholic town,
with a church dedicated to the Conception, should fall into
pagan hands.　It is a moving play—but once more with an
anti-climax (the bringing in of a ' *manes* ex machina ' to defeat
the enemy) for an end.　Of the three more directly ' religious '
plays, we can pass over the first, *La Devoción de la Cruz*, since
we have already referred to it, and in any case it is an early
work.　The other two, however, must be examined in some
detail, since they are probably Calderón's best-known plays
outside Spain[8]: *El Mágico Prodigioso* (1637), and *La Vida es
Sueño* (1634 or 1635, printed 1636.)

It is a little difficult at first to understand Shelley's enthusiasm
for the former, since the most impressive moments in it are, I

think, those which depend closely upon a theology that must
have been distasteful to him. But perhaps one critic's (Sr.
Ramón Silva's) account of Calderón's style helps to explain the
affinity: " The descriptions of natural beauty found in Calderón
give a feeling of lightness and airiness and at the same time
convey a sense of vagueness which never stoops so low as to
particularize. Calderón is the poet of the starry skies, of trim
gardens, sweet purling streams, crystalline fountains and multi-
coloured flowers."[9] Might not this pass for a description of
Shelley's own style? It is noteworthy that with characteristic
high seriousness Shelley in his fragmentary translation, like
FitzGerald after him,[10] entirely ignores the sub-plot—which is
really necessary to the play's balance, however little we may
appreciate the burlesque of the main theme by the *graciosos*
(buffoons). (Personally I find some of these buffooneries extremely funny.) No doubt it was the baroque elements in the
play that above all appealed to Shelley. He is obviously more
at home when he is translating, for example, the Demon's great
speech after the shipwreck when he appears in the form of a
castaway to Cipriano:

> Then I sailed
> Over the mighty fabric of the world,
> A pirate ambushed in its pathless sands,
> A lynx crouched watchfully among its caves
> And craggy shores . . . (etc.)

or when he is depicting, in Miltonic language, the Demon's
promethean pride:

> In my attributes I stood
> So high and so heroically great,
> In lineage so supreme, and with a genius
> Which penetrated with a glance the world
> Beneath my feet, that won by my high merit
> A king—whom I may call the king of kings . . .
> Named me his counsellor. But the high praise
> Stung me with pride and envy, and I rose
> In mighty competition, to ascend
> His seat and place my foot triumphantly
> Upon his subject thrones. . . .
>
> —(II, vii)

than he is when recounting the theological debating match
between Cipriano and the Demon:

CIPRIANO   Is it not indisputable
            That two contending wills can never lead
            To the same end? And being opposite,
            If one be good is not the other evil?
            Evil in God is inconceivable;
            But supreme goodness fails among the Gods
            Without their union.

DEMON   I deny your major.
            These responses are means towards some end
            Unfathomed by our intellectual beam . . .

CIPRIANO   Who made man
            Must have, methinks, the advantage of the others.
            If they are equal, might they not have risen
            In opposition to the work? . . .

DEMON   On impossible
            And false hypothesis there can be built
            No argument. . . . (etc.)
                                        —(I, iii)

Thus Shelley. Yet in its context this scene can be presented
with surprising power, especially when its echo is heard in the
last act where Cipriano is converted to Christianity by finding
visible evidence of the attributes of God that he here merely
argues for theoretically.

   I think we must agree with Shelley's estimate of the greatness
of this play, but on somewhat different grounds, and taking
more of it into account than he did. Indeed, it seems to me
(whatever qualifications we may have to add later) the one
example I know of a specifically Christian, indeed, theological,
drama of major stature. It is, of course, based on hagiological
legend; but Calderón has given his hero an ingenious Faustian
twist, and with effective inclusion of the terms of exact theological debate. Cipriano is a heathen philosopher, bent on studying cosmology.   But he has the misfortune (a misfortune
contrived by the Demon) to fall in love with a beautiful lady,
Justina, who is a Christian. Cipriano meets the Demon, who
designs to capture and use him. In a theological argument

Cipriano reaches the point of seeing through polytheism, and the devil has reluctantly to concede the force of his argument. However, passion is more important than theology, and Cipriano's real goal in life is to break down Justina's resistance to his love. In despair he cries out (not knowing that the devil is nearby):

CIPRIANO   My passion, alas! so tortures my thought
            And this torment of soul so sweeps my fancy along,
            That I would give—O foolish spite, which no
                warm-hearted breast
            Should gender—I would give to the most devilish
                sprite
            Yes, even to hell itself—would give my soul.

DEMON (off)   I accept. [*Thunder and lightning*].[11]

Then follows the magnificent scene (we have given a brief extract from it above in Shelley's rendering) in which the Demon, appearing as a shipwrecked traveller, describes his fall from Heaven in terms, partly, of a shipwreck. The Demon meanwhile does not despise more humble and more sordid methods, for Justina is as much his prey as Cipriano (this is clear from the original introduction to the play, which is not given in usual editions and translations).[12] He tries to incriminate Justina by disguising himself as a gallant and getting himself noticed as he climbs down from her bedroom. (Some have objected to the importation of a ' cloak and dagger ' motif into the play; but it is not inconsistent with the old conception of the devil.) Justina, however, remains pure and aloof. She has told Cipriano that she will never love him— short of death (II, ii); a prophetic utterance which will be taken up in the end. Cipriano is so desperate to win her that he signs a pact in his own blood, giving his soul to the Demon on condition that he is taught a magic which can bring Justina into his arms. (Though even at this stage he shows some scepticism as to the extent of such magic power: " For against free will I know no charms or enchantments " (II, xix). But the Demon brushes this aside.)

After studying under the Demon's tutelage for a year, Cipriano is ready to practise his magic. But first the Demon tries to break Justina's will by tempting her with amorous thoughts and songs; she stays firm, however. Here Shelley's translation is admirable:

JUSTINA　　　　　　　　　　　　　This agony
　　　　　　Of passion which afflicts my heart and soul
　　　　　　May sweep imagination in its storm;
　　　　　　The will is firm.

DEMON　　　　　　　　　　　　Already half is done
　　　　　　In the imagination of the act. . . .

JUSTINA　　　Although I thought it, and although 'tis true
　　　　　　That thought is but the prelude to the deed:
　　　　　　Thought is not in my power, but action is:
　　　　　　I will not move my foot to follow thee.

DEMON　　　But a far mightier wisdom than thine own
　　　　　　Exerts itself within thee . . . how will thou then
　　　　　　Resist, Justina?

JUSTINA　　　　　　　　　　　　By my free will.

DEMON　　　　　　　　　　　　　　　　　I
　　　　　　Must force thy will.

JUSTINA　　　　　　　　　　It is invincible;
　　　　　　It were not free if thou hadst power upon it.
　　　　　[*The Demon draws, but cannot move her.*]　　　(III, vi)[13]

Then Cipriano tries to summon Justina to him by his magic. Her figure appears, but when he tries to embrace it her veil falls and reveals—a skeleton. Cipriano questions the Demon about the failure of his magic; the Demon admits that it is because Justina is preserved by a higher Power. Cipriano begins to understand; he sees that this Power must correspond to the one God for whom he had argued at the beginning, and when told that it is the Christian God, determines to follow Him. The Demon tries now to trump him with his blood pact. But Cipriano argues that since the Demon has not fulfilled his condition in the pact—to bring Justina into his arms—he is free; and in any case, cannot the God who delivered Justina also deliver him?

We are now transported to the Governor's palace, where we learn that the Decian persecutions have begun. Justina is arrested and condemned as a Christian. Cipriano now arrives and declares himself a Christian. He and Justina have a brief and moving scene together. He is doubtful of his chances of salvation (though he has had himself baptized on his way to the palace), but she assures him of God's mercy. They are condemned together, and her closing words to him are:

JUSTINA   I told you that I would not love you until death,
           And since we are now to die together, Ciprian,
           See—I have kept my promise.   (III, xxv)

As they are beheaded there is an earthquake, and the Demon appears riding on a dragon to announce—reluctantly, but compelled by God to do so—that Cipriano has cancelled the blood with which he signed the devilish bond by the blood he has shed as a martyr (a fine touch, this), and that he and Justina have now gone to a better world. And the play ends with the thought that this last work of *el mágico prodigioso* is the magic of heaven.

★

La Vida es Sueño is an earlier play and less continuously concerned with Christian themes. The main theme, however, is this: how far can man control or over-ride his fate? With a subsidiary motif, that life is, after all, but a dream compared with the greater reality of eternity.[14] Basilio, King of Poland, has been warned by casting his son's horoscope that his son and heir, Segismundo, will grow up a brutal tyrant and will end by subjecting his own father, Basilio himself, to his will. Basilio therefore adopts the strange expedient of having Segismundo brought up in a lonely cell in the mountains, with a warden, Clotaldo, to keep him out of harm's way. But when the play opens we find Basilio doubtful whether he was right. True, he had thereby protected his country from the possibility of being subjected to a tyrant. But

> There is no law that says that we do right,
> In order to prevent a tyrant and oppressor,[15]
> Ourselves to tyrannize and oppress. . . .   (I, vi)

Moreover, should he, he asks himself, ever have submitted himself to the tyranny of a horoscope? Though Segismundo's fate is declared to be that of a wicked despot, might he not resist his fate?

> For the most evil destiny, the most powerful
> Inclination, the most implacable star,
> Can only sway the will, but cannot force it.   (*Ibid*)

So he resolves to give his son after all a chance to prove his power over destiny. Yet what if the experiment ends in disaster? Segismundo will then have to be forcibly returned to his mountain fastness; and will not this be more bitter for him than never having been given a chance at all? Basilio therefore resolves on an even stranger ruse than the first. Clotaldo is to drug Segismundo, then bring him to the palace, where, at first, while he is shown the trappings of royalty and paid the respect due to an heir, he will think he is dreaming it all.

> And if he did so understand, Clotaldo,
> He would do well, for in this world
> All those who live are dreaming,   (II, i)

Basilio remarks inconsequently. If the oracle wins, and Segismundo does turn out the predicted tyrant, then he can be transported swiftly back and 'wake up' in his cell, and can think that it was all a dream.

Thus it happens. Segismundo is successfully conveyed to the palace; he soon shows his mettle, threatens a valet, and later throws him over the balcony, loses his temper all around, and threatens his father. However, before the King has him forcibly returned to his cell, he falls in love with a lady, Rosaura. When he ' wakes up ', back in his cell, he thinks it may have all been a dream—except for this love for Rosaura, which remains and which is too vivid to have been dreamed. And now there is a further hitch in Basilio's plans; for a great part of the people and army of Poland, learning that there is a rightful heir, come to release Segismundo, in order to put him on the throne. The Prince accepts their fealty, and even if this should turn out but another bad dream, decides nevertheless to advance against his father. But his experiences have taught him that, indeed, life is but a dream, and therefore must be conducted with prudence, since one day we shall ' awake '.

> SEGISMUNDO . . . Since life so quickly closes,
>   Let us, even though this as false is,
>   Dream once more—this not forgotten,

> That we must at fittest hour
> Wake again, this brief joy over;
> For that known, the undeception
> Will not prove so sad nor costly.
> Then, promising only this,
> That this power, if true, belongeth
> Not to us, but merely lent is,
> To return unto its Owner,
> Let us venture upon all. . . .   (III, iii)[16]

Armed with this pious reservation, Segismundo now manages to take his passions in hand. He spares his victims, refuses retribution even where there is ample provocation. And when his father, fulfilling the prediction, throws himself at his son's feet, the Prince raises him up and now kneels before him in turn. Thanks to his newly acquired wisdom and self-mastery, he surrenders his loved one, Rosaura, to Astolfo, in order to right her honour, and accepts the hand of Estrella, and the play ends happily:

BASILIO   Your wisdom, son, is our astonishment. . . .

SEGISMUNDO   What is there here that can astonish you?
> A dream has been my teacher, and I fear
> E'en yet, and tremble, lest I must awake
> To find myself once more in narrow cell.
> And even if that should not come about,
> To dream it were enough to mend my ways:
> For I have learned by this that human joys
> At length will pass and vanish like a dream;
> And now [turning to audience] I want to use it well,
>   so long
> As it may last—in asking pardon for our faults,
> For 'tis a mark of noble souls to pardon them.
>   (III, xiv)

A summary like this cannot convey the effectiveness of much in the play, or its power to suspend our disbelief in the curious turns of the plot. The soliloquies, especially Segismundo's first soliloquy in prison, asking why he should have been denied the freedom given to all the lesser creatures of the earth, are admirable products of a romantic imagination combined with a reasoned syllogistic argument. And the unseen horoscope,

dominating the movement of events and waging its battle with
the human freedom to resist them, is a truly dramatic *tour de
force*. As in *El Mágico Prodigioso*, whatever qualifications we
may have later to add, we cannot refuse to salute this play as
a genuine, and unexpected, achievement.

★

The other pieces, the *autos sacramentales*, which should directly
concern us, must have briefer treatment, partly because they
are so numerous, and so many of them of such equivalent value,
that they would need a book to themselves[17]; and still more
because they are almost inaccessible in translation. But we
must glance at one or two to get their measure. We have said
that Calderón in his declining years devoted himself almost
exclusively to producing these short pieces, two a year, for royal
festivals and Corpus Christi (he wrote about seventy). They had
to be relatively simple, being performed in the open air on
moveable carts (though these were able to provide quite
complex staging),[18] and they had to give religious instruction.
There were *autos* based on the Bible; *autos* based on history or
lives of the saints; and *autos* allegorically representing Catholic
dogma—especially of the Blessed Sacrament—or illustrating
human life, sin and destiny. This might seem terribly to limit a
dramatist, but in fact it is astonishing what variety as well as
vigour he is able to achieve within these bounds.

He has, for instance, an *auto* with the same title as the play
we have just discussed, *La Vida es Sueño* (1673), which uses the
theme of the Man sleeping in the cave to even greater effect.
The four Elements are disputing for a crown of laurel: the
Trinity, under the forms of Power, Wisdom and Love, tell
them, the Elements, that they must work together, according
to the law of the first Creation. But there is a warning that the
second Creation will be rebellious; for the Shadow, with his
henchman, the Prince of Darkness, is abroad. Man is then
revealed, clad in skins, and comes forth from his cave-prison.
Man is, like Segismundo, transported to Paradise; but here he
begins to show pride and disobedience, and Shadow and the
Prince of Darkness drug him so that they may make Man eat
and fall. Man eats the drug—which is an apple—and the Fall
results; Man is put back in his cave-prison. But at length he

determines to seek the lost Paradise, and calls on Light to guide him. Instead of Light comes Shadow, who says she is Sin and will go with Man wherever he goes. Wisdom, however, comes to his rescue, takes off Man's fetters and puts them on Himself. Lucifer and Shadow then slay Wisdom; but an earthquake throws them to the ground, and Wisdom is found embracing a Cross. Man then accepts his Redemption, and—taking up the Segismundo theme again—cries, " If this be sleep, may I sleep never to wake again". Power (God the Father) gives him a final warning:

> And since this life of thine throughout is dream,
> For in the last result is life a dream,
> Lose not again a good so wholly precious:
> For if thou dost, mayhap thou'lt find thyself
> Again imprisoned in a straiter cell,
> If in the final sleep, the lethal dream,
> Thou should'st awake contaminate with sin.[19]

In spite of the abstractions there is real vividness and theatrical power in the dramatic conflicts of this *auto*.

Another rich and ingenious *auto* is that based on the book of Daniel, *La Cena del Rey Baltasar*. Instead of simply reproducing the Biblical story, he sets it within a wider allegorical frame. Daniel is discovered arguing with *Pensiamento*, Human Thought, as to the powers of the mind. Belshazzar has just espoused Idolatry (bigamously, since he is already married to Vanity!): but Daniel withstands the King's threats with the continually repeated refrain, " the hand of God". Death comes to claim Belshazzar's soul, and puts the King to sleep (and when he sleeps, *Pensiamento* must sleep too); but Daniel stays Death's hand until the King's time has come. The King wakes and recounts his dream, but, still unrepentant, commits blasphemy by drinking a sacramental toast to Moloch. The writing then appears on the wall, and only Daniel, representing not *Pensiamento* but the Wisdom of God, can interpret it. Death can now step in, and the King's career is ended. But the play ends with Daniel pointing forward to the true ' toast ', the true Feast of Bread and Wine in the Holy Sacrament. By moving thus on three planes at once—the ' naturalistic ' of the Bible story, the allegorical of the abstract characters, and the theological of Christian dogma—the play achieves a real depth and universality.[20]

Finally we must mention the most famous, the Spanish ' Everyman '—*El Gran Teatro del Mundo.* The whole play is a sort of extended metaphor, ' All the World's a Stage ', and it opens with the Author, who is, of course, God Himself, assigning their parts to various characters. Some complain that theirs are not important enough, but the Author replies:

> AUTHOR   In this play you act, he will
> As securely win my praise
> Who the part of beggar plays
> With true diligence and skill
> As who may the king's fulfil.
> Act your best, for God is God.[21]

And when they complain that their parts are not written out for them and so cannot be rehearsed, he replies that life cannot be made up and learned by heart and rehearsed beforehand. The World provides them with wardrobe and properties. The Author, who is now seen to be God, shows that the stage is bounded by two doors at the wings, a Cradle and a Tomb. Then the play within the play begins. The characters, Beauty, Discretion, the Beggar, the Rich Man, the Farmer, the King, etc., come in through the Cradle door. Some of them claim permanence, but each finds the Tomb door opening for him sooner or later. Beauty especially tries to remain, but a Voice sings:

> VOICE   Mortal flower in body thou,
> Though eternal in the soul.

(This is Trench's version. But he has inverted the more effective original—

> Que en el Alma eres eterna,
> y en el cuerpo mortal flor—

which might be translated

> Though in soul thou art eternal
> Mortal bloom in body thou.)

Then comes the judgment day, when the Author examines how they have played their parts. The World comes to claim back

the wardrobe and properties he has lent to the characters; their
time on earth is concluded. The Beggar, who has had least to
return, is able to sum up the theme.

> BEGGAR   Author of the earth and heaven,
> All thy company the players,
> Who that briefest comedy
> Played of human life so lately,
> Are arrived, of that thy promise
> Mindful, of that noble banquet.
> Let the curtains be drawn back,
> And thy glorious seat unveiled.

And so the play ends with the vision of God.

This brief account of one or two only of the *autos* is pitifully
inadequate, not least in that it fails to convey either the humour
or the extraordinary versatility of the author, playing such
extended and ingenious variations upon a few so simple themes.
It is surprising that with the rebirth of ' religious drama ', professional and amateur, from the 1930s onwards, no one has
been moved to attempt fresh translations and productions of
these brilliant brief plays. The experts assure us that some of
Calderón's most melodic and most vivid poetry has been
poured into them; and it is impossible but that some of this
should survive even in English and on a contemporary stage.

I V

Calderón has been frequently described as the poet of
certainty. He knows what he believes and exactly how to
express it. Perhaps one reason for his greatness is his combination of romantic, sometimes even wildly romantic, imagination
with the intellectual discipline and guidance of a clear theological belief. We are never left floundering for a meaning, and we
always have the impression that Calderón can not only answer
all the problems set within his plays, but could answer any
others we cared to put to him.

And yet it is in one sense this very certainty that limits him.
The certainty that ' beauty vanishes ', that the world passeth
away, that heaven is more real than earth, a waking compared

with a dreaming state—this certainly led him, first to confine himself more and more to directly religious, homiletic drama; and then, even within that drama, to subordinate life to immortality. Beauty, in *El Gran Teatro del Mundo*, complains pathetically that:

> It is a pitiful song that sings the dirge
> " Let beauty die ". No, no, let it not die,
> But blossom again into its primal bloom!
> And yet, alas, there is no budding rose
> That opens its petals, white or red, to the kiss
> Of the amorous sun, or to the flattering day—
> Which does not droop. Never a flower
> Can nestle back into its green bud again.
> Yet—what matter if these hints of dawn,
> These flowers, fade in the heat of the sun's embrace?
> Who would compare *me* to an ephemeral bloom
> Where death comes treading close upon life's heels?
> Nay—a flower of fadeless life am I:
> The sun who saw my birth shall never see
> My dying. Eternal, how can I ever die?—
> Say, Voice!

VOICE (*relentlessly*)   Though in soul thou art eternal,
                         Mortal bloom in body thou!

But the upshot of this platonic conclusion might well be Plato's own, that since the body is but a ' tomb ' there is no place for Beauty here.[22]

The good Archbishop Trench ascribes Calderón's limitation to his ' Romanism ', and begs some vast questions in so doing.

> A thoughtful man must, I think, be often deeply struck with the immeasurable advantage for being the poet of all humanity, of all ages and all people, which Shakespeare possessed in being a Protestant. At the first blush of the matter there is a temptation to conclude otherwise; to think of him as at a disadvantage, shut out, as he thus was, from the rich mythology, the gorgeous symbolism, the manifold legend, and from many other sources of interest which a poet of the Roman Catholic Church would command. . . . But if poetry be anything but a brain-sick dream, to bewail the vanishing of ought which, even while

we bewail, we [we Protestants] know to have been wholly
or partially untrue, is contradictory and idle. Are we not
bound to believe . . . that the truest will in the end be the
most beautiful and therefore the most poetical of all?[23]

He then praises the " stronger thinking and more earnest
doing " which is, he deems, characteristic of the Protestant
North, and which helps to set Shakespeare above all others;
but allows that Calderón is as great as any of the other Eliza-
bethans—and indeed, greater in one respect, " the entire
absence of grossness, of indelicacy, of *double entendre*, from his
plays ". Quite apart from the question whether Shakespeare
was a ' Protestant ', still more whether he was shut out from
any mythology, symbolism or legend he cared to use, this mode
of judgment reads oddly today. Yet if we could change
Trench's contrast between Protestant and Roman Catholic,
and substitute one between Catholic and Ultramontane (or
perhaps ' Seventeenth-century Spanish Jesuit '), there might
be some truth salvaged from the Archbishop's statement.
There is, indeed, an antinomian trend and a clericalist temper
in Calderón which does sometimes seem to us to prevent his
work from reaching a fully Catholic view of the world and its
destiny.

Anyway, the uncertainty about the real value of the world
and of beauty within it (which we have called platonic, but
which Calderón actually derives more directly from Seneca),[24]
certainly has the effect of complicating and perhaps even of
confusing the great play which takes this precisely as its theme,
La Vida es Sueño. Mr. Brenan goes so far as to say that " as an
allegorical drama, it is a muddle". First he complains that
" in the first act we naturally take [Segismundo] to represent
Man, condemned to unhappiness through no fault of his own:
we wonder whether the king, his father, is not God and the
astrologer's prediction the curse of original sin. The third act
undeceives us. Segismundo's pride, we learn here, is the result
of bad education, the king has been much to blame and the
astrologer's prediction is falsified: we return with a jar to the
plane of reality."[25] This, however, seems to me over-subtle,
and indeed to be a reading back into the earlier *comedia* of
allegorical themes only developed in the later *auto* of the same

name.[26] And in any case, the astrologer's prediction is wholly fulfilled; is not the whole point that the destiny is fulfilled (for Basilio does have to kneel at his son Segismundo's feet, as predicted) but that man can nevertheless use it, co-operate with it, so to speak, for good ends?

Mr. Brenan's second complaint is that " the reason Segismundo gives for dominating his evil impulses does not make sense, for if life is really a dream, then surely it is outside the dreamer's control, and the acts he performs in it have no moral consequences." There is a real difficulty here; but it is surely not the *automatism* of dreams so much as the unreality of dreams (representing, that is, the unreality of worldly values) that Calderón is stressing. It is not that man cannot choose, and so resist evil, in his dreaming; it is that if life is as unreal as a dream there does not seem much point in choosing or resisting. And there is no doubt that Segismundo's closing speech falls flat, dramatically, because it conveys a sense of a rather limp, almost grudging concession to life—as something to be ultimately despised but meanwhile to be tolerantly humoured with virtuous acts.

The word *dramatically* in the last sentence should be stressed, for this must be our criterion. It is not in the least axiomatic that the inclusion or employment of theological themes in a play necessarily and always leads to undramatic results. We have seen that the theological discussion between Cipriano and the Demon in *El Mágico Prodigioso* makes ' good theatre '. As a very different but equally interesting example of the same, we might cite a comic scene from one of Lope de Vega's plays, *Fuente Ovejuna*. There is a discussion on foot between three peasants, Frondoso and Barrildo against Mengo. Mengo has been maintaining that there is no such thing as love.

> MENGO   I say little, not being able to read, though I could learn, but if the elements make the world and our bodies are made of the elements which war against each other unceasingly, causing anger and discord, then where is love?
>
> BARRILDO   Mengo, the world is love, here and hereafter, not discord. Harmony is love. Love is a reaching out.

MENGO A pulling in, according to nature, which governs
all things through the resemblances that are.
Love is looking to its own, it's preservation. I
raise my hand to my face to prevent the blow,
I move my feet to remove them from danger
to my body, my eye-lids close to shield my
sight through the attraction of a mutual love.

PASCUALA (*a girl*) He admits it's love, so what then?
There's an end.

MENGO We love ourselves, no one else, that's flat.

PASCUALA Mengo, what a lie! And God forgive me.
The love a man bears for a woman, or a beast
for its mate, is a fierce, consuming passion.

MENGO Self-love, interest, not pure love. What is love? . . .

BARRILDO One day the priest preached in the village about
a man named Plato who had taught men how
to love, but what Plato loved, he said, was the
soul and the virtue that was hidden in it.
(I, ii)[27]

(This, which in the context of the whole play is much more
effective than it sounds in extract, comes straight out of St.
Thomas Aquinas.) But the weaknesses of the endings in
Calderón's plays are dramatic weaknesses which grow out of
theological ones. We have noticed already that in some of his
secular plays, notably *El Médico de su Honra* and *El Alcalde de
Zalamea* (and we might have added *A Secreto Agravia Secreto
Vengenza*, where the hero avenges himself on his wife's lover and
his wife by secret murder, but when the King in the last few
lines of the play discovers the secret he quite approves—" What
else could a man of honour do? "), what might have been
genuine tragedy is spoilt in the end by a bathetic applause for
violent deeds; as if *Othello* had ended, not with Othello's suicide,
but with a general approval and his promotion to be a field-
marshal. But the best example of this kind of bathos is provided by the ending of *El Mágico Prodigioso*, otherwise a great
play of Christian martyrdom. For consider Cipriano's great
speech when he declares himself a Christian.

CIPRIANO   It is the mighty God of the Christians that now
Openly I confess. For, although it is true
That I am now enslaved to Hell, and indeed
With my own blood I signed the covenant,
With my own blood I too will erase it
By a martyrdom for which I long . . .
                    Why then do you wait?
Let the executioner come, let him strike and sever
My head from my body—or test my endurance
With horrible torture. See, I am here and ready
To suffer a thousand deaths, since at last I believe
That without the great God whom I seek, whom I
        praise and adore,
All human glory is nothing but dust and vapour,
Ashes and wind.   (III, xxi)

It is noble, it is fine; but it is a little truculent. And his last
words, when Justina bids him show no weakness on the
scaffold, are in the same vein.

CIPRIANO   Faith have I, and ardour and courage. If I must pay
My life as a ransom for slavery—look you: he
Who gave up his life to the Demon for your sake,
What could he not do when he gives up his body
For God?   (III, xxv)

The end is determined—what else *can* happen? He has the
initiative, and, in effect, commands his own death. And the
declaration by the Demon at the end, that he and Justina are
enskied, announces a foregone conclusion. In other words,
this play, like the secular plays mentioned above, is not a
tragedy. The Christian hero has the card of immortality and
beatitude with which he can trump the last tricks of his
opponents, Paganism and Death. Heads may be severed from
bodies, but there is no suffering: what seems to be agony is
unreal because it is willed, not undergone—the victim remains
in control.

    There are those who will say that this is the inescapable lot
of the Christian writer; that belief in eternal life always must
rule out tragedy, and that that is why there may be Christian
comedy or Christian romance, but no Christian tragedy.[28] (Is
Murder in the Cathedral a tragedy? Is it not, strictly, a comedy
like *The Cocktail Party*?) We have seen, in fact, this very question

raised in the last chapter, in connection with the ' assimilation '
of the Christian devil to pagan themes. There it was suggested
that the ' pity ' we feel for the damned (Faust, Macbeth, as
well as the Devil) is not ' theologically justifiable '. Even
stated in these terms, this is, I think, an over-simplification.
For one thing, there has been a consistent—*marginal*, but never,
so far as I know, formally condemned—theological and
devotional tradition, starting from Origen, which has hoped
and prayed for the ultimate ' salvability ' of the devil! And
even if this were ruled out, it is important to notice that it is
not simply the eternal irrevocability of damnation beyond that
makes for tragedy, but the reality of damnation *quoad nos*. That
is, it is sufficient for us to know that Iago, Macbeth, Faust,
leave our stage for an infernal destination, to give us a tragic
situation (and even that requires qualification); what modification could be made ' off-stage ', so to speak, to that sentence is
not the play's concern—any more than it is the play's concern
to know, for example, how many children Miranda will have
or whether any later sorrows will come to disturb the marital
happiness of Hermione. And the view that the doctrine of
eternal life must always rule out tragedy (like the view, which
we shall examine in our last chapter, that the Christian can
only be a ' pilgrim ', never an ' explorer ') is one which, I
believe, misconceives the Christian doctrine of creation.
Briefly: only in a world where real tragedy is possible is redemption also possible. Perhaps the reverse is also true: only
in a world where redemption—and therefore damnation too—
is possible, is tragedy also possible. Thus it is not true that there
can be no genuine Christian tragic drama (we would prefer to
say, no genuine tragic drama within and compatible with a
Christian metaphysic); on the contrary, all genuine tragic
drama is material for Christian understanding. And to apply
this principle to Calderón: the final weakness of even his
greatest work is that he has not understood the genuine independence and validity of creaturehood.[29] Faith has tended
to eliminate sympathy, and instead of illuminating unbelief
it has had the effect of erasing it.

MANZONI'S *I PROMESSI SPOSI*, OR THE QUIESCENCE OF BELIEF

I

THE FACT that we have had to wait so many years in this country for a reprint[1] of Manzoni's great novel suggests a neglect such as must be a serious indictment of critical taste. In the last century it was a favourite in many quarters, and those not the least discerning. At Hursley Vicarage John Keble's little circle read books to each other, often at meals, and talked of books. "The authors most constantly read and beloved", says Miss Charlotte M. Yonge, one of the circle, "were, it seems to me, Dante, Spenser, Wordsworth, Scott and Manzoni."[2] Miss Yonge herself, we are told, translated the whole of it for her father, William Yonge.[3] Gladstone paid a visit to Manzoni in 1838. "He was a most interesting man, but was regarded, as I found, among the more fashionable priests in Milan as a *bacchetone* (hypocrite). In his own way he was, I think, a liberal and a nationalist, nor was alliance of such politics with strong religious convictions uncommon among the more eminent Italians of those days."[4] Later, however, Gladstone overcame any scruples he may have combined with his admiration, and paid him the tribute of translating his *Ode on the Death of Napoleon*.[5] Newman also tried to visit him in 1846, but was disappointed to find him out.[6] Scott is said to have pronounced Manzoni's novel "the best ever written".[7] Goethe's verdict is even more categorical. Manzoni, after an early addiction to classicism, threw himself wholly, both in his verse and his plays, into the romantic movement, and Goethe defended him from severe criticism by the *Quarterly Review*. But the novel, though no doubt showing strong traces of 'gothic' influence, is so strongly Christian and, indeed, Catholic (yet not obtrusively so) that it is surprising perhaps to find Goethe so enthusiastic.

I must announce to you [he said to Eckermann in 1827] that Manzoni's novel soars far above all that we know of the kind. I need say to you nothing more, except that the interior life—all that comes from the soul of the poet, is absolutely perfect; and that the outward—the delineation of localities, and the like, is no way inferior. That is saying something. The impression in reading is such, that we are constantly passing from emotion to admiration, and again from admiration to emotion; so that we are always subject to one of those great influences; higher than this, I think, one cannot go. In this novel we have first seen what Manzoni is. Here his perfect interior is exhibited, which he had no opportunity to display in his dramatic works. I will now read the best novel by Sir Walter Scott—perhaps *Waverley*, which I do not yet know—and I shall see how Manzoni will come out in comparison with this great English writer. . . . He has sentiment but is perfectly free from sentimentality; his feeling for every situation is manly and genuine. . . . Manzoni makes use of [the feeling of] alarm with wonderful felicity, by resolving it into emotion, and thus leading us to admiration. . . . There are four things which have contributed especially to the excellence of Manzoni's works. First, he is an excellent historian, and consequently gives his inventions a depth and dignity which raise them far above what are commonly called novels. Secondly, the Catholic religion is favourable to him giving him many poetical relations which he could not have had as a Protestant. Thirdly, it is to the advantage of the book that the author has suffered much in revolutionary collisions, which, if they did not affect him, have wounded his friends, and sometimes ruined them. Fourthly, it is in favour of the novel that the scene is laid in the charming country near Lake Como, which has been stamped on the poet's mind, from youth upwards, and which he therefore knows by heart. Hence arises also that distinguishing merit of the work—its distinctness and wonderful accuracy in describing localities.[8]

(I give the passage thus at some length, since it is apparently not very well known.) Goethe's only criticism of the novel is that it " suffers from too great a load of history ", and spends too long on descriptions of war, pestilence and famine, which are " repulsive ". It is possible to disagree with this criticism and yet to find Goethe's general verdict on Manzoni very perceptive. To come back to England: George Eliot, like Charlotte Yonge, read the novel aloud—it would have been interesting to have her opinion of it. " Aloud I have read Bright's speeches, and *I Promessi Sposi.*"[9]   (Strange combination!) Yet when we move into this century we find the novel comparatively unknown, until the last year or two, or if known, unappreciated.   Kathleen Mansfield read it and was bored; and it was, surprisingly enough (or not so surprising, in view of his frequently acute critical insight), D. H. Lawrence who defended it as a great work.[10] Finally, let us return to the nineteenth century for another tribute from an unexpected quarter.   On his Italian tour in 1856 Thomas Babington Macaulay noted: " I have finished Manzoni's novel, not without tears.   The scene between the Archbishop and Don Abbondio is one of the noblest I know.   The parting between the lovers and Father Cristoforo is most touching.   If the Church of Rome really were what Manzoni represents her to be I should be tempted to follow Newman's example."[11]

A novel that could evoke praise from such varied quarters cannot be negligible.

II

Alessandro Francesco Tommaso Antonio Manzoni was born in Milan on 7 March, 1785.   His father was a nobleman, and his mother was the daughter of a social historian and economist whose talent she had inherited.   The couple did not get on well together, and in the end Alessandro's mother went to live near Paris and resumed her maiden name.   As a result Alessandro himself was boarded out in a farmhouse in the hills near Como, and his foster-mother was a peasant with a lively gift of story-telling.   This no doubt helped to stock Alessandro's mind with rich folk-lore which he later was able to draw upon. As a schoolboy and student he was considered dull and preferred life and peasant pastimes in the country.   But he began to write poetry, and one of his early sonnets (which appeared in translation in *The Dublin Review* for October, 1882) showed promise. When his father died in 1805 he went for a time to live with his mother in France, and met some of the literary circle there. He returned to the neighbourhood of Bergamo in 1808 and there fell in love with Henriette Louise Blondel, daughter of a Genevese banker. They married in 1809, and Alessandro's mother, who was then anti-Catholic, was delighted, for the bride was a Protestant, and Alessandro himself had given up the Catholic faith, so that there was every likelihood that he would not return to it. But the young woman met some ardent Catholics in Paris who converted her; and bit by bit she influenced her husband to return to his old faith. Finally he gave way completely, and from then on became a keen champion of the Catholic cause—even winning his mother back to it.

He and his wife—and their now growing family—returned to live permanently in Italy. He started writing hymns (*Inni Sacri*, 1810) and also tragedies. He was nearly involved in difficulties when he supported the ardent desires for Italian liberation in 1821; he composed a patriotic ode, which could not be published till 1848, and himself took part in some preliminary stages of the abortive attempt at revolution in the early part of 1821. He also wrote the ode which Gladstone translated, on the death of Napoleon (*Il Cinque Maggio*), composed in the brief space of forty-eight hours.

But meanwhile he had embarked on his greatest work, *I Promessi Sposi*. It was partly based on the story of Bernardino Visconti in Ripamonte's *Storia Milanese*; but still more on a careful study of the social conditions of the people of Lombardy in the seventeenth century. It was begun on 24 April, 1821, and a rough copy was ready on 23 September, 1823. After criticism by friends, the first volume came out in 1825, and the second and third in 1826 and 1827. After that he wrote nothing, but spent much time revising the novel, in particular its style. The excessive regionalism of the Italian language at the time seemed to him to cry out for some kind of standardization; and he finally fixed on the Tuscan dialect as the nearest to a norm—for classical Italian was an academic language by then, and of no use for his purpose. The result in the long run was that Manzoni's style became the standard or fountain-spring of modern Italian literary writing. (Hence the excessive use of his great novel as a textbook for school work, and its neglect as a work of creative art.)

Meanwhile in his country retreat Manzoni occupied himself with rural pursuits—the improved breeding of silkworms, the grafting of olive and mulberry trees, and so forth. He endured many tragedies in the remainder of his life—the death of his wife, and later of his second wife, the death of all but two of his nine children. In 1859 he was delighted to be able to become a citizen of the new Italian kingdom, and he was appointed by the new Government President of the Royal Lombard Institution of Science and Arts, with a pension attached. He was nominated a Senator, and went to Turin to attend the first parliament; when he appeared leaning on the arm of Cavour, he was greeted with much enthusiasm. But he still spent most of his time in retirement. The death of his eldest son, Luigi, in 1872 was a terrible shock to him. He had already been weakened by a fall while coming out of church the previous winter, and now he became a pathetic figure, wandering through his house, calling for his son, talking to him; and finally he died on Ascension Day, 22 May, 1873. His funeral was almost a national occasion, attended by royal princes and delegations from Italian municipalities: and a now famous piece of music was composed for the occasion—the *Requiem* by his friend and admirer, Verdi.[12]

III

What is the novel ' about '? The plot is too intricate and extended for anything but the briefest of summaries. In its basic elements it is simple enough. A young man, Renzo, and a girl, Lucia, are betrothed; but their marriage is prevented by the jealousy of a local *bravo*, Don Rodrigo. They have to separate for a time, and the separation is prolonged by the coming of famine, food riots, war, enemy occupation, and finally—worst of all—the plague; in the end, however, they find each other; their persecutor, Don Rodrigo, has died—penitent—of the plague, and Don Rodrigo's still more powerful superior, ' the Unnamed ', has been converted from his evil life by the visit of a saintly bishop, Cardinal Borromeo; and so the couple are able at last to marry and settle down in reasonable comfort and great happiness.

But set in this simple frame there is a proliferation of other themes. There is a wonderfully complete picture of the social conditions of the time—the seventeenth century in Italy round about Milan and Bergamo. There are vivid descriptions of mass-movements and mass-tragedies; and at the same time there are delicate satirical and affectionate portraits of individuals, great and small. The plot, with its ramifications, and also its territorial divagations, as the unhappy couple move farther and farther away from each other and have to take refuge first in one spot and then another, became so complicated that it needed the most masterly handling. The author himself says that he feels like a child trying to cover a drove of little Indian pigs: " I have often watched a boy (a dear little lad, almost too high-spirited really, but showing every sign of growing up to be a decent citizen one day) busily driving his herd of Indian pigs into their pen towards evening, after letting them run around freely all day in a little orchard. He would try to get them all into the pen together, but it was waste labour. One would strike off to the right, and while the little drover was running to bring him back into the herd, another, or two, or three, would start off to the left, in every direction. . . . A similar game we are obliged to play with our characters " (p. 208).[13]

Yet he contrives to steer the fractious team with remarkable success. There are irrelevant episodes, and sections may seem a little top-heavy. The historical accounts of which Goethe, as we have seen, complained might seem to be cases in point. And yet they are so graphically presented that we would not be without them; and, more important, they lend a perspective depth to the novel which is one of its great qualities.

For it is clear that we are not being presented merely with a story of a few trivial incidents in the lives of insignificant and fictitious characters; nor, again, with a mere ' slice of history '. Manzoni is asking several fundamental questions: What can the simple, honest peasant do against the plots and resources of the powerful—of which not merely Don Rodrigo and his *brawes* are the symbol, but still more the tyrannical despots like ' the Unnamed '? What, again, can the Church do in the midst of tyranny, when she is bound to accept some degree of material provision and privileged position? How is it that the comparatively innocent may, through the slightest errors (for Lucia's mother, Agnese, and Renzo himself, had not behaved quite scrupulously when they first tried to arrange the latter's marriage with Lucia), be landed in disproportionate suffering? And, finally, behind all that, how can man meet the great natural afflictions, pestilence, famine, death?

The answers are not final or invariable. Yet there is, he seems to be saying, a moat of innocence which surrounds and protects the single-minded; and even the greatest and most villainous may have a weak point in their ramparts through which the besieging love of God may break. The terrifying figure of ' the Unnamed ', the tyrant in his castle, is softened and reduced to a shifty, sleepless night by the memory of the girl, Lucia, weeping in a huddle in the corner of a room; and this is the prelude to the great scene where he presents himself to the saintly Cardinal Federigo Borromeo and is converted. Again, the Church may have to compromise. The Capuchin friar, Father Christoforo, took pity on the unfortunate couple, Renzo and Lucia, and aided them in every way. Don Rodrigo complained of this interfering priest, and the Provincial of the Capuchins agreed to transfer Father Christoforo to another religious house at some distance away, where he could no longer help them; nor does Manzoni blame the Provincial for this, since the good friar may indeed have exceeded the bounds of religious precaution in thus shielding Lucia and Renzo. Yet at the same time the Church may not compromise through fear for her human safety. The parish priest, the fussy, terrified Don Abbondio, is taken as the sample of this. He had started the whole tragedy by refusing to marry Renzo to Lucia merely because he had been threatened by Don Rodrigo with dire punishment if he did. After the conversion of ' the Unnamed ' the Cardinal hears about the cowardice of Don Abbondio, and the contrast between the Cardinal's gentle and delicate hand-ling of the tyrant, and his severity, indeed anger, with the pettiness of the parish priest is given to the reader in a very uncompromising and significant lecture on the Church's call to heroism.

In the midst of suffering, too, Manzoni wishes to say, there can be seen glimpses of triumphant sacrifice. Father Christoforo's last words to Renzo and Lucia, when he knows that the plague is on him—he has been devotedly nursing and caring for the sick, and has now fallen victim himself—are tragic, perhaps, but not sorrowful: " It is now a long time ago since I besought of the Lord a very great mercy, that I might end my days in the service of my fellow-creatures. If He now vouchsafes to grant it me, I would wish all those who have any love for me, to assist me in praising Him " (p. 685).

Thus man can best meet life without too many pretensions. If he claims and demands absolute justice he will become a jealous and vengeful tyrant. When, for instance, Renzo, searching for his beloved among the victims of the plague, hears the rumour that she, Lucia, has contracted it too, his self-control breaks down for the first time in the book. He becomes wild with rage and despair, and vows that if he cannot find her he will instead hunt down the hated rival, Don Rodrigo. He is rash enough to say this to Father Christoforo, who is himself by now exhausted with nursing.

" If I find him," went on Renzo, furious with rage— " if the plague has not already meted out justice . . . The time is past when a coward surrounded by his bravoes could drive people to despair and get off free; the time has come when men must confront each other face to face; and . . . I'll minister my own justice, that I will! "

" Miserable wretch! " cried Father Christoforo, in a voice which had recovered all its former strength and resonance. " Miserable wretch! " And his head that had sunk into his chest now became erect again, his cheeks flushed with their former life, and the gleam in his eye was terrible. " Look, miserable wretch! " and with one hand he seized Renzo's arm and shook it fiercely, while with the other he swept round to cover all he could of the ghastly scene around. " Look and see who is the One who punishes. The One who judges and is not judged Himself. The One who chastises and who forgives. But you, worm of the earth, you want to minister justice, do you? Do you know what justice is? . . ."

As he said this, he flung Renzo's arm from him and began moving towards a hut full of sick people.

"Father!" said Renzo, following him with a look of supplication. "Do you want to send me away like this?"

"What!" said the Capuchin, his voice still as severe as ever. "Do you expect me to take time away from these afflicted people, people who are waiting for me to talk to them of God's forgiveness, to listen to your words of anger, your plans for vengeance? ..." (p. 640).

And Manzoni will not allow us to take refuge in excuses even when they are three-parts reasonable. At one point in her flight Lucia is boarded at a priory where there is a nun, Gertrude, 'the Signora', who because of her noble birth has a position of privilege (an abuse of the conventual life which was only too frequent in those days). This Gertrude, forced into the convent by her parents, has had an unhappy history; but she makes up for it, unfortunately, by wielding unchallenged authority over the priory, prioress and all. She is ill-tempered and resentful—and not unreasonably so. Yet even she, says Manzoni, might have surmounted this. For "it is one of the peculiar and incommunicable properties of the Christian religion, that she can afford guidance and repose to all who, under whatever circumstances . . . have recourse to her. . . . She teaches how to continue with discretion what is thoughtlessly undertaken; she inclines the mind to cleave steadfastly to what was imposed upon it by authority. . . . Here is a path so constructed that, let a man approach it by what labyrinth or precipice he may, he sets himself from that moment, to walk in it with security and readiness, and at once begins to draw towards a joyful end" (p. 188).

And this is not just a devotional platitude, thrown in for padding. It is exemplified time and again in the action of the novel itself. Is there not, indeed, a quiet note of triumph in the following passage, thrown in without comment and almost as an aside? Manzoni has spent much of the novel criticizing the clergy, but in his account of the plague he mentions, in passing, that the exertions of the clergy during this great test were so selfless that "more than sixty parish priests, in the city

alone, died of the contagion: about eight out of every nine "
(p. 593).

There are times when Manzoni appears scornful of the
crowd. He shows us their superstition and gullibility—for
example, about the mythical ' anointers ' who were said to
go about the city deliberately spreading the plague by smearing
houses with poison; their inability to hold a secret; their
frequent stupid adoption of plans which work to their own
detriment; their panic and thick-headedness. And yet he can
see them also with compassion—and more than that, he can
appreciate the positive virtues of gregariousness. Few contrasts
in the book are more striking than that between the loneliness
of ' the Unnamed ' before his conversion and the happy pur-
posiveness in the ordinary natural life of the village below his
castle. He is looking down on them from the window of his
castle, as they are gathering from all around for the festive
occasion of Cardinal Borromeo's visitation. And he muses,

" What the devil is up with these people? What reason
can there be for gaiety like this in this accursed country?
Where is all that mob going? " . . . The nobleman stood
there leaning on the window-sill, intent on the moving
spectacle below. There were men, women and children,
some in groups, some in couples, some alone; one man
would catch up with another in front of him and then
proceed in his company; another would join the first
person into whom he ran as he left his house; and they
would go on together, like friends bound on a common
journey. . . . He looked and looked, till he felt more than
common curiosity to know what could communicate so
unanimous a will, so general a festivity, to so many
different people (p. 391).

IV

The novel has been criticized as too artificial in its arrangement. But taken as a whole it does not seem so. No doubt the
parallelism that frequently occurs is carefully planned; but it
is never forced. There is, for example, a parallel in the opposi-
tion between Don Rodrigo and the good Father Christoforo at
one level, and at a higher level that between ' the Unnamed '

and the saintly Cardinal. Within the ecclesiastical frontiers, too, there is contrast, when after the tremendous scene of ' the Unnamed's ' conversion and the Cardinal's simple dignity as he witnesses the conversion, Don Abbondio, the pusillanimous parish priest, is brought bustling in, terrified, suspicious and self-exculpatory. And the contrasts or parallels extend to Nature herself. The awful oppressiveness of the weather stands for one mood: " In the country round, not a twig bent under a breath of air, not a bird was seen to alight or fly away. . . . It was one of those days in which, among a party of travellers, not one of them breaks the silence; and the hunter walks pensively along, with his eyes bent to the ground; and the peasant, digging in the field, pauses in his song, without being aware of it " (p. 652).

But this is followed by the coming of the rain, which not only washes away the pestilence but expresses the sense of easing and ' lift ' in the tone or feel of this section of the novel—when the fortunes of Renzo and Lucia are at last beginning to mend: " A few large and scattered drops began to fall, which lighting upon, and rebounding from, the white and parched road, stirred up a cloud of very fine dust; these soon multiplied into rain. . . . Renzo luxuriated in it, and enjoyed himself in that refreshing coolness, that murmur, that general motion of the grass and the leaves, shaking, dripping, revived, and glistening, as they were; he drew several deep and long breaths; and in that relenting of nature, felt more freely and more vividly, as it were, that which had been wrought in his own destiny " (p. 687).

It will be seen that Manzoni has great powers of description. Not only the more famous and unforgettable pictures of famine and the plague, but the simple sketches of scenery, the mountains and cultivated fields. The account of Renzo's little vineyard, when he returns after so long an absence, with its wild growth and saddening beauty, will do for an example: " There was a medley of stems, each trying to grow higher than the other, or to crawl past the other on the ground and get the lead at any cost. . . . There a red-berried bryony had twisted itself among the new shoots of a vine, which, seeking in vain a firmer support, had reciprocally entwined its tendrils around its companion, and, mingling their feeble stalks and their not very dissimilar leaves, they mutually drew each other upward, as often happens with the weak, who take one another for their stay " (p. 620).

Human beings, too, he can wonderfully portray in their little weaknesses and attractions. This is enough to justify the intrusion of one or two characters who are unnecessary to the plot, but whom we cannot but welcome all the same. There is Donna Praseda, for example, who gives Lucia refuge, a well-meaning but meddlesome person. She had five daughters, " . . . none of whom were at home, but who gave her much more to think about than if they had been. Three of these were nuns, two were married: hence Donna Praseda naturally found herself with three monasteries and two houses to super-intend; a vast and complicated undertaking, and the more arduous, because two husbands, backed by fathers, mothers and brothers; three abbesses, supported by other dignitaries, and by many nuns, would not accept her superintendence " (p. 500). A sly dig is even administered to the good-hearted tailor who with his wife gave asylum to Lucia and her mother, Agnese, after their release from ' the Unnamed's ' castle. The Archbishop visited Lucia at the tailor's house, and after that signal honour he obtained a portrait of his Grace " which he kept hung up on one of the door-posts, in veneration for the person, and also that he might be able to say to any visitor, that the portrait did not resemble him; for he himself had had opportunity of studying the Cardinal, close by, and at his leisure, in that very room " (p. 541).

His power of unusual and graphic simile has already been illustrated; but let us have one more example. Certain promul-gations issued against Renzo had lapsed, fortunately for him, because of the plague; and Manzoni comments that this " was a common occurrence in those days, that special as well as general orders against persons . . . often continued without taking effect, if they had not done so on their first promul-gation; like musket-balls, which, if they strike no blow, lie quietly upon the ground without giving molestation to any-one " (p. 697).

His account of Don Rodrigo's dream, when attacked by the plague, can almost be said, like some of Dostoevsky's descrip-tions of dreams, to anticipate Kafka. And, by contrast, for sheer quick-moving, romping comedy it would be hard to beat the scene when in the darkness three separate parties are all startled by the ringing of church bells. Renzo and Lucia are trying to slip into the priest's house and, taking him by surprise, to declare themselves man and wife in his presence and thus effect their own marriage; the parish priest himself, Don Abbondio, is in his room and does not know what is happening; and Don Rodrigo's *bravoes* have come to Lucia's house to kidnap her—all three groups are set at cross-purposes with each other by the sudden ringing of the church bells by a fourth party. The resulting confusion is glorious. Such are the varied circumstances and types that Manzoni's style has to encompass—and the experts tell us that its great virtue for this purpose is that flexibility and naturalness which has made it such a model for all subsequent writers of Italian.

v

I have entitled this chapter ' The Quiescence of Belief ', because it should be clear even from the foregoing extracts that nowhere does Manzoni parade his Christian faith in an aggressive or proselytizing manner. I take the word ' quiescence ' not in a negative sense but in the sense in which it was once used by D. H. Lawrence, in a very different context: " There is a brief time for sex, and a long time when sex is out of place. But when it is out of place as an activity there still should be a large and quiet space in the consciousness where it lives quiescent. Old people can have a lovely quiescent sort of sex, like apples, leaving the young free for their sort."[14] It is with this sense of belief as quiescent in the background that Manzoni can convey the ' moral ' element in his novel. Take, for instance, the great scene of the conversion of ' the Un-named '. The presentation of a religious conversion, indeed of supernatural charity of any kind, is a supremely difficult task for a novelist. It is apt to be either mawkish and unnatural or self-conscious and homiletic. But Manzoni approaches it with a humour and understanding, as well as an absence of cant or false simplicity, which result in a convincing and moving presentation. After his conversion ' the Unnamed ' returns to his castle and to his *bravoes* and addresses them with perfect poise, without contempt and yet without loss of dignity.

" My friends! the path we have hitherto followed leads to the depths of hell. . . . I revoke all the wicked commands you may any of you have received from me. . . . He who does not wish to remain shall receive what is due of his salary, and an additional gift: he may go away, but must never again set foot here, unless it be to change his life. . . ." Here he ceased, and all continued silent. . . . They were accustomed to receive the voice of their master as the declaration of a will from which there was no appeal: and that voice, announcing that the will was changed, in no wise denoted that it was enfeebled (p. 452).

It is one of the great ' conversion ' scenes in literature. And note that even the good Cardinal is not represented as perfect. He accepts too readily, for instance, some of the popular superstitions and suspicions about the plague—as Manzoni comments, " We should like to give that noble and beloved memory an even greater share of praise, and show that the good ecclesiastic was superior to most of his contemporaries in this matter as in everything else; but we are compelled instead to note in him another example of the power, even on the noblest minds, of public opinion " (p. 600). And if we want another example of Manzoni's restraint there is the charming bathos— a deliberately contrived bathos composed of understatement —by which he avoids the sentimentality of the ' happy ever after '. For man, he observes, " So long as he is in this world, is like a sick person lying upon a bed more or less uncomfortable, who sees around him other beds nicely made to outward appearance, smooth and level, and fancies that they must be more comfortable resting-places. He succeeds in making an exchange; but scarcely is he placed in another, before he begins, as he presses it down, to feel in one place a sharp point pricking him, in another a hard lump: in short, we come to almost the same story over again. And for this reason . . . we ought to aim rather at doing well, than being well " (p. 721).

For all the time we must remember that, though it is never unfairly obtruded, in Manzoni's conception of life, behind the story of man, behind the fiction as well as the historical fact, remains the Divine understanding. It is this perhaps that above all puts him in such a different category from other Catholic novelists—like M. Mauriac or Mr. Graham Greene in our own day—who have his convictions but none of his width of sympathy and fullness of human background. Would it be an exaggeration to call him the last of the Christian humanists? Perhaps we can find the best picture of the human showing itself at its most human in its awareness of divine dependence in Renzo's prayer. Here all that Manzoni wants to say ' macrocosmically ' is summed up ' microcosmically ', and without any false emphasis—merely in the gentlest hint of a contrast—in the scene where the young man, having searched in vain for his Lucia, and tormented lest she be dead of the plague, falls on his knees, " And there poured forth a prayer to God, or rather a crowd of unconnected expressions, broken sentences, ejaculations, entreaties, complaints, and promises; one of those addresses which are never made to men, because they have not sufficient quickness to understand them, nor patience to listen to them; they are not great enough to feel compassion without contempt " (p. 670).

5

DOSTOEVSKY AND THE AGONY OF BELIEF

WE HAVE SEEN in the last chapter that Manzoni is perhaps the last European writer to be able to take belief, unargued for, as the background to his picture of life. That is partly because he was from childhood soaked in Italian peasant Catholicism—though as an individual he had to struggle back to it in maturity—but also because he chose for the *mise en scène* of his great novel a period (seventeenth century) when such belief was simply there, given. There could scarcely be a sharper contrast than that between him and his Russian contemporary (more or less) Dostoevsky. We are frequently warned today of the danger of taking Dostoevsky as the ' typical nineteenth-century Russian ', still more as the typical Russian Orthodox believer; and of course he was too big as well as too strange a man to be typically anything. Nevertheless the greatness of any great writer is in part due to his ability to typify what he does not represent, that is, to give, as it were, prophetic recordings of states of mind which exist unrecognized in those who have them. In Dostoevsky we see the agony, both of belief and of disbelief; but we see it, not merely in his direct exposition of it, but also in those places in his novels where he is not directly considering belief at all but simply writing out of his imaginative experience of the poetry of life and thought. We need, that is to say, to learn to look in Dostoevsky, not merely at the well-known passages where, say, an Ivan Karamazov, a Shatov, or even a Raskolnikov, are arguing about faith and infidelity—the places where the usual ' interpretation of Dostoevsky ' is quarried—but at his work as a whole, in its style, its imagery, its preoccupations, and its technique as novel-writing.

I. THE NOVELIST

The trouble with criticism of Dostoevsky is that he has been regarded as *par excellence* the writer with a message. The message may vary much according to the type of reader or critic, but message of some sort there must be. He may be described explicitly as a ' prophet '.[1] Or he may be ransacked for an answer to ' the problem of evil '.[2] He may be defended as in essence a great Orthodox Christian writer.[3] Or he may be defended as, thank heavens, not a Christian at all.[4] Or, fitting neatly between these last two, he may be defended as the only kind of Christian which the critic can allow to be genuinely ' Christian '.[5] He may be studied as the portrayer of character,[6] or as the psychologist.[7] And no doubt there are many other messages which have been extracted from him in Russian, German and French studies with which the present writer is unfamiliar.

It is not that any of these approaches are necessarily invalid. Some, indeed, have been most rewarding. When, for instance, Vycheslav Ivanov defends Dostoevsky's orthodoxy, he categorically states that he has " an infallible criterion of this orthodoxy: the accord between what Dostoevsky had to teach and the living artistic imagery in which he clothed it."[8] This is a hopeful statement from a critic; and links on to his exposition of why it is that Dostoevsky can be so misleading: " The dialectical impetus of a spirit achieving awareness of itself is falsely interpreted, by some critics, as the expression of a radical scepticism and despair. . . . [But] this theory is tenable on grounds neither of biography nor of psychology (to Dostoevsky, with his passionate nature, irony of any sort is almost as foreign as it is to Dante), nor yet of logic; and it can be equally well refuted by a study either of the context of the particular passages in which the negative attitude is expressed, or of the great organic unity of Dostoevsky's work as a whole."[9]

Yet when M. Ivanov actually deals with the novels, though he has illuminating things to say about the Russian conceptions that lie behind them (especially the inward meaning of the names of many of Dostoevsky's characters), he says very little about them *as novels*. Another example of the limitation in an opposite direction of one-sided criticism of this sort is Mr. Curle's book on *The Characters of Dostoevsky*. Mr. Curle is very observant, and it goes without saying that some of his detective work throws considerable light on Dostoevsky's positive achievements. But his basic assumption can be gathered from the following remarks, about *The Possessed*: " The part Kirillov plays in the book matters but little, though his ideas are significant. But then with Dostoevsky the story in its entirety is of small consequence compared with the characterization. His novels are vast segments from the moving flood of life rather than co-ordinated episodes constructed round a central plan."[10] This can only mean, though Mr. Curle does not realize it, that Dostoevsky failed as a novelist. Mr. Curle will not draw this conclusion because to him characterization is a sufficient criterion. It leads him, as a result, to rank *The Brothers Karamazov* below the other major novels, simply on this ground. " Dostoevsky had passed his zenith when he came to write it, and, though his mind remained as alert as ever, his creative capacity, as almost always happens with an ageing novelist, had begun to wane. . . . [The fine passages] have little or nothing to do with its artistic unity and, above all, do not heighten our perception of the characters by those psychological touches which build up personality. . . . Dostoevsky used *The Brothers Karamazov* as a vehicle for his thoughts, not, as in previous novels, because they were the thoughts the characters concerned were bound to have, but because he was determined to utter them even if they had to be dragged in."[11]

This mode of criticism inevitably results in an assessment which runs counter to almost universal opinion on the status of Dostoevsky's last novel; that does not matter so much as the fact that it is a mode of assessment which would equally depreciate *War and Peace*, or *The Magic Mountain*, to take but two of the world's great novels. The idea that towards the end of his life a novelist might find his material bursting the usual bounds (in structure as well as in characterization) of the novel is ruled out. But we can see the weakness of this mode of assessment most clearly in Mr. Curle's account of Grushenka in *The Brothers Karamazov*. She would, he says, " have been, I judge, rather a censorious wife and a marvellous mother— kindness is as easily evoked in her as cattiness. . . ." And then, realizing that this is speculation, he adds hastily that a creative novelist " builds up a conception of his characters to a pitch where they have an existence beyond the framework of the narrative in which they occur, and one is surely entitled to speak of their future development with some degree of certitude."[12] This is the method of A. C. Bradley applied to Dostoevsky; the objections to one (see Professor L. C. Knights' *How Many Children Had Lady Macbeth?*) are valid against the other.

★

For a writer considered among the dozen or so greatest novelists in history it is indeed strange that so few studies, at least in English, have been concerned with him as novelist. Even the late André Gide's excellent little book (originally lectures) on him, though it shows the results of keen observation, tends to single out those preoccupations of Dostoevsky with which the sensitive author of *Les Faux Monnayeurs* was most in sympathy. We must therefore start with an examination of Dostoevsky's craft (with the necessary reservations that limitation of space and, above all, ignorance of the Russian language must impose).

The importance of starting from a literary-critical view of the novels as a whole lies also in this: that so often what is quoted from Dostoevsky is what is easily memorable, and what is easily memorable is what is extravagant. It is true that there is much that seems extravagant in the novels; but then there was much that seems extravagant in his life, and indeed in nineteenth-century Russia generally. We shall see later that undue concentration on these 'spot' passages can lead to misjudgment even of the strictly literary-critical kind. Let us start, therefore, with some passages in which the well-known obsession with the 'Russian soul' is entirely absent. Here, for instance, is the hero of *The Gambler* describing a meeting with the Englishman, Mr. Astley. They are both in love with Polina ('Pauline'), but Mr. Astley is much too polite and English to say so, and only betrays by his eyes what he is most anxious not to express by word or glance.

> Mr. Astley very often meets us out on walks. He takes off his hat and passes by, though, of course, he is dying to join us. If he is invited to do so, he immediately refuses. At places where we rest—at the Casino, by the bandstand, or before the fountain—he always stands somewhere not

far from our seat. . . . I fancy he is looking for an opportunity to have a conversation with me apart. This morning we met and exchanged a couple of words. He sometimes speaks very abruptly. Without saying " good-morning," he began by blurting out:

" Oh, Mlle Blanche! . . . I have seen a great many women like Mlle Blanche! "

He paused, looking at me significantly. What he meant to say by that I don't know. For on my asking what he meant, he shook his head with a sly smile, and added, " Oh, well, that's how it is. Is Mlle Pauline very fond of flowers? "

" I don't know: I don't know at all," I answered.

" What? You don't even know that! " he cried, with the utmost amazement.

" I don't know; I haven't even noticed at all," I repeated, laughing.

" Hm! That gives me a queer idea."

Then he shook his head and walked away. He looked pleased, though. We talked the most awful French together.[13]

There is a lightness of touch here, shown especially by the flick of the wrist in the last phrase, which reveals a deliberate intention to remain at this pleasant, bantering surface and not to plunge into the depths in which Dostoevsky is usually thought to dwell continually. Or we can find him going a little deeper, but still with the same sense of restraint, of careful control, as in the meeting of Velchaninov with Pavel Pavlovitch after the death of little Liza, the girl whom Velchaninov had by Pavel Pavlovitch's wife. Pavel behaved shockingly towards the little girl. He claimed to be fond of her, but in fact was too drunk to look after her. When Velchaninov undertook to have her cared for, Pavel let her go, and when later she died did not even turn up at the funeral. Some weeks after, Velchaninov meets him, after having paid an affectionate visit to her little grave. The way in which they avoid talking of what is uppermost in both minds, what in fact leads to their violent hatred for each other, is brilliantly conveyed. Pavel, actually sober for once, overtakes Velchaninov.

" Good evening," he said.

" Good evening," answered Velchaninov. . . .

" What an agreeable evening," observed Pavel Pavlovitch, looking into his face.

" You've not gone away yet," Velchaninov observed, not by way of a question, but simply making that reflection aloud as he walked on.

" Things have dragged on, but—I've obtained a post with an increase of salary. I shall be going away the day after tomorrow for certain."

" You've got a post? " he said, this time asking a question.

" Why shouldn't I? " Pavel Pavlovitch screwed up his face.

" Oh, I only asked . . ." Velchaninov said, disclaiming the insinuation, and, with a frown, he looked askance at Pavel Pavlovitch. . . .

" I was intending, Alexey Ivanovitch [Velchaninov], to communicate with you on a subject for rejoicing," Pavel Pavlovitch began again.

" Rejoicing? "

" I'm going to get married."

" What? "

" After sorrow comes rejoicing, so it is always in life; I should be so gratified, Alexey Ivanovitch, if . . . but— I don't know, perhaps you're in a hurry now, for you appear to be . . ."

" Yes, I am in a hurry . . . and I'm unwell too."

He felt a sudden and intense desire to get rid of him. . . .

" I should have liked . . ."

Pavel Pavlovitch did not say what he would have liked; Velchaninov was silent.

" In that case it must be later on, if only we meet again. . . ."

" Yes, yes, later on," Velchaninov muttered rapidly, without stopping or looking at him.

They were both silent again for a minute; Pavel Pavlovitch went on walking beside him.

" In that case, good-bye till we meet again," Pavel Pavlovitch brought out at last.[14]

The relationship between these two rivals—sometimes polite, sometimes almost effusive, but with always an undercurrent of real hatred—is superbly carried all the way through the novel. For a very different, but equally sure, handling of a relationship, we may instance the fateful interview between the engaged couple in *Crime and Punishment*. Dounia, Raskolnikov's sister, is engaged to Luzhin, a successful and hard business man. Raskolnikov, who in spite of his crime is fond of his family, is dubious about the match, and insists on being present at the interview between the betrothed, although Luzhin, anticipating trouble, has expressly asked that he shall not be. In the middle, bewilderingly trying to keep the peace, is the mother of Dounia and Raskolnikov, Pulcheria Alexandrovna. Bit by bit Luzhin's meanness and trickery are brought to the surface; bit by bit the frightened mother has to give way and to see that this hopeful and advantageous match is a failure; and finally the conversation flares up, after a particularly nasty and insinuating remark by the intending bridegroom, Luzhin.

Razumihin [Raskolnikov's friend, who takes their side— and who will one day himself marry Dounia] could not sit still on his chair.

" Aren't you ashamed now, sister? " asked Raskolnikov.

" I am ashamed, Rodya [Raskolnikov]," said Dounia. " Pyotr Petrovitch [Luzhin], go away," she turned to him, white with anger.

Pyotr Petrovitch had apparently not at all expected such a conclusion. He had too much confidence in himself, in his power and in the helplessness of his victims. He could not believe it even now. He turned pale, and his lips quivered.

" Avdotya Romanovna [Dounia], if I go out of this door now, after such a dismissal, then, you may reckon on it, I will never come back. Consider what you are doing. My word is not to be shaken."

" What insolence! " cried Dounia, springing up from her seat. " I don't want you to come back again."

" What! So that's how it stands! " cried Luzhin, utterly unable to the last moment to believe in the rupture and so completely thrown out of his reckoning now. " So that's how it stands! But do you know, Avdotya Romanovna, that I might protest."

" What right have you to speak to her like that? " Pulcheria Alexandrovna [the mother, at last plucking up courage] intervened hotly. " And what can you protest about? What rights have you? Am I to give my Dounia to a man like you? Go away, leave us altogether! We are to blame for having agreed to a wrong action, and I above all. . . ."

" But you have bound me, Pulcheria Alexandrovna," Luzhin stormed in a frenzy, " by your promise, and now you deny it and . . . besides . . . I have been led on account of that into expenses. . . ."

This last complaint was so characteristic of Pyotr Petrovitch that Raskolnikov, pale with anger and with the effort of restraining it, could not help breaking into laughter.[15]

And for a last example of Dostoevsky's skill in handling relationships, especially, in this case, of dialogue and crowded scenes, we may take the meeting of the conspirators from *The Possessed*. This illustrates also Dostoevsky's satire, which can at times be very keen, though sometimes it is a trifle crude and cruel. There is no need to identify the particular speakers; all we need to know is that it is a group of ' progressive ' friends of Pyotr Verhovensky and Nikolay Stavrogin who are meeting to discuss possible revolutionary plans.

" I'll venture to ask one question," said the lame teacher suavely. He had been sitting particularly decorously and had not spoken till then. " I should like to know, are we some sort of meeting, or are we simply a gathering of ordinary mortals paying a visit? I ask simply for the sake of order and so as not to remain in ignorance."

This ' sly ' question made an impression. People looked at each other, everyone expecting someone else to answer, and suddenly all, as though at a word of command, turned their eyes to Verhovensky and Stavrogin.

" I suggest our voting on the answer to the question

whether we are a meeting or not," said Madame Virginsky.

" I entirely agree with the suggestion," Liputin chimed in, " though the question is rather vague."

" I agree too." " And so do I," cried voices.

" I too think it would make our proceedings more in order," confirmed Virginsky.

(They then ask Lyamshin to play loudly on the piano so as to drown the noise of political discussion and make it sound like a party, in case of eavesdroppers.)

" I tell you one must always be on one's guard. I mean in case there should be spies," she [Madame Virginsky] explained to Verhovensky. . . .

" Hang it all! " Lyamshin swore, and sitting down to the piano, began strumming a valse, banging on the keys almost with his fists, at random.

" I propose that those who want it to be a meeting should put up their right hands," Madame Virginsky proposed.

Some put them up, others did not. Some held them up and then put them down again and then held them up again.

" Foo! I don't understand it at all," one officer shouted.

" I don't either," cried the other.

" Oh, I understand," cried a third. " If it's *yes*, you hold your hand up."

" But what does ' yes ' mean? "

" Means a meeting."

" No, it means not a meeting." . . .

" Mr. Lyamshin, excuse me, but you are thumping so that no one can hear anything," observed the lame teacher. . . .

" But what does ' meeting ' mean? " cried a voice.

No one answered.[16]

This last passage illustrates Dostoevsky's skill at conveying character through event. We have said that it is not so much in Dostoevsky's direct discussions of faith and unbelief that we get the clue to his real mind. So, too, we often learn more about one of his creatures through some chance confrontation with another, through a dialogue or a psychological reaction, than when the author is, so to speak, standing the character up in front of the reader and giving his own description. Here is a quarrel that occurs at the ' funeral party ' for Katerina Ivanovna's dead husband, Marmaladov. Poor Katerina, though prostrate with grief and herself in the advanced stage of T.B., tries to keep up the dignity necessary to the occasion's hostess; but her landlady, Amalia Ivanovna, resents the attention being given to her. Gradually they become more heated with each other. Katerina has been describing the school she is hoping to open, as a way of making her living, for the daughters of gentlemen.

At that moment Amalia Ivanovna, deeply aggrieved at taking no part in the conversation, and not being listened to, made one last effort, and with secret misgivings ventured on an exceedingly deep and weighty observation, that " in the future boarding-school she would have to pay attention particularly to *die Wäsche*, and that there certainly must be a good *Dame*, to look after the linen, and secondly that the young ladies must not novels at night read."

Katerina Ivanovna, who certainly was upset and very tired, as well as heartily sick of the dinner, at once cut short Amalia Ivanovna, saying " she knew nothing about it and was talking nonsense, that it was the business of the laundry maid, and not of the directress of a high-class boarding-school to look after *die Wäsche*, and as for novel-reading, that was simply rudeness, and she begged her to be silent." Amalia Ivanovna fired up and getting angry observed that she only " meant her good " . . . and that " it was long since she had paid her *gold* for the lodgings."

Katerina Ivanovna at once " set her down ", saying that it was a lie to say she wished her good, because only yesterday when her dead husband was lying on the table, she had worried her about the lodgings. To this Amalia Ivanovna very appropriately observed that she had invited those ladies [some guests about whom there had been an earlier argument], but " those ladies had not come, because those ladies *are* ladies and cannot come to a lady who is not a lady ". Katerina Ivanovna at once pointed out to her that as she was a slut she could not judge what made one really a lady. Amalia Ivanovna at once declared that her " *Vater aus Berlin* was a very, very important man, and both hands in pocket went, and always used to say: ' Poof! poof! ' " and she leapt up from the table to represent her father. . . .

But this was too much for Katerina Ivanovna, and she at once declared, so that all could hear, that Amalia Ivanovna probably never had a father, but was simply a drunken Petersburg Finn, and had certainly once been a cook and probably something worse. . . .

Amalia Ivanovna ran about the room, shouting at the top of her voice that she was mistress of the house and that Katerina Ivanovna should leave the lodgings that minute; then she rushed for some reason to collect the silver spoons from the table. There was a great outcry and uproar, the children began crying. Sonia ran to restrain Katerina Ivanovna, but when Amalia Ivanovna shouted something about " the yellow ticket ", Katerina pushed Sonia away, and rushed at the landlady to carry out her threat.[17]

The setting of this tragi-comic scene, just at the moment when the Marmaladovs' fortunes are most precarious—it is soon to be followed by the almost unbearable account of Katerina Marmaladov's madness, when she leads the whole family out and makes them dance and beg for money in the streets—is no doubt a trifle obvious. It is, indeed, as we shall show later, a very Dickensian receipt, using a little comedy to wring the last ounce of tears out of pathos. But it is effective in its ' build-up ' and in the way it tells us more of Katerina herself, including her weaknesses, through the clash of personalities.

Dostoevsky's fondness for children, and use of them as a catalytic to adult character, so to speak, in his stories, is well known. But one of the best studies of the meeting, and mutual illumination, of two persons occurs in a study of two children which is not at all well known. The heroine of the unfinished story, *Nyetochka Nyezvanov*, is an orphan girl, taken in out of kindness by ' Prince X ' and his family. She has been ill, but is at last well enough to do lessons with the Prince's daughter, Katya. Here she meets Katya for the first time.

Towards the end of the lesson Madame Leotard [the Governess] was really angry with Katya.

" Look at her! " she said, indicating me [Nyetochka]. " The child is ill and is having her first lesson, and yet she has done ten times as much as you. Aren't you ashamed? "

" Does she know more than I do? " Katya asked in astonishment.

" How long did it take you to learn the alphabet? "

" Three lessons."

" And she has learnt it in one. So she learns three times as quickly as you do, and will soon catch you up."

Katya pondered a little and turned suddenly fiery red. . . . But she said nothing, merely looked at me as though she would burn me with her eyes. . . . When we left Madame Leotard I began to speak, hoping to soften her vexation and to show that I was not to blame for the governess' words, but Katya remained mute as though she had not heard me.

An hour later she came into the room where I was sitting over a book. . . . She looked at me from under her brows, sat down as usual on the sofa, and for half an hour did not take her eyes off me. At last I could bear it no longer, and glanced at her enquiringly.

" Can you dance? " asked Katya.

" No, I can't."

" I can."

Silence.

" And can you play the piano? "

" No, I can't do that, either."

" I can. That's very difficult to learn."

I said nothing.

" Madame Leotard says you are cleverer than I am."

" Madame Leotard is angry with you," I said.

" And will father be angry too? "

" I don't know," I answered.

Silence again; Katya tapped the floor with her little foot in impatience.

" So you are going to laugh at me because you are quicker at learning than I am? " she asked at last, unable to restrain her annoyance.

" Oh, no, no," I cried, and I jumped up from my place to rush and hug her.

For two days Katya sulks; and then they have a flare-up, after which the Prince orders his daughter to apologize.

" Go to her at once and beg her forgiveness," said the prince, indicating me.

The little princess stood as white as a handkerchief and did not budge.

" Well? " said the prince.

" I won't," Katya brought out at last in a low voice, with a most determined air.

" Katya! "

" No, I won't, I won't! " she cried suddenly, with flashing eyes, and she stamped. " I won't beg forgiveness, papa. I don't like her. I won't live with her. . . . It's not my fault she cries all day. I don't want to. I don't want to! "

" Come with me," said the prince, taking her by the hand. " Nyetochka, go upstairs." And he led her away into the study. . . .

At last she came back, and without saying a word passed by me and sat down in a corner. Her eyes looked red and her cheeks were swollen from crying. . . .

Exactly three days after our quarrel she came suddenly after dinner into my room and shyly drew near me.

" Papa has ordered me to beg your forgiveness," she said. " Do you forgive me? "

I clutched Katya by both hands quickly, and breathless with excitement, I said—

" Yes, yes."

" Papa has ordered me to kiss you. Will you kiss me? "

In reply I began to kiss her hands, wetting them with my tears. Glancing at Katya, I saw in her an extraordinary change. Her lips were faintly moving, her chin was twitching, her eyes were moist; but she instantly mastered her emotion and a smile came for a second on her lips.

" I will go and tell father that I have kissed you and begged your forgiveness," she said softly, as though reflecting to herself. " I haven't seen him for three days; he forbade me to go in to him till I had," she added after a brief pause.[18]

For sheer descriptive genius alone it would be hard to beat this. But it is more than novelettish description. It is brilliant employment of dramatic suspense. There is another instance of similar, indeed even more intense, dramatic suspense a little later in the same story, which is worth quoting for another reason. This time the confrontation is not between the two little girls but between Katya and the bulldog, Falstaff. Katya could not bear to think that there was even an animal in the house which did not recognize her authority and give way to her. So she determined to try and conquer Falstaff.

One day, when we were both sitting downstairs in one of the big drawing-rooms after dinner, the bulldog was lying stretched out in the middle of the room, enjoying his after-dinner siesta. . . . Katya began cautiously on tiptoe to approach him, coaxing him, calling him the most endearing names, and beckoning to him ingratiatingly. But even before she got near him, Falstaff showed his terrible teeth; the little princess stood still. . . . Seeing that she could not approach him all at once, Katya walked around her enemy in perplexity. Falstaff did not budge. Katya made another circle, considerably diminishing its diameter, then a third, but when she reached a spot which Falstaff seemed to regard as the forbidden limit, he showed his teeth again. The little princess stamped her foot, walked away in annoyance and hesitation, and sat down on the sofa.

Ten minutes later she devised a new method of seduction, she went out and returned with a supply of biscuits and cakes. . . . But Falstaff was indifferent, probably because he already had had enough to eat. . . . When Katya again reached the forbidden line . . . Falstaff raised

his head, bared his teeth, gave a faint growl and made a
slight movement as though he were preparing to leap
up. Katya turned crimson with anger, threw down
the cakes, and sat down on the sofa again.

She was unmistakably excited. . . . Her little foot
tapped on the carpet, her cheeks were flaming, and there
were actually tears of vexation in her eyes. . . . She jumped
up from her seat resolutely, and with a firm step went
straight to the fierce dog.

Perhaps astonishment had a powerful effect on Falstaff
this time. He let his enemy cross the boundary, and only
when Katya was two paces away greeted her with the
most malignant growl. Katya stopped for a minute, but
only for a minute, and resolutely advanced. I was almost
fainting with terror. Katya was roused as I'd never seen
her before, her eyes were flashing, with victory, with
triumph. She would have made a wonderful picture. She
fearlessly faced the menacing eyes of the furious bulldog,
and did not flinch at the sight of his terrible jaws. He sat
up, a fearful growl broke from his hairy chest; in another
minute he would have torn her to pieces. But the princess*
proudly laid her little hand upon him and three times
stroked his back in triumph. For one instant the bulldog
hesitated. That moment was the most awful; but all at
once he moved, got up heavily, stretched, and probably
reflecting that it was not worth while having anything to
do with children, walked calmly out of the room. Katya
stood in triumph on the field of battle and glanced at me
with an indescribable look in her eyes, a look full of the
joy and intoxication of victory. I was as white as a sheet;
she noticed it with a smile. But a deathly pallor over-
spread her cheeks too. She could hardly reach the sofa,
and sank on it almost fainting.[19]

Some may say that this is overdone; that a storm has been
brewed in an afternoon tea-cup. But I do not think so.
Dostoevsky is well aware that it is often, indeed perhaps
usually, in quite trivial matters that the occasion arises for

* For euphony I have omitted ' little ' in Constance Garnett's version, which is
quite unnecessary; the close occurrence of two ' littles ' does not, I am informed,
occur in the Russian.

profound and lasting decisions, and the power with which he is able to convey the tension of those moments of crucial psychological or emotional strain is unique among novelists. We shall discuss the significance of this in the next two sections of this essay. Meanwhile let us have a last example of the same type—the dramatic element in human relationships. It is the famous scene in *The Possessed* when Shatov strikes Stavrogin. The preparation for the blow is carefully described, and the blow itself, a very heavy blow. " The whole scene did not last more than ten seconds. Yet a very great deal happened in those seconds." And then, with the skill of a tantalizer, Dostoevsky breaks off the narrative to remind us of Stavrogin's fearlessness, cool self-possession, etc.: " Stavrogin would have shot his opponent in a duel, and would have defended himself from a brigand in the forest . . . but it would be without the slightest thrill of enjoyment, languidly, listlessly, even with *ennui* and entirely from unpleasant necessity." All this prepares us for the description of his reaction to Shatov's blow.

> In the present, what happened was something different and amazing.
> He had scarcely regained his balance after being almost knocked over in this humiliating way, and the horrible, as it were, sodden thud of the blow in the face had scarcely died away in the room when he seized Shatov by the shoulders with both hands, but at once, almost at the same instant, pulled both hands away and clasped them behind his back. He did not speak, but looked at Shatov, and turned as white as his shirt. But, strange to say, the light in his eyes seemed to die out. Ten seconds later his eyes looked cold, and I'm sure I'm not lying—calm. Only he was terribly pale. . . .

And we get a further sense of the tension of that moment when we feel how it is eased—eased by Shatov's withdrawal.

> Shatov was the first to drop his eyes, and evidently because he was unable to go on facing him; then he turned slowly and walked out of the room, but with a very different step. He withdrew quietly, with peculiar awkwardness, with his shoulder hunched, his head hanging as

though he was inwardly pondering something. I believe he was whispering something. He made his way to the door carefully, without stumbling against anything or knocking anything over; he opened the door a very little way and squeezed through almost sideways. As he went out his shock of hair standing on end at the back of his head was particularly noticeable.[20]

II. THE MELODRAMATIST

In the last section we mentioned *en passant* the influence of Dickens. That influence is very widespread (it is well known how enthusiastically Dostoevsky read him) and not always to the good. The madness of Katerina Ivanovna Marmaladov in *Crime and Punishment*, for instance, plucks a little too persistently at the heart-strings. There is a similar excess in the picture of little Marie, in *The Idiot*, befriended by Prince Myshkin. She had been seduced by a French commercial traveller, and when she returned people who had been kind to her before now had no sympathy with her.

They all stared at her, as though she were a reptile; the old people blamed and upbraided her, the young people laughed; the women reviled and abused her and looked at her with loathing, as though she had been a spider. Her mother allowed it all; she sat there nodding her head and approving. The mother was very ill at the time and almost dying: two months later she did die. . . . Marie bathed her legs every day and waited on her. . . . When the old mother was completely bedridden, the old women of the village came to sit up with her in turns, as their custom is. Then they gave up feeding Marie altogether, and in the village everyone drove her away and no one would even give her work. . . . She had begun to spit blood at the time. At last her clothes were in absolute tatters, so that she was ashamed to show herself in the village. . . . When her mother died the pastor did not scruple to heap shame on Marie in church before all the people. Marie stood crying by the coffin. . . . Then the pastor—he was a young man, and his whole ambition was to become a great preacher—pointed to Marie and, addressing them all, said: " Here you see the cause of this worthy woman's death . . . here she stands before you and dares not look at you, for she has been marked out by the finger of God; here she is, barefoot and ragged—a warning to all who lose their virtue! Who is she? Her daughter! " . . . And, would you believe it, this infamy pleased almost everyone.[21]

Or let us examine the following passage from that frequently too melodramatic novel *Crime and Punishment*: Raskolnikov and Sonia are together and the former suddenly orders Sonia to read from the Bible. She reads about the raising of Lazarus, until emotion overcomes her. " She could read no more, closed the book and got up from her chair quickly. ' That is all about the raising of Lazarus,' she whispered severely and abruptly, and turning away she stood motionless, not daring to raise her eyes to him. She still trembled feverishly. The candle-end was flickering out in the battered candlestick, dimly lighting up in the poverty-stricken room the murderer and the harlot who had so strangely been reading together the eternal book."[22]

What is wrong with this is that it has first been posed in a Rembrandtesque *chiaroscuro*, and then matters have been made worse by Dostoevsky's sudden interposition (' the murderer and the harlot '—whose comment is that but the author's?) in the narrative. We might say that *Crime and Punishment* is an early novel; but Dostoevsky's harmful intrusions into his novels are not confined to the immature ones. In *The Idiot*, for instance, we find a passage of rather crude satirical comment such as this: " Even with our nurses the rank of general has been considered the highest pinnacle of Russian happiness, and so has been the most popular national ideal of peaceful and contented bliss. And, indeed, after passing an examination without distinction and serving thirty-five years, who can fail to become at last a general and to have invested a decent sum in the bank? "[23]

This, it is true, occurs in one of those long preambles to a chapter, in which it is usually legitimate for the author to make his own general comments on society, preparatory to some illustrative incident in the novel. There is less excuse for his sarcastic intrusion into the description, for instance, of the political meeting (from which we have already quoted an admirable passage) in *The Possessed*. The speakers have been decrying Russia and lauding the West, and one of them " raised his fist, waved it ecstatically and menacingly over his head and suddenly brought it down furiously, as though pounding an adversary to powder. A frantic yell rose from the whole hall, there was a deafening roar of applause; almost half the audience was applauding: their enthusiasm was excusable. Russia was being put to shame publicly, before everyone. Who could fail to roar with delight? "[24]

This is in the vein of his journalistic contributions such as we find in *The Diary of a Writer*; in a novel it will not do. It reveals a weakness which is correlative to the internal kind of weakness displayed in the actual technique of story-telling. Here, for instance, is Raskolnikov's soliloquy, after he has had a charming encounter with little Polenka Marmaladov, Sonia's sister.

Raskolnikov told her his name and address and promised to be sure to come next day. The child went away quite enchanted with him. It was past ten when he came out into the street. In five minutes he was standing on the bridge at the spot where the woman had jumped in.

" Enough," he pronounced resolutely and triumphantly. " I've done with fancies, imaginary terrors and phantoms! Life is real! Haven't I lived just now? My life has not yet died with that old woman! The Kingdom of Heaven to her—and now enough, madam, leave me in peace! Now for the reign of reason and light . . . and of will, and of strength . . . and now we will see! We will try our strength! " . . .

" I am very weak at this moment, but . . . I believe my illness is all over. I knew it would be over when I went out. By the way, Potchinkov's house is only a few steps away. I certainly must go to Razumihin even if it were not close by. . . ."[25]

This is, of course, intended to convey the semi-delirious wanderings of the neurotic murderer; and no doubt this is one of those many sections in Dostoevsky's novels in which a con-

vincing English translation is almost impossible.* Nevertheless it is difficult not to feel that when an author has decided
to adopt a clumsy and crude technique like this, he shows
evidence at this point of some failure of connection, some lack
of spontaneous flow between the novelist and his material.

★

To draw a line between these deviations into sheer melo-
drama and such passages as those quoted at the end of the last
section where Dostoevsky is supremely successful at conveying
dramatic tension is very hard. And there are those who would
contend that no such line can be drawn—that even in the
passages I have called supremely successful there is an element
of strain, of hectic temperature, which betrays something
essentially unhealthy in the novels as a whole. This criticism
has been cogently stated in an article contributed to *The
Criterion* some sixteen years ago[26] by that keen and perceptive
critic Mr. D. A. Traversi. It is very little known, and has
never, so far as I am aware, been controverted by Dostoevsky's
defenders. It is a long and subtle article, and a summary is
bound to distort the argument somewhat. He starts from an
analysis of two passages in which he shows Dostoevsky, as he
says, trying to " transcend experience and stretch the capacity
of the mind beyond the limit of the conceivable. . . . We feel
that our senses are continually being mobilized to the furthest
limit of their intensity, only to be driven beyond the frontiers
of the palpable, until we break down before the prospect of
an infinite voyage into nonentity." As distinct from the great
European tradition (e.g. Shakespeare), where the writer is
concerned to " press the utmost out of sensible experience ",
to use bodily and sensible means to " show the life of the
whole man in its richest inter-relation and fullest function ",
Dostoevsky " sought to use the sensible simply as an instrument
to attain independence from everything distinctively human.
He tried to transcend sensible experience without having
first extracted its full value, and so he tended to a purely
abstract universality. . . . This accounts for a strange vortex-
like movement in his writing, as though we felt the life he

* Father Tweedy informs me that the prose only begins to be incoherent
and delirious in the Russian after the words ' The Kingdom of Heaven to her '.

was considering circling faster and faster until, at the crucial moment, it collapsed."

Mr. Traversi instances the famous account of Prince Mysh-kin's ' mystical ' experiences (at the moment of his epileptic fits), and shows how they grow out of the author's " peculiar desire to transcend normal feeling ", and so lead to anarchy. Myshkin, he says, is " reaching after an impossible abstraction of self-awareness ", and so " the fragile compound of humanity is torn between two incompatible forces, and falls into epi-lepsy ". He contrasts this with Catholic mysticism: " in *The Spiritual Canticle* [of St. John of the Cross] we see the flame of soul transfiguring the mere inert matter of the body in its ascent to God: but there is no suggestion of an inconceivable flame bursting in a vacuum ". As a further example he shows how humility in Dostoevsky often becomes an expression of egoism—" humiliation in the novels is simply sadism on a spiritual plane, and this accounts for the positive pleasure which Dostoevsky derives from it ". (In parenthesis we might confirm Mr. Traversi's thesis at this point by reference to the story of Dostoevsky's famous interview with Turgenyev: after Dostoevsky had prostrated himself in abject apology before the great rival, and had his melodramatic self-humiliation coldly received, he suddenly flared up and departed in an almost paranoiac fury.)

Mr. Traversi then analyses the movement in each of the main novels; and he points out that in *The Brothers Karamazov*, which should be the culminating novel and bring a resolution of the conflicts in the earlier ones, there is a failure to bring the broken world of good and evil together: " The most striking point about Alyosha seems to be the complete discontinuity between his virtue and the general characteristics of the *Karamazov* world. It is, in fact, pasted on to the main body of the work." It is significant, too, that

> . . . the supposedly ' Christian ' teaching of Alyosha hardly contains a word of the Incarnation. . . . It is a purely personal mysticism, often using Christian termino-logy, but rather sentimental and pantheistic in its force. It lays stress upon " watering the earth with your tears ", but the reader is troubled by lack of feeling for the real

earth of creation; Dostoevsky's earth is merely there to be wept upon. His lack of sympathy for the sensible and the tangible lands him finally in a sentimental weakness.

And so Mr. Traversi's conclusion is that Dostoevsky is

> . . . unrivalled in his exploration of certain aspects of modern disorder. His very 'metaphysical' keenness enables him to express most clearly the way in which humanity is being cut off from a full and integrated experience. . . . Placed in a world which had reached this stage of denial [denial of the sacramental nature of, for example, marriage and culture] he explored its consequences to the full, and his findings are written in his novels. In them a man is revealed with quite extraordinary discriminations of feeling, but with these directed to an impossible end. . . . The finding of criticism, I suggest, is that Dostoevsky was the master of all explorers of physical and spiritual disorder, and that his findings expose an erring adventure in human experience—the experiment, ultimately, of replacing the true balance of living by the despotic activity of the independent mind.

This is criticism of a serious and penetrating kind, beside which the average belle-lettristic eulogies look amateurishly feeble. It is a criticism which is the more serious in that it is not merely a criticism of Dostoevsky's 'ideas', but of how those ideas work out in the actual writing—the imagery, even the style—of the novels. That there is justice in the criticism I think we must admit; indeed my own rather different criticisms above of his technique, melodrama, etc., are a sort of independent endorsement of it. But the positive evidence of achievement I have tried to present in the first section of this essay suggests that this cannot be the whole story. Dostoevsky, as his letters and notebooks show, was after all painfully aware of his failure to present, either in Prince Myshkin or even in Alyosha, the 'perfectly good man';[27] but this is surely not to be taken merely as a theological deficiency—for what writer (Dante? Shakespeare?) has ever brought off this supremely difficult feat? We shall in our last section try to present an account of Dostoevsky's 'sacramental' approach to nature in a way that makes him out much nearer to the traditional Catholic position than Mr. Traversi allows. It would, however, be possible to quote passages from his novels and from occasional writings (*Letters from the Underworld*, for instance, which can hardly be classed as a novel) which show how deeply and keenly Dostoevsky sensed that what Mr. Traversi calls " the despotic activity of the independent mind " was precisely responsible for the most serious problems of modern man. But what is more to the point than Dostoevsky's theoretical awareness of this is the effect of that awareness in his actual novels. For it is open to Mr. Traversi to say that here the evidence is all against Dostoevsky. It is perfectly true that in the best-known, indeed, the most spectacular passages in the great novels there are marks of the unbalance that Mr. Traversi speaks of. But these passages need to be judged in relation to the novels as a whole, and particularly to those passages (such as those quoted in our first section above) in which Dostoevsky shows a control and a handling of his human material which only an extremely balanced writer could achieve. It is true that sometimes, indeed often, Dostoevsky in his exploration of extreme states of consciousness seems to lose his head, to grow dizzy in the midst of the ' vortex-like ' movement which he is studying. Few writers have ever penetrated so deeply into these movements (as Mr. Traversi admits), and it is not to be wondered at that the effort became so often vertiginous. What is, I believe, amazing, is rather the extent to which Dostoevsky did manage to keep his head in the midst of it, that he has in the long run such a constant awareness of the dangers involved. In a novel like *A Raw Youth*, for instance (which Mr. Traversi does not study), it is remarkable that the whirling and almost neurotic development of Versilov's character and the ' Raw Youth's ' own reactions to it should be so coolly placed, and, as it were, steadied, by the framework of the novel itself—viz. the mental history and growth of the boy through whose eyes the story is seen. There is, perhaps, just a suggestion, in Mr. Traversi's criticism, of the ' personal heresy ', the biographical replacing the literary-critical. He is, of course, too good a critic to take the crude view such as was taken by, for example, Strakhov, who believed that Stavrogin's ' Confessions ' (the confession that he had raped a little girl, which Dostoevsky cut

out of *The Possessed* in deference to his friend's criticism) was a
piece of autobiography—an insinuation which is now rejected
by all the best authorities.[28] But a hint nevertheless remains in
Mr. Traversi's essay that Dostoevsky has too closely identified
his own personal doubts and lack of grip upon the central
Catholic tradition with the themes of the novels. If one were
in fact discussing the personal issue, there would, I think, be
something to be said, as Vycheslav Ivanov has contended[29],
on behalf of Dostoevsky's essential and ultimate orthodoxy—
taking into account, of course, the ' romantic ' divagations of
his time, which affected Catholic writers too. But at the level
of the novelist's art, what wants saying is that Dostoevsky is
always in the end aware of what he is doing. A deep-sea diver,
he is in constant danger of succumbing to the pressures at the
levels which he reaches; but always, I believe, we are conscious
of the steadying pull of the rope and the constant presence of
the air-pipe line.

★

Let me conclude this section by trying to justify the above
claims for Dostoevsky through an indication of his artistic
steersmanship, not this time so much in individual passages of
brilliance as in the larger shape of his themes as a whole. I have
mentioned *A Raw Youth* for its effectiveness of total direction
(whatever its internal weaknesses and occasional tedium).
This requires to be made more explicit. The novel opens thus:

> I cannot resist sitting down to write the history of the
> first steps in my career, though I might very well abstain
> from doing so. . . . I know one thing for certain: I shall
> never again sit down to write my autobiography even if I
> live to be a hundred. One must be too disgustingly in love
> with self to be able without shame to write about oneself.
> . . . I am not a professional writer and don't want to be,
> and to drag forth into the literary market-place the inmost
> secrets of my soul and an artistic description of my feelings
> I should regard as indecent and contemptible. . . .
> I am beginning—or rather, I should like to begin—
> these notes from the 19th of September of last year, that is,
> from the first day I first met . . .

But to explain so prematurely who it was I met before anything else is known would be cheap; in fact, I believe my tone is cheap. I vowed I would eschew all literary graces, and here at the first sentence I am being seduced by them. . . . I am now reading over what I have written, and I see that I am much cleverer than what I have written. How is it that what is expressed by a clever man is much more stupid than what is left in him? I have more than once during this momentous year noticed this with myself in my relations with people, and have been very worried by it.[30]

Normally this kind of self-conscious, apologetic introduction to a novel, in which the author makes the protagonist of the novel disclaim all pretensions to being a novelist, rings crude and insincere. But in reference to what is to follow, and the curious, circular, fumbling movement of the whole novel, so expressive of the Youth's development (the development, that is, which comes from suddenly plunging immaturity into the midst of subtle and advanced experiences), it seems to me that the opening turns out to be masterly. And this is confirmed by the conclusion of the novel. At first it appears to be the traditional kind of conclusion—the rapid and rather summary tying up of a number of loose ends—till we suddenly come across this paragraph:

Katerina Nikolaevna he [Versilov, the ' Raw Youth's ' father] seems to have completely forgotten and has never once mentioned. Nothing has been said of marriage with my mother so far, either. They did think of taking him abroad for the summer; but Tatyana Pavlovna strongly opposed it, and he did not desire it himself. . . . By the way we are all still living at the expense of Tatya Pavlovna [his aunt]. One thing I will add: I am dreadfully sorry that I have several times in this narrative allowed myself to take up a disrespectful and superior attitude in regard to Versilov. But as I wrote I imagined myself precisely at each of the moments I was describing. As I finish the narrative and write the last lines, I suddenly feel by the very process of recalling and recording, I have re-educated myself. I regret a great deal I have written, especially the

tone of certain sentences and pages, but I will not cross
them out or correct a single word.[31]

This conclusion seems to me to be borne out by the actual
writing in the course of the novel itself, and testifies quite
remarkably to what I have called the sense of control that
Dostoevsky, often unsuspectedly, is able to exercise over his
creation.

A much slighter and perhaps even a flippant example may
be taken from the end of a very different type of story, *The
Eternal Husband*. Here we are, astonishingly, in the world of
(almost) light farce, the farce of the eternal triangle. (Only
' almost ', because the novel has its sudden passionate depths,
in the scenes of hatred between Pavel Pavlovitch and Velchaninov, especially the famous scene in which they are sleeping
together and the former, having nursed the latter through
sickness, attempts immediately after to murder him.) In the
last chapter we are whisked back from the tenser atmosphere
into the light play of sexual rivalry. Two years after the
devastating events that form the centre of the story, Velchaninov has an accidental encounter with his old rival Pavel
Pavlovitch on a railway station on the way to Odessa. This time
the latter is married to a pretty young girl. By chance Velchaninov has been able to render service to the young wife,
without knowing who she is, and when Pavel Pavlovitch
appears on the scene this very indebtedness resuscitates the old
rivalry. Pavel Pavlovitch is a born cuckold; and his heart
sinks when he finds that his new young wife is inviting Velchaninov to come and stay with them—for he foresees the old
story starting up all over again. Pavel Pavlovitch is waiting for
their train to start, so that he can get away from his rival.

> Pavel Pavlovitch promptly appeared before him with an
> uneasy expression in his face and whole figure. Vel-
> chaninov laughed, took him by the elbow in a friendly way,
> led him to the nearest bench, sat down himself, and made
> him sit down beside him. He remained silent; he wanted
> Pavel Pavlovitch to be the first to speak.
> " So you are coming to us? " faltered the latter, going
> straight to the point.
> " I knew that would be it! You haven't changed in the

least! " laughed Velchaninov. " Why, do you mean to say "—he slapped him again on the shoulder—" do you mean to say you could seriously imagine for a moment that I could actually come and stay with you, and for a whole month too—ha-ha? "

Pavel Pavlovitch was all of a twitter.

" So you—are not coming! " he cried, not in the least disguising his relief.

" I'm not coming, I'm not coming! " Velchaninov laughed complacently.[32]

For a moment, however, the scene becomes tense again, as Velchaninov suddenly threatens to tell Pavel Pavlovitch's new wife about their previous rivalry—how Pavel Pavlovitch had nearly murdered him because he had taken his first wife as a lover—but all is solved by the last train whistle going; Pavel Pavlovitch has to rush to catch it, while his young wife, who is already aboard, shrieks for him.

> Pavel Pavlovitch roused himself, flung up his hands and ran full speed to the train; the train was already in motion, but he managed to hang on somehow, and went flying to his compartment. Velchaninov remained at the station and only in the evening set off on his original route in another train. He did not turn off to the right to see his fair friend [a lady friend whom he had been travelling to Odessa to see]—he felt too much out of humour. And how he regretted it afterwards.[33]

With those words, rather in the vein of a short story by Mr. Somerset Maugham, the novel ends. It is slight, but extremely skilful and shows not only Dostoevsky's versatility but also his supreme control.

For a final example of the ' control ', we will turn back to a novel which we have found plenty of reasons for criticizing on other grounds. Mr. Traversi, indeed, singles out the end of *Crime and Punishment* as an example of sentimentality doing duty for genuine resolution: " not all the talk about ' regeneration ' at the end of the book can conceal that Dostoevsky's deepest, almost unconscious, interests were elsewhere ".[34] This seems to me not wholly fair. If one compares the end of the novel with the almost word-for-word identical scenes in *The House of the Dead*, where Dostoevsky is undisguisedly describing his own experience of, and 'regeneration' in, the Siberian prison camp, one cannot be left in doubt as to the genuineness of the interest. However, it is not the end of the novel, which in its picture of Sonia has perhaps something of the sentimentality of a Dickens conclusion, but an earlier passage that I wish to use for illustration. It is the brilliant and heart-rending scene—here not, I think, exaggerated to melodramatic proportions—between Raskolnikov and Sonia Marmaladov, when the former visits her flat after her father's death. The scene is long, yet never long drawn out. We can only quote the central section.

" So you pray to God a great deal, Sonia? " he asked her.

Sonia did not speak, he stood beside her waiting for an answer.

" What should I be without God? " she whispered rapidly, forcibly, glancing at him with suddenly flashing eyes, and squeezing his hand.

" Ah, so that is it! " he thought.

" And what does God do for you? " he asked, probing her further.

Sonia was silent a long while, as though she could not answer. Her weak chest kept heaving with emotion. . . . There was a book lying on the chest of drawers. He had noticed it every time he paced up and down the room. Now he took it up and looked at it. It was the New Testament in the Russian translation. It was bound in leather, old and worn.

" Where did you get that? " he called to her across the room. . . .

" It was brought to me," she answered, as it were unwillingly, not looking at him.

" Who brought it? "

" Lizaveta, I asked her for it." [The old pedlar whom Raskolnikov had murdered.]

" Lizaveta! Strange! " he thought. . . .

" Where is the story of Lazarus? " he asked suddenly.

Sonia looked obstinately at the ground and would not answer. She was standing sideways to the table. . . .

" Find it and read it to me," he said. . . .

Sonia heard Raskolnikov's request distrustfully and moved hesitating to the table. She took the book, however.

" Haven't you read it? " she asked, looking up at him across the table.

Her voice became sterner and sterner.

" Long ago. . . . When I was at school. Read! "

" And haven't you heard it in church? "

" I . . . haven't been. Do you often go? "

" N-no," whispered Sonia.

Raskolnikov smiled.

" I understand. . . . And you won't go to your father's funeral tomorrow? "

" Yes, I shall. I was at church last week, too. . . . I had a requiem service."

" For whom? "

" For Lizaveta. She was killed with an axe."

His nerves were more and more strained. His head began to go round.

" Were you friends with Lizaveta? "

" Yes. . . . She was good . . . she used to come . . . not often . . . she couldn't. . . . We used to read together and . . . talk. She will see God."[35]

We could have quoted instead of this passage the more famous, perhaps more spectacular, ending of *The Idiot*, with its superb quiet of reconciliation between Myshkin and Rogozhin, in the presence of Nastasya's dead body. But the above passage from *Crime and Punishment*, with its sincerity and tact keeping the dramatic arrangement (the sudden mention of a requiem for Lizaveta) in rein, shows better than almost any other passage from the novels how Dostoevsky, for all his utter commitment to the characters in their deepest plunges, remains in control. Or perhaps we may say that, because of his essential humility (a different thing from the masochistic self-humiliation which Mr. Traversi criticizes, which remains nearer the surface), because of the absence in such passages of all personal dogmatism, Dostoevsky shows himself not imperiously standing above the struggles of his creatures, on the contrary involved in their very depths, and yet aware that there is higher ground, not of his making, where final judgment is passed—of which his own judgment, as artistic creator and novelist, is but a pale though genuine analogy.

III. DOSTOEVSKY AND THE DOCTRINE OF 'NATURE'

The element of ' strain ' which we have seen adduced as a weakness in Dostoevsky's novels is inseparable from both his vocation as a writer and his experience as a nineteenth-century believer in the midst of unbelief. We know well enough how he poured himself, his questionings and doubtings, his reassurances and flashes of certainty, into his characters. " The main question which will be pursued in all the sections of this book ", he said himself of *The Brothers Karamazov*, " is the very one which has tormented me, consciously or unconsciously, all my life: the existence of God." And we cannot doubt that the same is true of Raskolnikov's soliloquies, of Shatov, of old Makar Ivanovitch of *The Raw Youth*, and even of Kirillov. But the truest test of a writer's integrity of belief is to be found in his total creations. We have tried to vindicate his skill and control as a creator. We will now conclude by looking at one particularly revealing element in his creation; his attitude to, and use of, the natural world.

★

A cursory reading of at least the major novels of Dostoevsky leaves most people, one suspects, with the impression of a very voluble and excited conversation between two or three gesticulating travellers in the third-class compartment of a rather dingy express train rushing through countryside which none of the travellers ever takes a moment to observe through the window. I had myself formed this impression from the novels before ever I came across the remarks about Dostoevsky made by his friend Strakhov. He said in his Memoirs: " All his [Dostoevsky's] attention was upon people, and all his efforts were directed towards understanding their nature and character. People, their temperament, way of living, feelings, thoughts, these were his sole preoccupation." And again, describing Dostoevsky's visits abroad, " He did not take much count either of natural beauty or historical memories or of works of art."[36]

On the other hand we are brought up short when we read in Dostoevsky's Diary an account of his childhood, when he was nine years old.

> [I recalled] the month of August in our village: a dry and clear day, though somewhat chilly and windy; the summer was coming to an end, and soon I should have to go to Moscow, again to be wearied all the winter over French lessons; and I was so sad over the fact that I would have to leave the country. I went beyond the barns and, having descended to a ravine, I climbed up the ' Losk '— this was the name given to a thick shrubbery on the far side of the ravine, which extended as far as the grove. Presently I plunged deeper in the bushes. . . . I was absorbed in my task: I was trying to break off a walnut whip for myself, to hit frogs with; walnut whips are so pretty though not solid—no comparison with birch ones! I was interested in insects and beetles; I was collecting them—among them there are very neat ones. I was also fond of little agile lizards with tiny black dots; but I was afraid of little snakes; these, however, were found far more rarely than lizards. Here, there were a few mushrooms— to find mushrooms one had to go to the birch grove, and I intended to go on there. And in all my life I have loved nothing so much as the forest, with its mushrooms and wild berries, its insects and birds and little hedgehogs and squirrels; its damp odour of dead leaves, which I so adored. Even now, as I am writing these lines, it seems that I can smell the odour of our country birch grove: these impressions remain intact throughout one's whole life.[37]

Does not this passage suggest a rather different view? Or at least, if it is true that in his childhood Dostoevsky had a great love of ' nature ', how is it that so little of this seems to survive and find its way in his major creative works?[38]

NATURE AS THERAPY

Even this passage from his Diary, however, is set in a qualifying context which is important. For the passage we have just quoted precedes the famous account of his meeting with the peasant Matvei. Dostoevsky, in fact, had been discussing his own 'discovery' of the simple faith of the Russian peasant, of which he first became fully aware during his imprisonment in Siberia. And to illustrate this he tells us how it brought back to him a forgotten incident in early childhood. He had wandered into the country (here follows the passage we have quoted). Then he was suddenly startled by the imaginary fear of a wolf. He ran along, screaming with fright; and it was at this point that the old peasant, Matvei, found him and comforted him with that gentle piety and illiterate wisdom which Dostoevsky was later to admire so much (and to depict in Makar Ivanovitch of *A Raw Youth*).

Now it is significant that in many of his novels some of the descriptions of 'nature' occur thus at the centre-point of passages of emotional disturbance. Sometimes 'nature' simply acts as a sedative to spiritual turmoil. It is obvious how this could happen in the prison camp. For instance, here is Dostoevsky's account of the work the prisoners had to do in the summer—far harder than in the winter. He had to carry bricks, for building, 160 yards from the River Irtish to the barracks that were being constructed—150 pounds' weight of bricks at a time, with the cord cutting his shoulder. Yet, he says,

> I liked carrying bricks because the work took me to the bank of the Irtish. I speak of the river bank so often because it was only from there one had a view of God's world, of the pure clear distance, of the free solitary steppes, the emptiness of which made a strange impression on me. . . . Everything there was sweet and precious in my eyes, the hot brilliant sun in the fathomless blue sky and the far-away song of the Kirghiz floating from the farther bank. One gazes into the distance and makes out at last the poor smoke-blackened tent of some Kirghiz. One discerns the smoke rising from the tent, the Kirghiz woman busy with her two sheep. It is all poor and barbarous, but

it is free. One descries a bird in the limpid blue air and for
a long time one watches its flight: now it darts over the
water, now it vanishes in the blue depths, now it reappears
again, a speck flitting in the distance. . . . Even the poor
sickly flower which I found early in spring in a crevice of
the rocky bank drew my attention almost painfully.[39]

Sometimes the therapeutic power of the natural scene is
more subtly and less overtly conveyed. There is an interesting
example in the witty, long-short novel from which we have
quoted earlier (since it is not very well known), *The Eternal
Husband*. Velchaninov has arranged for the adoption of his
natural daughter, Liza. Velchaninov is not a mere 'rake';
it is that some husbands are simply fated to have unfaithful
wives, and Pavel Pavlovitch Trusotsky is such a husband. It
is by Trusotsky's wife, Natalya Vassilyevna, that Velchaninov
has this little girl, Liza—though he only learns about it with
surprise some years later. Natalya, the mother, has died of
consumption and Pavel Pavlovitch turns up with Liza, whom
he maltreats. Velchaninov then, finding that Liza is ill, and
that Pavel Pavlovitch is in too drunken a state to care for her,
takes her away to some friends in the country. There, on a
beautiful summer evening at sunset, Liza dies. Velchaninov is
prostrate with grief—in the short time he had come to love the
little girl.

After the funeral Velchaninov left the villa. For a whole
fortnight he wandered about the town aimless and alone,
so lost in thought that he stumbled against people in the
street. Sometimes he would lie stretched out on his sofa
for days together, forgetting the commonest things of
everyday life. . . . One day, scarcely conscious of where
he was going, he wandered into the cemetery where Liza
was buried and found her little grave. He had not been to
the cemetery since the funeral; he had always fancied it
would be too great an agony, and had been afraid to go.
But strange to say, when he had found her little grave and
kissed it, his heart felt easier. It was a fine evening, the
sun was setting; all around the graves the lush green grass
was growing; the bees were humming in a wild rose close
by; the flowers and wreaths left by the children . . . on

Liza's grave were lying there with the petals half dropping. There was a gleam of something like hope in his heart after many days.

" How serene! " he thought, feeling the stillness of the cemetery, and looking at the clear, peaceful sky.

A rush of pure, calm faith flooded his soul.

" Liza has sent me this, it's Liza speaking to me," he thought.[40]

The action of kissing the grave links with another element in Dostoevsky's attitude to nature which we shall discuss later (we have already noticed Mr. Traversi's comments on it). What is to be observed here is that even the faded flowers, symbols of Liza's mortality, do not undermine the dominant hopefulness of the scene.

THE UNDERWORLD

There is one sentence in the passage from the Diary which we quoted at the beginning of this section which gives us a clue in another direction. " I was interested in insects and beetles; I was collecting them . . ." Plenty of children have done so before without sinister implications; but when we take into account Dostoevsky's later preoccupations it may be more significant in his case (especially when linked with the element of sadism implied in the fact that he was making himself a walnut whip ' to hit frogs with '). It is interesting that in the title *Letters from the Underworld*, the word translated ' underworld ' (*podpolye*) is, we are told, one used to describe the cellar or the space under the floor-boards where the spiders and beetles lurk. And in these letters when he talks about the ' man of sensibility ', the man who is different, independent, who will not sit down under the boredom and inertia of the commonplace, is compared to a mouse—" a very sensitive mouse, it is true, yet none the less a mouse ". This man of sensibility will, no doubt, be insulted by the normal run of mankind, as a result of which " nothing will be left for the mouse to do but to make a disdainful gesture with its little paw, indulge in a smile of deprecatory contempt . . . and retire shamefacedly into its hole. There, in its dirty, stinking underworld, our poor insulted, brow-beaten mouse will soon have immersed itself in a state of cold, malignant, perpetual rancour. . . ."[41] But he (the ' mouse-man ' of sensibility) will even so be better off than the normal man, for he will at least have the consolation of his independence; and his bitterness and desire for revenge will be better than the state of mere monotonous, naturalistic, predictable existence. (This leads up to the often-quoted passage in which Dostoevsky, with astonishing foresight, predicts the coming of scientific materialism, of the ' brave new world ' of statistical efficiency and determinism, against which, he says, even wicked originality will be a healthy, because a natural, reaction.)

In one form or another the ' underworld ' constantly recurs in the novels. There is one passage which may, I think, have given Kafka some ideas for his terrible story, *Metamorphosis*. It is the dream of the tubercular boy, Ippolit Terentyev, in *The Idiot*. Here is a section of it:

> I fell asleep and dreamt that I was in a room, but not my own. . . . In the room I noticed an awful animal, a sort of monster. It was like a scorpion, but was not a scorpion, it was more disgusting, and much more horrible, and it seemed it was so, just because there was nothing like it in nature, and that it had come *expressly* to me. . . . It was brown, and was covered with shell, a crawling reptile, seven inches long, tapering down to the tail. . . . Almost two inches from the head, at an angle of forty-five degrees to the body, grew two legs, one on each side, nearly four inches long, so that the whole creature was in the shape of a trident, if looked at from above. I couldn't make out the head, but I saw two whiskers, short, and also brown, looking like two strong needles. . . . The beast was running about the room, very quickly, on its legs and its tail, and, when it ran, the body and legs wriggled like little snakes. . . . I was awfully afraid it would sting me; I had been told it was poisonous. . . . It hid under the chest of drawers, under the cupboard, crawled into corners. I sat on a chair, and drew my legs up under me. . . . Suddenly I heard behind me, almost at my head, a sort of scraping rustle. I looked round and saw that the reptile was

crawling up the wall, and was already on a level with
my head and was positively touching my hair with its
tail. . . . My mother came into the room with some
friend of hers. They began trying to catch the creature,
but were cooler than I was, and were not, in fact, afraid
of it. . . . Then, my mother opened the door and called
Norma, our dog—a huge, shaggy, black Newfoundland;
it died five years ago. It rushed into the room and
stopped short before the reptile. . . . All at once she
(Norma) slowly bared her terrible teeth and opened her
huge red jaws, crouched, prepared for a spring . . . and
suddenly seized the creature with her teeth. . . . Its shell
cracked between her teeth, the tail and legs hanging out
of the mouth, moved at a tremendous rate. All at once
Norma gave a piteous squeal: the reptile had managed to
sting her tongue. Whining and yelping she opened her
mouth from the pain, and I saw that the creature, though
bitten in two, was still wriggling in her mouth, and was
emitting, from its crushed body, on to the dog's tongue, a
quantity of white fluid such as comes out of a squashed
black-beetle. . . . Then I waked up and the prince
came in.[42]

The symbol of the spider, the cockroach, the insect or the
germ is of frequent occurrence, especially in the uglier sections
of the novels. A curious, bludgeoning, self-opinionated character in *The Possessed*, Captain Lebiadkin, observes in his incoherent way that: " That little word ' why ' has run through all the
universe from the first day of creation, and all nature cries
every minute to its Creator: ' Why? ' And for 7,000 years it
has had no answer. . . ." And he goes on to illustrate this
would-be profound remark by a stupid—yet revealing—fable
in verse called ' The Cockroach '. A cockroach fell into a glass
full of flies, collected there in summertime. The flies resent the
cockroach's presence, and there is a fight. At that moment a
' fine old man ', Nikifor, comes in. " Nikifor takes the glass,
and in spite of their outcry empties away the whole stew, flies,
beetles and all, into the pig-pail, which ought to have been
done long ago. But observe, madam, observe, the cockroach
doesn't complain. That's the answer to your question, ' Why? '

he cried triumphantly. ' The cockroach does not complain.'
As for Nikifor, he typifies nature."[43]

When in *The Idiot* Prince Myshkin is describing the maltreat-
ment of the girl Marie by the villagers, who blamed her because
she had been seduced by a French commercial traveller, he
says: " When they all ran in, she hid her face in her dishevelled
hair and lay face downwards on the floor. They all stared at
her, as though she were a reptile; the old people blamed and
upbraided her, the young people laughed; the women reviled
and abused her and looked at her with loathing, as though
she had been a spider."[44]

Even more significant are two conversations, one from *The
Possessed*, the other from *Crime and Punishment*. In the former
Stavrogin is talking to the atheist, intending-suicide, Kirillov:

"You don't say prayers yourself? "
" I pray to everything. You see the spider crawling on
the wall, I look at it and thank it for crawling."[45]

In the latter Svidrigailov is talking to the murderer.

" I don't believe in a future life ", said Raskolnikov.
Svidrigailov sat lost in thought.
" And what if there are only spiders there, or something
of that sort? " he asked suddenly.
" He is a madman ", thought Raskolnikov.
" We always imagine eternity as something beyond our
conception, something vast, vast! But why must it be vast?
Instead of all that, what if it's one little room, like a bath
house in the country, black and grimy and spiders in every
corner, and that's all eternity is? I sometimes fancy it like
that."[46]

Svidrigailov, like Kirillov, shoots himself: but without the
latter's clear deliberation; and the difference in their respective
attitudes to ' the spider on the wall ' is the difference in their
natures. Finally we may take another instance from *Crime
and Punishment*. When Raskolnikov is taken ill in the
Siberian prison to which he has been sentenced for his murder,
he has a dream which is expressed in somewhat similar imagery.

He dreamt that the whole world was condemned to a
terrible new strange plague that had come to Europe from

the depths of Asia. All were to be destroyed except a very
few chosen. Some new sorts of microbes were attacking
the bodies of men, but these microbes were endowed with
intelligence and will. Men attacked by them became at
once mad and furious. But never had men considered
themselves so intellectual and so completely in possession
of the truth as these sufferers, never had they considered
their decisions, their scientific conclusions, their moral
convictions so infallible. Whole villages, whole towns and
peoples went mad from the infection. . . . Men killed each
other in a sort of senseless spite. They gathered together
in armies against one another, but even on the march the
armies would begin attacking each other, the ranks would
be broken and the soldiers would fall on each other, stab-
bing and cutting, biting and devouring each other. . . .
There were conflagrations and famine. The plague spread
and moved farther and farther. Only a few men could be
saved in the whole world. . . .[47]

Here we have a variant of the theme of *Letters from the
Underworld*, already mentioned: the coming of a new, efficient,
scientific totalitarianism which will claim to answer all problems but will end by setting men against one another.* So vile
and corrupt nature is used to symbolize the evil in man. But
there is also another use of nature: to symbolize that which
most contrasts with man.

MAN THE EXILE

We have quoted from Ippolit's mad dream in *The Idiot*. But
to understand that dream fully we must see it in its context. It
is quoted in a long article he has written, which he calls *Après
moi le déluge*, and which he insists on reading aloud to the
assembled company, and which ends with an apologia for his
intended suicide. He thinks he has only a few weeks to live
in any case, owing to his consumption. Prince Myshkin has
tried to make his last few weeks on earth more comfortable by

---

* Of course, as Mrs. Cross has pointed out to me, the insects symbolize much
more than this. See also Renato Poggioli on " Kafka and Dostoevsky " in A. Flores,
The Kafka Problem (New Directions, 1946).

moving him into pleasanter surroundings, with the trees of
the Pavlovsk park to look at. But Ippolit resents this.

> What does he want to bring in his ridiculous ' trees of
> Pavlovsk ' for? To soften the last hours of my life? . . .
> What use to me is your nature, your Pavlovsk park, your
> sunrises and sunsets, your blue sky, your contented faces,
> when all this endless festival has begun by my being
> excluded from it? What is there for me in this beauty
> when, every minute, every second, I am obliged, forced,
> to recognize that even the tiny fly, buzzing in the sunlight
> beside me, has its share in the banquet and chorus, knows
> its place, loves it and is happy; and I alone am an outcast,
> and only my cowardice has made me refuse to realize it
> till now.[48]

Actually Ippolit does not kill himself. But Myshkin remembers this passage vividly later on. He is in the park, and is
about to have a fatal encounter with Aglaia, when he suddenly
remembers Ippolit's saying. " In a tree overhead a bird was
singing, and he began looking for it among the leaves. All at
once the bird darted out of the tree, and at the same instant
he recalled the ' fly in the warm sunshine ', of which Ippolit
had written, that ' it knew its place and took part in the
general chorus, but he alone was an outcast '. The phrase had
struck him at the time; and he recalled it now. One long-
forgotten memory stirred within him, and suddenly rose up
clear before him." What he suddenly recalls is a similar
experience of his own, when he had been in Switzerland, an
invalid suffering from epilepsy.

> He once went up into the mountain-side, on a bright,
> sunny day, and walked a long time, his mind possessed
> with an agonizing but unformulated idea. Before him was
> the brilliant sky, below, the lake, and all around a horizon,
> bright and boundless, which seemed to have no ending.
> He gazed a long time in distress. He remembered now
> how he had stretched out his hands to that bright, infinite
> blue, and had shed tears. What tortured him was that he
> was utterly outside all this. What was this festival? what
> was this grand, everlasting pageant to which there was no

end, to which he had always, from his earliest childhood,
been drawn and in which he could never take part?
Every morning the same bright sun rises, every morning
the same rainbow in the waterfall; every evening that highest snow mountain glows, with a flush of purple against
the distant sky. . . . Every blade of grass grows and is
happy! Everything has its path, and everything knows its
path, and with a song goes forth, and with a song returns.
Only he knows nothing, and understands nothing, neither
men nor sounds; he is outside it all, and an outcast. Oh,
of course he could not say it then in those words, could
not utter his question. He suffered dumbly, not
comprehending. [49]

We notice the reference to his childhood—and can scarcely
forbear to link it with Dostoevsky's own reference to his childhood in his *Journal*. But the passage also has another
significance. If we keep it, along with Ippolit's remarks, in
mind, we shall find that it illuminates the brilliant and terrible
scene at the end of the same novel, when Myshkin calls on
Rogozhin and finds Nastasya Filippovna dead, killed by
Rogozhin. The scene, which we forbore to quote in our
last section, is too important to omit, even though it is so
famous.

Myshkin took a step nearer, then a second, and stood
still. He stood still and looked for a minute or two.
Neither of them uttered a word all the while they stood by
the bedside. Myshkin's heart beat so violently that it
seemed as though it were audible in the death-like stillness
of the room. Someone lay asleep on it [the bed], in a
perfectly motionless sleep; not the faintest stir, not the
faintest breath could be heard. The sleeper was covered
over from head to foot with a white sheet and the limbs
were vaguely defined; all that could be seen was that a
human figure lay there, stretched at full length. All
around . . . clothes had been flung in disorder; a rich
white silk dress, flowers and ribbons. On a little table at
the head of the bed there was a glitter of diamonds that
had been taken off and thrown down. At the end of the

bed there was a crumpled heap of lace and on the white lace the toes of a foot peeped out from under the sheet; it seemed as though it had been carved out of marble and it was horribly still. Myshkin looked and felt that as he looked, the room became more and more still and death-like. Suddenly there was the buzz of a fly which flew over the bed and settled on the pillow. Myshkin started.[50]

The marvellous economy of this scene is shown by the double work of that fly. It is never expressly stated that the ' sleeping ' figure of Nastasya is dead, but we are prepared for it by the 'death-like' nature of the silence and the room; and then suddenly the fly, gently hinting at the imminent corruption which is already beginning to attract it, appears to announce, with its buzz, the word ' death '.[51] At the same time, the fly that alights on the pillow, after a free flight through the air, represents that part of nature's ' festival ' from which man is excluded—until he takes up a humbler rôle in it, as carrion. All this helps to explain the power and purity of this *Act Five* of the tragedy, which has something of the horror and yet delicacy of the closing scene of *Lear*. And, significantly, what follows in *The Idiot* is that Myshkin, always unbalanced, now goes completely mad, and is taken back again to Dr. Schneider's institute in Switzerland—the scene of his first sudden awareness of man's exile from nature.

NATURE AS SACRAMENTAL

In the passage quoted above from *The Eternal Husband*, where Velchaninov visits Liza's grave, we noted his action in kissing the grave. There are other incidents of this sort in the novels; and no doubt they do not appear so demonstrative to the Russian, with his ceremonial attitude to *things*, as they do to us. The prostrations and osculations of the Eastern rite provide a background of familiarity for some of the gestures of Dostoevsky's characters, and suggest a modification of Mr. Traversi's criticism that ' the earth only exists to be wept upon '.[52] There is, for instance, Raskolnikov's sudden reaction in the presence of Sonia Marmaladov, the girl who had been reduced to prostitution to keep her family alive.

He paced up and down the room in silence, not looking at her. At last he went up to her; his eyes glittered. He put his two hands on her shoulders and looked straight into her tearful face. His eyes were hard, feverish and piercing, his lips were twitching. All at once he bent down quickly and dropping to the ground, kissed her foot. Sonia drew back from him as from a madman. And certainly he looked like a madman.

" What are you doing to me? " she muttered, turning pale, and a sudden anguish clutched at her heart.

He stood up at once.

" I did not bow down to you, I bowed down to all the suffering of humanity," he said wildly and walked away to the window.[53]

In *The Brothers Karamazov* there is a strikingly similar gesture —striking precisely because this time it is in the opposite sense; instead of a murderer kissing the foot of a saint, it is a saint kissing the foot of a (prospective) murderer. In Father Zossima's cell the visitors have been behaving badly, especially the old Karamazov, Fyodor Pavlovitch. " But this unseemly scene was cut short in a most unexpected way. Father Zossima rose suddenly from his seat ... moved towards Dmitri [Karamazov] and reaching him sank on his knees before him. Alyosha thought that he had fallen from weakness, but this was not so. The elder distinctly and deliberately bowed down at Dmitri's feet till his forehead touched the floor."[54] Later Zossima explains his action to Alyosha: " Make haste to find him [Dmitri], go again tomorrow and make haste, leave everything and make haste. Perhaps you may still have time to prevent something terrible. I bowed down yesterday to the great suffering in store for him."[55] This helps us to understand the apparently extravagant gesture which Sonia imposes upon Raskolnikov, when he shall confess his crime. " Raskolnikov suddenly recalled Sonia's words, ' Go to the crossroads, bow down to the people, kiss the earth, for you have sinned against it too, and say aloud to the whole world, " I am a murderer " ' . He trembled, remembering that. ... Everything in him softened at once and the tears started into his eyes. He fell to the earth on the spot. ... He knelt down in the middle of the square, bowed down to the earth, and kissed that filthy earth with bliss and rapture."[56]

Father Zossima's own teaching is in line with this. " Love to throw yourself on the earth (he pleads) and kiss it. Kiss the earth and love it with an unceasing, consuming love. . . . Water the earth with the tears of your joy and love those tears."[57] And his own death illustrates his teaching. " He seemed suddenly to feel an acute pain in his chest, he turned pale and pressed his hands to his heart. All rose from their seats and hastened to him. But though suffering, he still looked at them with a smile, sank slowly from his chair on to his knees, then bowed his face to the ground, stretching out his arms and as though in joyful ecstasy, praying and kissing the ground, quietly and joyfully gave up his soul to God."[58]

It is either the simple or the penitent who have this vision of the earth's place in God's kingdom. For the simple, the best example is the mad old woman in the convent who was doing penance for her sins, of whom Marya Timofyevna tells the company in *The Possessed*. This old woman, says Marya Timofyevna,

> . . . whispered to me as she was coming out of church: " What is the mother of God? What do you think? " " The great mother," I answer, " the hope of the human race." " Yes," she answered, " the mother of God is the great mother—the damp earth, and therein lies great joy for men. And every earthly woe and every earthly tear is a joy for us; and when you water the earth with your tears a foot deep, you will rejoice at everything at once, and your sorrow will be no more, such is the prophecy." That word sank into my heart at the time. Since then when I bow down to the ground at my prayers, I've taken to kissing the earth. I kiss it and weep. . . . I used to go out to the shores of the lake; on one side was our convent and on the other the pointed mountain, they call it the Peak. I used to go up that mountain, facing the east, fall down to the ground, and weep and weep, and I don't know how long I wept, and I don't remember or know anything about it. . . .[59]

Of the penitent we may take two examples. Father Zossima's

young brother, who had for a time been a sceptic, in his last illness returns to the Orthodox faith.

> The windows of his room looked out into the garden, and our garden was a shady one, with the old trees in it which were coming into bud. The first birds of spring were flitting in the branches, chirruping and singing at the windows. And looking at them and admiring them, he began suddenly begging their forgiveness too. " Birds of heaven, happy birds, forgive me, for I have sinned against you too." None of us could understand that at the time, but he shed tears of joy. " Yes," he said, " there was such a glory of God all about me; birds, trees, meadows, sky, only I lived in shame and dishonoured it all and did not notice the beauty and glory."[60]

Similarly it is as a result of his purgation in the Siberian prison that Raskolnikov can see nature pure and whole again. The passage in which he goes out to work on the river bank and meets Sonia, and finally accepts his punishment as a mere momentary interruption to their future happiness, is simply the working into the novel of the almost identical passage from Dostoevsky's own experience on the Irtish river bank, given above. For a final example of this awareness of nature as sacramental we may turn to a very different novel, *The Raw Youth*. The semi-literate, but deeply wise old peasant-monk, Makar Ivanovitch, is talking to the ' raw youth ', whose guardian he once was:

> You're wrong, my dear, not to pray [he says]. It is a good thing, it cheers the heart before sleep, and rising up from sleep and awakening in the night. . . . Let me tell you this. In the summer we were hastening to the monastery of our Lady for the holy festival. . . . We spent the night, brother, in the open country, and I waked up early in the morning when all was still sleeping and the dear sun had not yet peeped out from behind the forest. I lifted up my head, dear, I gazed about me and sighed. Everywhere beauty passing utterance! All was still, the air was light; the grass grows—Grow, grass of God, the bird sings—Sing, bird of God, the babe cries in the woman's arms—God be

with you, little man; grow and be happy, little babe! And
it seemed that only then for the first time in my life I took
it all in. . . . Life is sweet, dear! If I were better, I should
like to go out again in the spring.[61]

All this is not Dostoevsky's invention, for it is there in the
Russian Orthodox tradition. There are close affinities between
the Franciscan attitude to nature and that of some Russian
saints—even extending, for instance in the case of St. Seraphim,
to a hypnotic power over wild animals. And we know, too,
that Dostoevsky had a great veneration for St. Tikhon Zadonsky—he complains in his Diary that men have forgotten St.
Tikhon; he visited his monastery, and drew on memoirs of him
for the picture of Father Zossima. Here, then, is a passage from
one of St. Tikhon's writings, comparing the spring with the
Resurrection:

> Spring has burst out; it reveals a new treasury of divine
> gifts . . . the womb of the earth brings forth its riches; the
> fruit of seeds and roots appears and offers itself for the use
> of all; the meadows, the cornfields, the woods deck them-
> selves with green, they adorn themselves with flowers and
> pour out fragrance; the springs flow and the impetuosity
> of the rivers gladdens not the sight alone but also the
> hearing; everywhere the diverse voices of a variety of birds
> make sweet melody; the cattle stray over meadows and
> steppes, no longer asking food from us but fed and satisfied
> with what the hand of God spreads before them—they eat
> and play as though thanking God for His mercies; in a
> word, all things under heaven change into a new, beautiful
> and gladsome form; both animate and inanimate creation
> is so to speak born anew.[62]

This is not pantheism. And cannot we recognize this authentic
voice of orthodox sacramentalism in the speeches of some of
Dostoevsky's most sympathetic characters?

CONCLUSION

As we read these passages we are surely led to qualify the
superficial and common impression that Dostoevsky walked

about with his eyes closed to the natural scene around him. But we note that what he is supremely sensitive to is the ' moods ' of nature as appropriate backgrounds, as tonal accompaniments to man's own moods. The sultry air in the garden before one of Prince Myshkin's fits; the rain that falls and falls relentlessly at a gloomy period in *A Raw Youth*, etc.— these are reminiscent of Shakespeare's use of weather in his tragedies. But also we become gradually aware that where Dostoevsky is recording the happiness, the beauty, the ' success ' of the natural scene, he does so very *imprecisely*. He gives us usually ' trees ', ' birds ', ' sunsets ', and the usual common-places of ' nature '; there is nothing here of that sharpness and clarity, that sometimes shocking specificity, of his pictures of evil nature, of crawling, squirming, threatening things.[63] We have seen, in our second section, that Dostoevsky fails ultimately in his attempt to present ' perfection '; but what we now can see is that he is not even interested in ' perfection ' for long— his mind switches back relentlessly to the present plight of man. Father Zossima, speaking of his early days as an officer, tells how in the middle of a duel he suddenly sees the futility of it all. " ' Gentlemen,' I cried suddenly, speaking straight from my heart, ' look around you at the gifts of God, the clear sky, the pure air, the tender grass, the birds; nature is beautiful and sinless, and we, only we, are sinful and foolish, and we don't understand that life is heaven, for we only have to understand that and it will at once be fulfilled in all its beauty, we shall embrace each other and weep.' "[64] We can believe, reading him, in this contrast between sinful man and sinless nature: but we cannot believe in the abolition of the contrast. And though Dostoevsky believes in it in theory, he cannot envisage it or show it us. This is not failure on his part; it is an awareness of his proper talent and task.

It is with these considerations in mind that we should come to those passages where Dostoevsky more directly discusses his great preoccupation, the ' agony of belief '. That we detect in them his own agony, his long, hard pilgrimage to recovery of faith and his constant struggle to retain it, is obvious enough. Kirillov's strange logic, by which the proof that God does not exist and that I am God leads directly to the conclusion that I must take my own life to show my power over it; that is indeed

part of the logic of Dostoevsky's own mind. Ivan's terrible out-
burst against the providence of God which permits the suffering
of children—

> " Listen! If all must suffer to pay for the eternal har-
> mony, what have children to do with it, tell me, please?
> It's beyond all comprehension why they should suffer, and
> why they should pay for the harmony. Oh Alyosha, I'm
> not blaspheming! I understand, of course, what an
> upheaval of the universe it will be, when everything in
> heaven and earth blends in one hymn of praise. . . . But
> what pulls me up here is that I can't accept that harmony.
> I renounce the higher harmony altogether. It's not worth
> the tears of that one tortured child who beat itself on the
> breast with its little fists and prayed in its stinking out-
> house. . . . Too high a price is asked for harmony; it's
> beyond our means to pay so much to enter on it. And so
> I hasten to give back my entrance ticket. . . . It's not God
> that I don't accept, Alyosha, only I most respectfully
> return Him the ticket. . . ."[65]

—this has been thought through by one who knows the
agonizing problem in its depths. Shatov, muttering, in reply
to the direct question whether he believes in God, " I—I will
believe," speaks too out of a genuine sceptical centre in
Dostoevsky's heart. But to leave it like that would be to turn
the novels into autobiography. The point is, as we said in the
second section, that though Dostoevsky is deeply in these
passages, he is also above them. When Shatov, representing a
mystical view of life, argues with the midwife, Arina Pro-
horovna, representing the scientific-materialist view, he is not
made to triumph—Shatov is sentimental and effusive compared with her tough masculinity. Or when the old peasant,
Makar Ivanovitch, tries to counter the self-confident scientific
arrogance of the ' raw youth ', with an appeal to the ' mystery '
in nature, he is as simple-minded and laughable, almost, as the
youth is cocky and assured. And it is, very significantly, into
the mouth of the unsatisfactory person, Rogozhin, the ' villain ',
almost, of *The Idiot*, that one of the profoundest discussions of
faith is placed.

As to' the question of faith, I had four different conversations in two days last week. I came in the morning by
the new railways and talked for four hours with a man in
the train. He really is a very learned man. He doesn't
believe in God. Only, one thing struck me: that he seemed
not to be talking about that at all, the whole time; and it
struck me just because whenever I have met unbelievers
before, or read their books, it always seemed to me that
they were speaking and writing in their books about
something quite different, although it seemed to be about
that on the surface.

In the evening I stopped for the night at a provincial
hotel, and a murder had been committed there the night
before. Two peasants had been there. One of them had
noticed that the other was wearing a silver watch on a
yellow bead chain. He was so taken with that watch and
so fascinated by it that at last he could not restrain himself.
He took a knife, and when his friend had turned away, he
approached him cautiously from behind, took aim, turned
his eyes heavenwards, crossed himself, and praying fer-
vently " God forgive me for Christ's sake! " he cut his
friend's throat at one stroke like a sheep and took his
watch.

Next morning I went out to walk about the town. I saw
a drunken soldier in a terribly disorderly state, staggering
about the wooden pavement. He came up to me. " Buy
a silver cross, sir? " said he. " I'll let you have it for
twenty kopecks. It's silver." I took out twenty kopecks and
gave them to him; and I could see from his face how glad
he was that he had cheated a stupid gentleman, and he
went off immediately to drink what he got for it. I walked
on, thinking, " Well, I'll put off judging that man who
sold his Christ. God only knows what's hidden in those
weak and drunken hearts."

An hour later I came upon a peasant woman with a
tiny baby in her arms. She was quite a young woman and
the baby was about six weeks old. The baby smiled at her
for the first time in its life. I saw her crossing herself with
great devotion. " What are you doing, my dear? " I
asked. She replied, "God has just such gladness every time

he sees from heaven that a sinner is praying to Him with all his heart, as a mother has when she sees the first smile on her baby's face."[66]

In the mouth of Rogozhin this is not sentimentality—it is too self-aware for that. And behind it is, as we have said, Dostoevsky's amazingly mature self-awareness as a writer. That he knows his own talent, in its strength and weakness, is, I believe, most clearly shown in the moving little story that suddenly appears tucked away in a corner of his *Diary of a Writer*—the not very well-known tale " The Dream of a Ridiculous Man ". A man has discovered, one gloomy November (the atmosphere is again well conveyed), that he no longer cares about anything in life. He returns home resolved to shoot himself that night—why not, since nothing now matters? On the way home a girl rushes up to him and tries to get him to go with her—her mother is dying; she is very incoherent, breathless and desperate. The man shakes her off brutally and returns home. But now he cannot get her off his mind; he has been gratuitously cruel to her, and this nags at his consciousness; he no longer feels indifferent about everything, and now he cannot shoot himself. Then he falls asleep, and dreams he is on another planet, in a paradise where there is no sin, no evil.

> Everything was exactly as it is with us, but it seemed as if everything shone festively and had the air of great holiness, of ceremonial finally achieved. A gentle emerald sea washed softly on the shores and caressed them with a love which was apparent, visible, and almost perceptible. Beautiful tall trees stood in the full splendour of their hues, and I was convinced that their numberless leaves welcomed me with their gentle noise and seemed to mouth loving words. Flocks of birds crossed in the air and did not fear me but perched on my shoulders and hands, joyfully beating their gentle fluttering wings. . . .

He finds difficulty in explaining to the inhabitants of this paradise how pain can be mixed with joy on this earth, since they had never known evil. And the dream and happiness might never have come to an end if it had not been for the fact that " I ruined them all! Yes, yes, finally, I ruined them all. . . . How that happened I don't know, but I remember it clearly. The dream flew over thousands of years, and merely left me with the sensation of completeness. I only know I was the cause of their falling into sin. I infected with my presence a land that had been happy and innocent before my coming, like . . . an atom of plague which destroys whole kingdoms." Hatred, cruelty and war spread among them, until finally—the man wakes up! But what he wakes up to is the realization that it is sin, paradoxically, that has saved him. If it had not been for his cruel refusal of the little girl's sobbing request, he would have killed himself that night. It is the remorse for that that awakens in him the realization that some things *do* matter—and that therefore he cannot take his life. In a wider sense we may take this superbly told story as a symbol for Dostoevsky's own talent. It is sin that saves the artist in him. That is, the shadowy, somewhat cliché-strewn, picture of the paradisal planet is shattered into reality by the coming of the infectious, but *live*, sinful man. (Note again Dostoevsky's imagery of the plague, to which we drew attention above.) And so the ' ridiculous man '—and the novelist—returns to life, and to a purposeful life, where there is sin and sorrow but also possibility of redemption.

I raised my arms and invoked eternal truth; not invoked but wept; ecstasy, a boundless ecstasy, inspired my whole being. Yes, life and—preaching! I decided to preach that moment and, of course, for life! I go to preach, I wish to preach—what? Truth, since I have seen it, and seen it with my own eyes, seen it in all its glory! . . .

I have found that little girl. . . . And I will go on![67]

6

C. F. RAMUZ, OR THE ANALOGY OF BELIEF

I

BEYOND Dostoevsky's agony of belief it would be hard to go much farther in the same direction. Indeed, it might be said that Dostoevsky's writings, which, like those of Søren Kierkegaard in this respect, are a " defence of belief separated only by a hair's breadth from an attack on it ", have exhausted the modes of fruitful doubt. All that could be left, it would seem, for a writer to do after his time would be to advance either towards aggressive unbelief or militant faith, or else to abandon the debate between belief and unbelief as unprofitable and develop an eclectic humanism. All these ways, and others, have in fact been tried since his day, and we shall be considering some of them in the last chapter. But there is one path, somewhat aside from the main road, which is worth examination: the re-presentation of belief, not in direct statement but by way of analogy. It is not a thickly populated route, but those who have explored it have been informative. And of them I know none better than C. F. Ramuz. I shall not pretend that he is a writer of a stature comparable with some of the great names we have been considering. But he is powerful as well as pure in his deliberately self-limited way; and the fact that—though he is a wide reader and, as his essays show, not in the least deaf to the voices of his time—his writings seem almost entirely uninfluenced by contemporary fashions and experiments, in his particular case stands in his favour.

★

C. F. Ramuz, born in 1878 at Lausanne, died on 24 May, 1947, at the age of sixty-nine. He had scarcely been heard of in this country until the appearance of *The Triumph of Death*, the translation of *Présence de la Mort* (1922), in 1946.[1] The tepidity with which the book was received by reviewers shows that his particular distinction as a writer was not perceived; and since then, though there have been two more of his books translated (and those not at all the most significant), there has been little sign that his measure has been taken. In France, too, Ramuz was slow in achieving recognition, though from the first he had the discriminating support of his publisher, Bernard Grasset, and also of such writers as Claudel, Thomas Mann and Denis de Rougemont (who wrote an excellent introduction to the first English translation mentioned above).

I have said that he stands a little apart from his contemporary world, and this is both a deliberate personal choice and a characteristic of the Switzerland in which he was brought up. As early as 1896 he writes in his diary (10 December) " I have a terrible fear of morally and intellectually resembling anyone else. To read much perhaps gives you ideas—but personal ideas, no. I seek. . . . I seek."[2] And in 1908 (3 April) he looks back at his development as a writer and notes: " Examining myself carefully and deeply, I must do myself the justice of saying that I have never, at least consciously, *imitated*. Since the age of twenty-three, if I remember correctly, that is to say, since my second stay in Paris, I have never, in writing, had any model before my eyes or in my head. That is partly why my progress, if I have made any, has been so painful and so slow. . . . My ideas come from my eyes—if I have any masters, it is among the painters."[3]

But something of this is true of his countrymen. We are, he says,

> a people who are always mocking, because we are scared of being fooled. We are peasants, and the peasant is naturally distrustful, because he lacks self-confidence. . . .
> To that we must add, in our case, a total lack of experience. We are a too peaceful country, a country which has remained always a stranger to the great fevers which have agitated Europe. We are a country, not of arteries but of veins, and our sluggish blood drifts softly and always behindhand. We have been put to sleep by centuries of neutrality, and of all kinds of neutralities, and on top of that has come pacifist preaching. . . . And so it is that

when this war [1914] which we had been told was quite
impossible, was finally declared, there were first of all
smiles among us (we still didn't believe it) and then
followed stupor.[4]

Ramuz himself shows something of a similar neutrality with
regard to religious affiliation. Brought up a reformed Protestant
(he notes on a visit to Germany in 1896 that the Protestants of
Carlsruhe, with whom he worships, are not Lutherans as he
had expected but ' evangelicals ' like his own people),[5] he
writes frequently, and with sympathy, about the life of Catholic
villages; and once he remarks in his diary that " Catholicism
has understood that everything needs a *culminating point* (the
elevation), without which nothing counts."[6] But this must not
be taken as a total religious neutrality. In 1904 he suddenly
makes an interim statement of faith, in his diary:

Nothing is eternally new except that which is eternally
old. Nothing is inexhaustible except the commonplace.
There are only two things which really matter: love and
death. Every *subject* which departs from everyday life
deserves no attention. One must be narrow and authori-
tarian. That's the condition of strength. In art it is only
its *strength* which is the exact measure of a man. This
strength comes from the passion to feel; that's why detachment is so hateful. I have too long played the dilettante
towards things; but that time is past. Scepticism was like
a feather I wore in my cap; the wind has carried it away.
One must *believe*. There is no truth except in faith.[7]

All this is not irrelevant to his search for himself as a writer.
In his *Salutation Paysanne* (1929) he writes, as a foreword, a
letter to his publisher, Bernard Grasset, which is the most
revealing account of his struggles. He is defending himself
against the accusation of critics that he writes ' bad French ';
and to do so he gives us his history. He has always, he says,
felt " an imperious need of submission, of submission to that
which is, of submission to that which I am ". The conditions
to which he has to submit are those of being a Vaudois, with
the Vaudois' history and the Vaudois' language—" so that my
first orientation has not been, as with many other young men,

political or metaphysical, but topographical, geographical, geological, that is to say entirely concrete." At first, he says, he did not realize what this imperative need meant. When he started trying to write he thought he must try and write ' correct ' French. Indeed, it was a struggle to find himself a writer at all; none of his countrymen ever imagined that writing could be a vocation, and he was quite ashamed of his ambition. In fact he tried to hide it from his parents, especially his mother; and when at home, doing his Latin exercises, he had a dodge by which he kept a piece of sliding paper ready to cover up the poetry he wrote, when she came into the room— always being careful to leave his exercise not quite finished so that he could show her that he was still busy on it. For long he felt separated from ' them ', while he wrote octosyllabics and alexandrines in the traditional manner; until " having gone down deeper into myself,' and there having come to a self that was more truly myself, at the very same moment I rejoined them. They were no longer outside me. The distance which separated me from them had been abolished. There was no longer any contradiction between them and me, because I had set myself to be like them. They had recognized me; I was speaking their language. . . ."

And so he came to write their own language, the vigorous countryman's language of the Swiss peasant; not a mere patois, as it had once been (a kind of Franco-Provençal, " une espèce de Savoyard "), but a genuine French with the old patois pronunciation and turn of phrase. This discovery of his true vocation was, he says, no self-conscious ' turning back ', no artificial attempt to turn himself into a peasant; indeed, the accusation itself, he declares, comes from those who think that by becoming educated, a graduate, one has thus become a member of a class, a ' lettered ' individual, a bourgeois, an ' intellectual '; " which implies that an intellectual is neces- sarily *superior* to a non-intellectual in that he has *learnt* more things ". In fact, he found himself, at the age of twenty-two, faced with two ' traditions ', written and oral. What he wanted to show was that the old, classical, written tradition got its strength precisely from being also ' lived ', i.e. also an oral tradition; that this no longer obtained; and that therefore the oral tradition must be reintegrated into the written. It was precisely when he tried to write correct French, like a ' good pupil ', that he felt himself most artificial, self-conscious; the traditions of his folk, the very land of his people, were far deeper and more ineradicable. And so he deliberately rejected the ' classical ' style—which he admired—believing that a new and genuine classic could only be achieved, at least in the case of his people, by that rejection, that is by a return to the tradition from which it first arose.

He departed, too, from the classical rules—the ' period ' and so forth; and from the normal shape of the novel—some of his tales are merely called *récits*. He adopted a spoken language; when he began to be recognized he was given an opportunity for public readings of his works, which clarified much for him. It also, as he points out, brought him strangely and unasked into the *avant-garde*, for he thus fitted in with the techniques of broadcasting; and his stress on the gesture-language of the countrymen, " where logic gives way to the very rhythm of the images ", brought him close to the technique of the film. (It is surprising, by the way, that one of his most charming stories, *Farinet, ou la Fausse-Monnaie*, has never been filmed; it would be a gift to the Italian directors.) One of his numerous and penetrating aphorisms reads: " The whole secret of art is perhaps to know how to bring order to disordered emotions, but to order them in such a way that you make people all the more clearly sense the disorder."[8] And he soon discovered that his " goût de l'élémentaire " was very closely related to the " goût de l'universel ". Far from his adoption of a particular language and place leading to isolation, to the impossibility of communication with those of other traditions, he found that it was an emancipation and a widening of his understanding: this language " being simple, being elementary, being in movement, being essentially ' dynamic ', and because this elementariness, certain elementary movements, a kind of dynamism, are common to all men—is very suitable, it seems, for translation . . . very suitable for communication even through translation, and thus suitable to remain intelligible to readers of the most distant regions and races."[9] (He was delighted to receive a letter from a working man, a Parisian, son of a working man, with no ambitions to be anything but a working man, who yet—in spite of different backgrounds and ideas—had found himself appreciating Ramuz' writings.) Right towards the end of his life (April, 1942) he notes in his *Journal*, " I no longer love conversations except with men who have a trade and love their trade. Direct contact between them and things. Direct contact in that way between them and me."[10]

It is interesting, too, to find that he instinctively felt the need for the bringing together again of the sundered arts and expressions of man (an ambition which has been shared by some of the greatest exponents of poetic drama in our time): and that his charming little play (to call it that), *Histoire du Soldat*, which is a sort of mediæval miracle play in modern (dialect) verse, containing mime and dancing as well as ballad-poetry, was given music by Igor Stravinsky and performed in September, 1918.

★

His early works were, as we have seen, in the classical tradition—and his novels in the naturalistic. Even as late in his development as 1913 we find a story like *Vie de Samuel Belet*, which is a straightforward tale (in the form of an autobiography) of a Swiss who wandered, lived, settled down, lost, wandered again, and finally settled down again into a sort of philosophical resignation. It is only the conclusion (apart, of course, from the flashes of brilliant description and observation which are never absent from any of his work) that suggests the genuine Ramuz. And even here there is a somewhat obtrusive pantheism which is under much more careful control in his greater writings.

> Everything has changed [muses Samuel, towards the end of his life], and I am no longer the same. . . . I have become the real Samuel, and now I love you, Louise [his dead wife]. And this is why nothing separates us any longer when I lean over and look towards you, and towards all my living past in this clear water where you dwell. . . .
> For all is confused. Distance and time are suspended. There is neither life nor death, only that great image of the world in which all is contained and from which nothing escapes and nothing is destroyed. It is one more degree to be crossed. But you see rising before you that visage, which

is the visage of God. I have also learnt to love and to know
Him. I know He is everything and everywhere, and only
He remains. . . . When I row in my boat I move forward
in Him, when I come alongside I come to Him, He is
above, below, on all sides; He is here and there; He is this
tree, He is the mountain; the lake is only a morsel of Him
and the sun another, and everything is but a morsel of
Him, from the shuttle of the fallen net to the pebble
rounded by the waves.[11]

It should be evident, I think, that at this stage Ramuz had still
much to unlearn. What is extraordinary is that only three
years or so later he could produce such integral and moving
works as *La Guérison des Maladies*.

There are one or two of his other novels, of varying dates,
which can be regarded as coming mid-way between these
early traditional stories, like *Samuel Belet, Aline, Jean-Luc
Persécuté*, etc., and the type more characteristic of, indeed
peculiar to, Ramuz, which we shall be considering later.
There is the charming and amusing *Farinet* (1932) already
mentioned, in which the hero finds a way of making gold
coins, and then is astonished to discover that the circulation
of them is not welcomed by the authorities; he is gaoled
several times, and finally becomes a fugitive from justice—
assisted by his faithful mistress, Josephine; when he is given a
chance of freedom on condition he undertakes never to coin
again, he refuses because he is still obstinately convinced that
since his gold coins are of purer gold than the official currency
his ought to be given preference; in the end he is surrounded,
among the mountains, and shot dead defending himself. There
is *La Beauté sur la Terre*, in which Ramuz describes the effect
upon the villagers of the coming of a beautiful young woman
from America to their village. Here an erotic theme is handled
with great delicacy (which does not mean with prudery), and
all the time the theme is there, below the surface—that beauty
gives meaning to life yet does not last in life. Another novel
takes this theme a stage farther. *Le Garçon Savoyard* (1937) is
a Swiss youth who has his head turned by a dancer—a trapeze
artist—in a circus. Joseph is engaged to Georgette, and their
marriage is to take place quite soon. But he becomes restless,

because the sight of the dancer, flying up and up on her cord, up into the roof of the tent, up and away (it seems) into the clouds, convinces him that there is something better, more transcendent, than the dull petty life of work, marriage and the narrow circle of village life. First he loses his job; then he is tempted to spend the night with the local Circe, the barmaid. But that isn't it, and still he searches for the unattainable. Georgette and his future mother-in-law see there is something wrong, and try to hurry on the marriage. But once again he is beguiled by the barmaid, Mercedes, to go to her bedroom, and there she tries to show that she is as beautiful and attractive as the dancer he had seen at the circus. She draws him into her arms and—he strangles her. He takes refuge in the mountain, and his fiancée, Georgette, suspecting what has happened, tracks him down and makes plans to get him to safety. But he is distrait, and doesn't seem interested in escaping. In an attempt to pin him down, Georgette persuades him to sleep with her in a cabin up in the mountains.

> Once again he was there, on a straw mattress, lying by a woman. The dawn came.
> It made everything pink in the room. He thought: " It isn't her either."
> He couldn't know whether she was asleep, because he didn't look at her, and lying on his back it was the ceiling he was looking at. He saw the ceiling, a ceiling made of planks, turn a light pink colour.
> Two women, and it wasn't either this one or the other.[12]

He tries to explain to Georgette that there is another—a woman in the air, above the world, nameless. . . . And when she still tries to persuade him to make for safety, he runs back to the village. He is chased, and he steals a boat and rows out on to the lake. He is evidently a bit ' fey ' by now. The police and others follow him, but he takes no notice and rows on towards the reflections of the clouds in the lake—

> He goes where the clouds go. A light morning breeze propels him in the direction they themselves are propelled. He tests with his hand the planks which serve for the

bottom of the boat; he feels them decayed and soft under his hand. He sees that he is going where ' she ' is: it's to rejoin her. A cloud. A pretty cloud up there. A pretty cloud above you. The blade sinks with one blow into the planks, and then he makes it turn against itself in his hand. . . .

Up there and down here, it's the same thing. Once more he makes the blade of his knife turn on itself; and she flies before him, but he too flies after her, and so he is going to rejoin her.

She soars up, she weighs nothing now. She has escaped death, but through her I shall escape death too.

He turns his knife in the hole which he has gradually hollowed out in the thickness of the plank.

She is upright standing on a fine shred of air, on a column of vapour, on a cloud; and, at the moment that he goes down and sinks, he sees that he gets even nearer to her; while they still shout after him, but he doesn't hear.

She goes up, he sinks towards her.

And she is seen no longer, but he too is seen no longer, because he has parted the waters at the very moment she parts the air.[13]

Finally, in this semi-naturalistic, semi-fantastic vein, there are the novels about the mountains. *La Grande Peur dans la Montagne* (1925), in which among the mists of the Swiss peaks and escarpments terror overcomes the simple, superstitious shepherds; *La Guerre dans le Haut-Pays* (1915), in which a war breaks out between two cantons, and the hero, being in love with a girl in the other village, is torn in his allegiance and is finally shot, mistakenly, as a traitor—while his fiancée, Félicie, wanders for the rest of her life in the mountains, looking for him.

All is calm again in the village. There are women around the fountain; little frightened girls, when you approach them, hide their heads in their aprons. . . .

But perhaps you ought to climb up higher, where it is still more beautiful and still calmer. If ever you come to us, come at the beginning of May. May, that's the month of flowers in the mountain, everywhere round you they will have bloomed, blue ones, white, red, yellow. If by chance you lift your eyes you'll see a little cloud come. It will slide by, it will go off, and the great sky will be empty again; just so our lives, just like up there, after all this noise and these wars; but what do they matter to the ramparts of the hills? And nothing has ever stained the pure blue of the gentian, which has just opened like a little eye.[14]

The philosophic conclusion is commonplace enough, and we shall see that Ramuz can delve much more profoundly than this; but within the limits of this kind of tale it will do. Perhaps the best example of this *genre*, which will serve to point its achievements, is *Derborence* (1936).[15] The plot is taken from a sentence in a geographical dictionary, describing how a shepherd, missing and believed dead, lived for several weeks entombed in a chalet, overwhelmed by an avalanche, feeding on bread and cheese. But behind the simple plot Ramuz shows us the village, the people, their traditional hopes and fears, their stupidity as well as their courage. Hidden in the mountains, the peasants believe, is the devil and his army; when he is in a bad mood, he declares war, and the result is an avalanche. So when, after more than seven weeks' absence, the young shepherd, Antoine, reappears, haggard and pale, they think at first that he is a ghost. No one knows what to do; some of them run away, some of them take up forks, sticks, flails, ready for anything; then someone goes and fetches the Curé. He comes out. " He is white and black. He holds in front of him Our Lord, who glitters. A choir-boy, who is red and white, carries the cross. . . ." The villagers kneel. What will the strange figure do? If he is a ghost, we shall know now. The little procession advances. The figure sways a little, like a drunken man. " Is it you, Antoine Pont? " He bends his knee and then kneels down. It is he! Antoine is taken by the President of the village and questioned, and then the men bring him to the *maison de commune*, where, after several drinks, he slowly comes to and tells his story—how he was in the hut, sleeping, when the mountain fell; buried, he tried to find a way out, but day after day he explored holes between the rocks without success, living on the fodder stored in the chalet, and

drinking water from a melted glacier; until at last he saw
daylight and squeezed his way through.

Early next morning, when he wakes up still rather dazed, he
suddenly remembers that an old shepherd had been with him
in the hut—Seraphin. He goes back resolutely to search for
him, madly hunting among the boulders. None of the villagers
dares follow him back into that dangerous zone; but his wife,
Thérèse, only married a few months before and now pregnant,
goes after him. She shouts up to him, among the rocks, but he
does not pay attention to her; he still goes on in his fruitless
search. The peasants dare not move, they watch from a distance. But she goes on, climbing the rocks till she reaches him.
" Right in front of the five men was the mountain with its
ramparts and its immense towers, and it is wicked, it is all-
powerful—but look, a feeble woman has challenged it and
beaten it, because she loved, because she dared. Having life,
she has been there where there was still life, and brings back
what is living from the midst of what is dead." They come back
together, husband and wife, he helping her over the rough
stones. That is all.

★

We have had some indication already of Ramuz' powers of
observation. The simple style matches the simple themes and
the simple clarity of the painting. The dignity and courage of
man in face of huge obstacles; the overhanging fate; the
specificity of little things, little actions—that is what his novels
are about. The tramp lies down and rubs his bristling chin
and ponders the strangeness of life.

He thinks with a part of himself. Funny how little notice
things take of you. . . . Anyway, we ourselves, what are
we? There are five or six parts of you at least which are
you; each one goes its own way. Your head thinks without
you. Your stomach is hungry without you. Your beard
grows without you. . . . It's grown a good finger-and-a-
half's length without asking your permission. It's grown,
it's grown. That's its job, it does its job. . . .

What are we? Which is the part of you that is you? Is
it the part which thinks in you which is you? The part

which enjoys pleasures which is you? . . . He moved his legs; is it your legs which are you? Where do we begin, where do we end? Is it my arms which are me, is it my blood which is me? But my beard (as he said to himself), that's nourished by my blood. He looks, he looks inside himself; and, in there, nothing obeys him.

The tramp is lying in a meadow by the stream.

A branch sticks up in the sky like a feather in a hat. . . . the water does not sing here, as it often does. You would think it was someone tapping with his fingers on a cardboard box; little irregular taps, sometimes stronger and more marked, sometimes so feebly that you can hardly hear them. . . . The dragonfly is a little blue twig which goes up and down in jerks, as if it was hung by a thread which was suddenly pulled up.

There is the mole-catcher; the vine-dressers; the boy and girl in the woods; the ferry-boat on the Rhône, the men playing cards below-deck; Pinget, the sand-collector, with his rickety old boat which sinks in the harbour entrance; a hairdresser whose hobby is collecting—collecting bits of everything, primitive weapons, coconuts, sabres, képis, insects, butterflies.[16]

She looked over her shoulder, she looked once more towards the lake: a second wave is born, a second wave stretches itself towards her before letting itself fall forwards on its paws, like a cat.[17]

In the square there were still cows drinking; you could still make them out clearly in what was left of the daylight. No noise. They drew from the smooth surface of the water without disturbing it with the least ripple, while their flanks touched each other in the middle in the same motionless space.[18]

A baby is expected:

To these five months we only have to add four more: January, February March, April—that's practically right round the year. It'll be when the birds begin to sing and there are little green points in the hedges, as if they'd been pushed up with your finger-nails.[19]

The child begins to grow:

> He suddenly stretches out his arms, closing his fists like
> a boxer, then pulls them in to him, and you can see that
> he's looking for his mouth. He misses it. . . . He can't
> distinguish an object, he only distinguishes the movement
> of objects (just like the blackbird who is pecking at bits of
> bread behind the window-pane and I'm two paces from
> it, but it doesn't move as long as I don't move). He can't
> add yet; he doesn't see two, he sees one. He doesn't see,
> for instance, that there are three persons round him. He
> sees one, and then when he sees another and because he
> sees another, the former exists no more. The three people
> only make one. For him the world is so far only a succes-
> sion of units, and a motionless succession, each of these
> units only imposing itself on him by the disappearance of
> the preceding one. We ourselves have no memory of this
> time, because it's a time without memory.[20]

All these *aperçus*, which lie about Ramuz' works everywhere
like sequins, are not mere illustrations of the commonplace
' descriptive genius '; they are his theme. For " You can only
make poetry out of the anti-poetic. You can only make music
out of the anti-musical. Our true friends are working-men, not
those people called artists. . . . Art—you know what that is:
a grafting on what has already been grafted. . . . But all
grafters know you can only graft on to what grows wild: that
is how *we* graft." And Ramuz knew the ' wild ' so well that he
greets it like a personal friend. The native of the place, coming
back after an absence, greets everything anew: " Salut, les
gens! salut, les champs! salut, le ciel! salut, l'arbre! salut
tout! "

For it is all a part of him: " Well then, this hill, down there,
isn't it more like his shoulder? And is it really still a hill, that
lovely shoulder down there? That curve in front of us, isn't
that his arm? . . . For where are you, and who are you? The
lake stirs and makes a movement like his chest when it goes up
and down. . . . You, you, you, everywhere, you here, you
there. And so Hullo you! Hullo everything! It's the same
thing."[21]

★

Yet so far we have only presented a Ramuz who might be any kind of 'nature writer'—a Swiss Jean Giono, a pantheistic Hudson writing a self-consciously 'peasant' French. It is the combination of these obvious earthy gifts with a rare metaphysical imagination that makes the real distinction of his writing. And this distinction is shown above all in four works which deserve to be much more widely known than they are, and which, however distinct, have some remarkable qualities in common.

We shall not pause long over the first of this group, *Le Règne de l'Esprit Malin* (written 1914, published 1917), though it is a striking work of fantasy. A stranger comes to the village, and turns out to be a cobbler. The last cobbler has just died, so the new man, Branchu, who seems to be quite well off, takes over his shop. But gradually things begin to go wrong in the village. Branchu is a superb craftsman, and never seems to charge much for the shoes he makes or mends; and gradually he gets the villagers into his power. He even seems to have the power of healing, and some begin to think he is the Lord come to His own. But slowly his influence begins to work for evil. Peasants begin to take to drink, families are broken, the Church is deserted, and the priest gives up, and finally life seems to leave the village—except for a group of sodden drunken revellers. But in the end they are delivered because of the repentance of one of them and the perseverance of his daughter, the girl Marie. The conclusion is a trifle melodramatic. The Man (Branchu) appears:

He looked around him; he did not seem as much at ease as usual. He smiled, but his smile was forced. They all made way before Marie, no one stopped her as she went. As for him, he went to meet her. He did not walk as quickly as one would have believed. And now his skin became curiously folded on his neck, his hands, his face; it creased up still more; now it hung all round him, it detached itself from him like a garment which is going to fall. And then there was a colossal clap of thunder. That is at least what the old people say, and they got it from the lips of their grandparents. The sun all at once disappeared behind a veil. The sky was cleft through the middle, where the lightning flashed violet like a vein in marble. The earth which is our support left us for a moment, the walls fled under our hands. . . .[22]

The devil, for so of course he was, disappears, and order is restored in the village; but it isn't till the following winter that they discover the Curé hanging in a maple tree: " He had two red holes in the place where his eyes were, because the crows had come, and they know their job."

Thus crudely summarized the story sounds uncomfortably like one of the ' supernatural thrillers ' of the late Charles Williams; but it is much less sophisticated and much more convincing than these uneasy combinations of detective story and conjuring-trick. The nearest equivalent in English writing is rather the late T. F. Powys, but without the element of cynicism that sometimes marks his works.

In *Présence de la Mort* we see more clearly Ramuz' power of presenting a supernatural context within which his love of the particular is given its true precision and value. The primary theme, as usual, is simple enough: one day the news reaches the Swiss village that something has gone wrong with the law of gravity: " The earth is rapidly falling towards the sun, rushing to rejoin it. So all life will come to an end. The temperature will go up. It will become too hot for anything to go on living . . . everything will rapidly die."

At first nothing happens, except a drought; but nobody minds, because the weather is so lovely—the sky is so blue, " as if the painters had come and two or three coats are applied, but the good workman, never satisfied, says: ' Another won't hurt '."

The gardener, watering the beds, finds the hose-pipe dwindle to a trickle and then stop—now there is only a little circle of fine white dust about the base of the sprinkler. But still people won't believe the news. The papers have headlines about it, but it is so hot that everyone has gone bathing, and when they come home they do not look at the papers at first. " On an old green bench up against the barn wall, the master, having finished his work, begins to read: but no, he has not understood. No, it is too big. It is not for us, it is too big. Our own world is quite small. Our own world only goes where our eyes go; it is our eyes that make it. The master having read, looks about him, a little worried perhaps in the beginning; the worry passes away."

When someone does begin to take it seriously, to point out what it means, there is a general silence, and another says, " Shut up, do you hear! "—with a nasty voice, like someone who is afraid. Gavillet the stockbroker goes to the cinema, and lets the world of the cinema pass dully over him. Afterwards he buys a paper and looks at the headlines; he does not bother about them, and goes back to bed. Only in bed, when the light is out and the inner light is turned on, does he realize its meaning; " and suddenly life was there, but at the same time death was there, which he had never yet known, because he had not yet known life ". Some of the men react to it merely by thinking: " The only difference is that we'll all go together, instead of each of us going his own way. . . . Maybe it'll be better that way, who knows? " A guard is placed in front of the National Bank; the Government have posters put up, reassuring and appealing to the good sense of the citizens —" but there, it is precisely the thing that ought to reassure you that makes you more alarmed ". Meanwhile it gets hotter every day; in the lake water-weeds grow, " the sun comes and drinks, the sun sips through its straws, the sun comes with two lips, and constantly sucks up. . . ." But the level of the water begins to rise, for the lake is filled from the melting glaciers in the mountains. The man and his wife, faced by death, find that they do not know each other, or now know each other for the first time; that their unity is broken, they are two not one, they do not love—and then that they do love after all, that they can come together again, really this time, " and Death can come now, because this is good, this is sweet ". A revolt begins to spread. A man tries to pray, but his little boy, put to bed, does the praying instead—" and then come the words which he believes simply because they are there, as when the wind comes to the tree ".

Some villages are burnt in the rebellion; men form a new society with goods in common; each village forms its own republic, and defends itself against all comers: " there is still a bit of sky for them, they want to keep it for themselves ". Gavillet the stockbroker " looks in the mirror at Gavillet; there is nothing else to be seen but he himself, when he looks and sees himself. Already there is neither time nor space. There is nothing but the very small space of a room, and the still smaller space of oneself. Death has reduced everything to one's own size, which is about five feet eight by a foot and a half ". Gavillet opens the dresser drawer and takes out the revolver. . . .

The drought gets more intense, and people die waterless. Then the opposite; the lake overflows, houses are flooded. Now people begin to take refuge high up in the mountains. A party of eight young people push right up to the heights, to a chalet 2,700 yards up. But others follow them and ambush them; they are driven from their chalet by the newcomers. But they return and, having tied the door of the chalet from outside, set fire to the building: as the men inside try to escape through a trapdoor in the roof they are shot. They are so pleased with their successful revenge that they scarcely notice how the thermometer is still creeping up—115, 117, 120 degrees on the ice up there and the uninhabited snows. And then the glacier above them begins to bend a little, " like a bow against the knee. It sounded as though hundreds of artillery guns were being shot off together. A great whirlwind went up, and at the same moment a gust of wind, lifting with both hands the men and cattle, throwing them over one another, sprawling pell-mell down the slope, carrying away the roof of the chalet ".

Finally, as the end approaches, another little party climbs up to a tiny village up on a promontory of the mountain, past another village perched on an escarpment—" and we asked ourselves how it held, how it had not already slid down the slope, sitting there like a man sitting down on a sled and barely able to hold back with his feet ". Up there the bell-ringer with difficulty clambered up the slope to the church and rang the bell. And the folk all gathered at the summoning of the bell—" And now, you can fall down, mountains, you can fall upon them: they no longer fear you, they have escaped you." In the church the bell rings once, and they see imperfect space open out for them before the other space; it rings again, saying " Are you coming? " It rings the third time—

And, in their new bodies, they then stand forth. Some-one was standing before them on the cheap lace cloth, between the earthly flowers that fade, among the flickering of the tiny lights—suddenly. Someone rose, rising alone, and He began to walk; He said " Are you coming? " And, in their new bodies, they moved forward. . . .

The light struck them so strongly that their eyes melted away, their former eyes, that knew night. . . . At that instant their courage failed them, they stopped in their tracks, they stood motionless; they then saw that now they no longer knew how to walk.

He had to ask them again, " Come! " and again: " Are you coming? " Then they tried once more, and they saw that they could, they saw that they had learned how to walk again. . . .

For a long time they looked about, turning to the left and the right: they were quite astonished. . . .

As though it were new, yet at the same time it was the same: as though in seeing it, they recognized: and at first they hesitated, and then they hesitated no longer.

They nodded their heads.

Because, then, after all, they had not been deceived! Because they had not, then, done wrong, in being attached to the earth, they were right in loving it, in spite of all!

And they said:

" But we're home! "[23]

After this work of singular power Ramuz attempts something even more difficult—a sequel.* *Joie dans le Ciel* (1925) is meant to be a picture of the blessed realm which man reaches after ' the end of all men '. A description of heaven, sustained through 150 pages, is a remarkable feat, and it is worth seeing how he brings it off. The work bears some resemblances to the short story of Dostoevsky at which we glanced in the last chapter, *The Dream of a Ridiculous Man*; except that the picture of paradise is not so romantic as in the latter, and the ending is different. It opens abruptly: " Then those who were called stood up out of their tombs. With the nape of their necks they pushed the earth back; with their foreheads they pierced through the earth as when the seed sprouts, pushing up its green tip; they had got bodies again."

* Only a sequel in its *theme*; the same characters do not appear.

A mother meets her child again, two lovers come together once more after being parted; the joiner no longer makes coffins—now he paints pictures on wood instead; Phémie still gardens, but with less pain and more success. Bé, who was born blind, now finds that he can see.

> There were two of them who held him, one on each arm. Every now and then Bé stopped; he stood still like someone who has got asthma. . . . He kept his eyes closed.
> Suddenly he opened them again; he said, " And that white spot? "
> " That's at Produit's, it's the wall of Produit's stable."
> And Bé started to stretch out his hand towards the thing to grasp it, while the other two laughed and said, " You can't, look! it's too far off! " and then for a few moments he made night-time again for himself, like when one goes into one's house to rest. . . .
> He only raised his pupils gently this time and with great caution, taking in a little store of things, and then letting his pupil fall once more. He only let a few things enter at once, having first of all to set them in order. . . .
> Now Bé kept his eyes wide open, he didn't shut them any more. He asked Delacuisine and Besson to let him go; they said, "D'you think we can? "—and then they did let him go all the same. And so he went along all by himself, and so they turned round, having the village in front of them now. And Bé saw this little world coming in the midst of the world—among all the other bits of the world this tiny bit of the world, while he went on all by himself; and he only occasionally stretched out his hand from habit, feeling the air, only occasionally his foot before coming down interrogated the ground.[24]

Bonvin the hunter somehow finds that even here his expertise is not wasted—though he says that " formerly our pleasure was in destroying; now our pleasure is in seeing that nothing can any more be destroyed ".[25]

But in spite of the perfection and joy everywhere things begin to go wrong. " Their happiness left them because the earth left them; their happiness departed because the earth departed. They had come with their memories, but their memories were now used up. They had come with their stories, they had told them to each other: they had fallen from them as the fruit falls from the tree, and then the tree has no more fruit. . . ."[26]

As they drank they savoured the liquor, and " it was imposs- ible to imagine a more perfect taste; and so they started nod- ding their heads, in an approving way; yet perhaps one missed the pleasure of surprise, perhaps this perfection itself was too much expected for one to be able to enjoy it as one would have wished ".[27]

The real break in the idyllic monotony (" One thing alone we lack—that it can't change "[28]) comes when Thérèse Min, the woman goatherd, loses one of the goats, one called la Blanche who belongs to Phémie; la Blanche goes off down a steep gorge and disappears. From that moment the smooth order is upset. Thérèse and Phémie go off to look for the missing la Blanche; but the land begins to be covered with smoke or fog, and a starless night descends upon them. Then a red glare comes up and the houses begin to tremble. ' They ' begin to approach, coming up from the fissure in the mountain, with a noise like wind.

> They flowed out through all the holes, all the crevices, all the fissures, the tiniest cracks. As when a main bursts, when a hose-pipe gives, when there is too much pressure. . . . Those from down there, from below! Those from below us, the condemned! Those we thought no more about! Those who are in torment for ever, while we were in happiness for ever, and yet they came. In fact they came from all sides. They pulled themselves up in clusters, one after another, they fell in twos and threes; they rolled in twos and threes on the slope. . . .

So they advance, and the inhabitants of this village paradise stand terrified, thinking that it is the end.

> They turned and looked back with sorrow at their happiness, and thought " It's all over ".
> But—No! for there is order. For they are the con- demned, so they are powerless. At a given moment they were held back; they were hauled back.

They were hauled back by means of themselves and by means of their own passions. Not from outside but from inside.

They got in each other's way. They destroyed each other.

You could see some who pulled each other back out of jealousy.[29]

And so order was restored, and there was only the memory of the menace. But it was even better now. " It was only that this thing had to come again, so that they might possess all the heavens. Finally they had all the heavens when they had all the earth once more; they had all joy when suffering returned to take its place alongside it. . . ."[30]

And so Chemin, who had found that his painting had been going badly, now finds that the colours will ' take ' once more, that he can apply himself to the work, and now among the colours on his palette there appears for the first time—black.

Ramuz' ' Paradiso ' is a courageous experiment, and remarkably successful considering the difficulty of the task. When, however, we turn to a greater work, perhaps his greatest, *La Guérison des Maladies* (1915-17) we can see that he has an easier task here—indeed, it may be the only task suitable to fallen man: to convey, not paradise beyond the earth, but an analogy on the earth for a perfection that lies beyond it.

The novel opens with a superb description of old Grin, returning home drunk:

A low sky in March, and windy. He wasn't walking very straight, and he was making a lot of noise; it's this song he's singing. Our happiness is incomplete when we're the only ones to be happy. So I've got to give testimony to those who are my brothers and sisters at heart. Was he heard or not? He didn't care—he went on singing. . . .

Now began the business of the stairs, no small business either. And he absorbed himself in the job, silently (for a long time nothing in the darkness but his breath, rather short too). A tough job, as you can see, but the occasion all the same for a new pleasure, because each step was like someone he was holding forth to: " Ah! It's you—all right, come on! " And in fact, they did come on, one after the other, although they came rather slowly.[31]

Then we meet Marie, Grin's daughter, who has to work from seven in the morning till eleven at night to help her mother with her wages, since Grin drinks away all his. A young Parisian comes to the village. At first he takes up with a ' girl of loose morals ', La Brûlée (so called because there is a brown scar on her cheek where she once burned herself on a red-hot iron). But suddenly he begins to reform, paint up his attic room, dresses neatly, ceases to drink so heavily: he has fallen in love with Marie. But Madame Grin objects to the marriage, and Marie fails to keep tryst with him. He is repulsed by Grin *père* also, who for all his faults sees that his daughter is something very special—" My poor friend," he says to the Parisian, "don't imagine that she takes any notice of you; she is far above those things! And you look much too tiny from where she is for you to exist for her any more, much too tiny, my poor friend, much too tiny! "[32]

Disheartened, the Parisian goes off and commits suicide. Grin is full of remorse when he hears, and Marie falls ill.

But now the strange development commences. Marie remains completely silent and the doctor cannot discover what is wrong with her. But some of the village folk come to visit her, and feel curiously strengthened by merely being in her room. Then sick people come to see her and go away finding their sicknesses cured. But Marie herself contracts each sickness of which they are cured. Grin himself becomes her great advocate, showing her off, and bringing all sorts of people to her, confident that they will be healed. He even persuades La Brûlée to come and see her—reluctantly, humbly, and as a penitent. Marie, saying nothing, kisses her on the cheek. La Brûlée goes away a different person, but Marie begins to develop a burn-mark on her face. Two villagers are discussing the visit of a blind man to her room, and his recovery of sight:

" When he came it was he who couldn't see; when he went away, it was her. . . ."

" Mon Dieu! . . ."

" Only he was so happy about it. He said, ' How

beautiful everything is! Isn't the sun beautiful, and even the women are beautiful! Though at my age . . .' And then he laughed. And he wouldn't allow those who had brought him to accompany him on the way back, because he said, ' I want everyone to know that I can get along all by myself now. . . .' "

" And she—did she know what would happen to her if she healed him? "

" Certainly."

" Beforehand? "

" Yes, beforehand."

" And what did she say? "

" She was even happier about it than he. She said, ' It's within that one sees '. And she also said, ' How beautiful everything is! ' So they both of them said the same, one because she couldn't see any more, the other because he could see all over again. . . ."[33]

The village authorities, M. Guicherat and M. Bolle, are sceptical, and also disturbed at the possible social upset that wi'l result. They determine to suppress this practice of unorthodox medicine; Grin is arrested for debt, and an ambulance is sent to convey Marie away to a hospital far from the village. Marie is lying still in bed, and in the stillness of the room even the noise of a pipe dripping in the garden can be heard:

Tic-tac, it beat the measure of time, and that was all that could be heard in the silence, with a movement sometimes quicker, sometimes more slowly, as the rain became heavier or lighter.

Tiny things, all of these, but they became vastly important because of the emptiness all round. This drop, as it fell, gave a solemn hollow sound, and then one watched for the next. Madame Deléglise sat as usual at Marie's bedside, more motionless, it seemed, and stiffer than the back of her chair. And in the bed there was the same motionlessness: she who could not see any more, could not move any more, could hardly speak any more; more devastated, more dead each day because more alive; every day more withdrawn from any kind of communication because of another language.

She held her hands crossed on the sheet. The drop still
fell into the watering-can. At one moment a barrel rolled
in the road. The noise came over the roof-tops, drew
near, swelled, then began slowly to die away. A fly
settled on the counterpane covered with red cotton
material to look like satin; it rubbed its feet against each
other.[34]

The villagers get wind that the ambulance is coming to take
her, and they surround her door. But as the stretcher bearing
Marie reaches the door, instead of blocking its way, as they
had intended, they suddenly fall back—for she herself has
raised her hand and whispered that she wishes to go. So the
ambulance drives off from the village, and the inhabitants
mutter that " they have taken away our sun and put out the
light ".

The next day is a grey day, and the leaden weight that seems
to lie on the hearts of the people even affects the crops; among
the vines there is canker-worm, ' oïdium ', mildew. And worse
is to come; the sky lowers and there is the threat of a hailstorm
which will ruin the vine crops altogether. The villagers rush
out and fire the guns that are supposed to divert the storm; the
explosion of the guns is echoed by the claps of thunder. But
suddenly, just as the storm is working up to its worst, the wind
falls and the sun comes out. They say to each other, " She has
come back to us ". And later they realize that it is true; for it
was at that very moment that she died, on her hospital bed,
" in order to be altogether ours ". M. Guicherat and M. Bolle
are very complacent about the result, but as they talk they
stop short in the middle of a sentence: for they see La
Brûlée, kneeling silently on the quay. She is dressed all in
black. . . .

It is hard to do justice, in a brief summary, to this exquisite
tale. The style is, as always, simple, unaffected, colloquial and
immensely graphic. There is no attempt to bludgeon the
reader into belief—the story is merely told, straightforwardly,
unselfconsciously, and with the countryman's keen eye for
detail, colour and change. Even when the ' supernatural ' (if
that is the word) occurs, it is described in the most matter-of-
fact tone without any thought of rubbing it in. It is the old

drunkard, Grin, who first sees the point of it all; it is not those who come to Marie, but Marie herself who is healed—" Elle est guérie—guérie de la terre et des maux de la terre, guérie des maux de l'âme et des choses d'en bas."[35]

It is Ramuz' great gift to steer to the very edge of sentimentalism but always, like an expert skater, to swerve away at the last moment. This is because he preserves the exact proportion between the large and the small, the local and the universal. In one of his books he describes his return to ' nature '—not of course to mere picturesque ' nature '— " Nature is not a *décor* for me; it is essentially the opposite of a *décor*. A *décor* is something which takes its place around an action, but which remains independent of it. On the contrary, nature has always been closely intermingled with my life and has always played an active part in it." And so his rediscovery of his locality and people was not a narrowing process;

> For I had the sense that I was participating not only in a little human collectivity, but beyond it, in a total life, which some call God, which I daren't give a name to, but whose presence I felt, being glad to lose myself in its dimensions beyond time and space. Far from diminishing myself by it, I felt myself enlarged as it were, because I felt myself now loved and protected. A great sense of interdependence, a sense also (not a very Christian one, I fear) of close lineage. I reintegrated my family, pouring myself anew into a kind of common destiny, from which I had become separated, into a universal life which ran from the beast to me, from the insect to me, from the tree to me, from the stone to me; and in which there were no longer things, where there were only beings, for all took on life here. . . .[36]

This near-pantheism is corrected by his continual sense of the limits of ' nature ', and, especially in his novels, by the sense that personal relations can be analogies of the divine. And analogy is for the writer—perhaps for all of us—the securest way to point to what lies beyond the horizon of our vision. When the women come to see for themselves whether the story about Marie's healing power is true or not, the analogy is for once made explicit; and it is significant of Ramuz' control that he resists the temptation to make it more, or more frequently, so: " On avait voulu venir voir, parce que la nature de l'homme est méfiante, parce que c'est un besoin chez lui de toucher et de constater (et tel déjà n'avait pas voulu croire avant d'avoir mis le doigt dans les trous des Mains et des Pieds)."[37]

7

PILGRIMS OR EXPLORERS?

I

THE MAJOR PROBLEM which faces the creative writer in the twentieth century is the erosion of the imaginative soil. It is this more than anything that has caused the death of the contemporary novel. Joyce and Lawrence not only saw this but in their writings put down a solid road-block in the way of the traditional novelist, with a signpost annexed: ' No further advance down this road '. The erosion has spread more widely than most people are aware. It has been a common charge against the Believer that the area where his supernatural faith can still relevantly operate has shrunk to absurdly insignificant dimensions; the rest of the land has been taken over and exploited by other firms—the natural sciences, psychology, anthropology, etc. Even if the charge is true, it is not only the man of religion who feels—or is told he ought to feel—this shrinkage. It was not wholly in light-hearted mood that a young philosopher remarked recently: " Philosophy was once conceived as the study of Reality, but was displaced by the application of empirical methods in the physical sciences; it was also conceived . . . as the *a priori* study of Mind . . . or Knowledge, but is being gradually but firmly replaced by the application of empirical methods in psychology, it is now generally conceived as the *a priori* study of Language. . . ." But even this is not the last stronghold, for, he says, soon we shall find ourselves turning, for this last purpose, " to a methodical study of the facts, to comparative linguistics and semantics, only recently discernible as sciences. It seems historically to be the function of philosophy to initiate genuine science by speculation; in all its phases (outside pure logic) it is pre-science ".[1]

The shrinkage of imaginative terrain is more obvious, however, when we consider the invasions of psychology.

Perhaps it is the critics who have suffered most. In the realm of the visual arts, for instance, there has been a tendency to assessment of painting from a pragmatic, social point of view; as merely a form of occupational therapy. Sir Herbert Read is doubtless not to blame if the theme of his book *Education Through Art* has led to an over-emphasis upon this aspect. We would not be thought to decry the interesting and sometimes very moving exhibitions of paintings by sub-normal children, epileptics, psychotics, etc. Of course art is therapeutic. So is prayer. But a painting looked at or executed *solely* for the sake of coping with a manic-depressive mood is not likely to be very good painting; any more than a prayer offered *merely* to escape spiritual aridity is likely to effect its end. And literary criticism from a psycho-analytical point of view is even more barren. When we are given (as we have been from time to time) a detailed and technical examination of the psychology of *Hamlet* (man and play) we may perhaps be getting something useful; we may be gaining professional confirmation for what we knew intuitively all along: that Shakespeare was, among other things, a brilliant ' psychologist '. But if it is thereby suggested that this is to be the touchstone of Shakespeare's genius, then we see that psychology has intruded beyond its own sphere. Indeed, what the psycho-analytical critic usually does not realize is that a play like *Hamlet*, which provides him with such excellent material for his own technique, may often be a worse play the better its psychology is done; precisely because a great drama must be more than an accurate case-history. One does not need to agree with all the contentions of Professor E. E. Stoll and the other exponents of Shakespearean ' conventions ' to maintain this.

   If we wish to see a cautionary example of the smudging of literary criticism by psychology, there is one ready to hand. An interesting study was written recently of the novels, and person, of Franz Kafka.[2] It contains much useful information, especially biographical. But its major claim is to have discovered ' the secret meaning ' of Kafka's works. Mr. Neider, the author, is emphatic that those critics who have detected theological themes in his novels are looking awry. (But then, Mr. Neider spoils a not very good case by, implicitly and sometimes explicitly, denying that theology can have any objective reference anyway. The result is a curious paralogism. As if one were to argue that there are no musical references in Milton: because all music is basically mathematical; therefore all overtly musical themes are really comments on Euclid; therefore all musical references in Milton are in fact Euclidian; therefore there are no musical references in Milton.) Having disposed of theological views, Mr. Neider proceeds to disclose the ' key ' he has discovered to Kafka's work. The key is: that Kafka's novels contain a "web of symbols that are mostly sexual in nature—those symbols common to dreams, folklore, and the unconscious . . ."; that they "present in detail the dynamics of the Œdipus complex ", and that they " contain a web of nomenclatural symbolism ". Using the symbols of Venus (♀) and Mars (♂) as female and male symbols respectively, Mr. Neider then proceeds to analyse certain passages in the novels. For instance in *The Castle* we find, says Mr. Neider, mythical symbolism and symbolic action.

> A castle, like a village, town, citadel, and fortress, is a symbol of woman and mother. A count is a father symbol, like emperor, king, and president. The count's permission is necessary for K. to enter the castle; i.e. the father's permission is necessary for the son to possess his mother incestuously. Land, too, is a symbol of woman and mother, as indicated by the expression ' mother earth '. A land surveyor is therefore one who measures the mother—the incestuous implication is obvious. K.'s surveying apparatus, an obvious symbol of his masculinity, never arrives; i.e. he is not adequate sexually, although he has unusual sexual drives. K. telephones the castle (the old-fashioned telephone is a male symbol) and later discovers that there is no real connection with the castle. The lack of sexual connection is an important theme of the novel.[3]

Thus armed, he proceeds to examine some passages in detail. We give one example:

> At the superintendent's, K. witnesses a mass of symbols, the superintendent's gouty leg (♂), the candles (♂), cabinet (♀), shed (♀), chest (♀), the rolls (♂) of paper (♂)

documents (paper is derived from papyrus, a long-stemmed plant with a spray on top). The Bridge Inn landlady has retained three (♂) [Neider notes that according to psycho-analysts the sacred number three is a mythical symbol of the whole male genitalia] keepsakes from Klamm, who sent for her three (♂) times. In the school-room there are gymnastic apparatus (♂), wood (♀), shed (♀), sausage (♂), stove (♀), candle (♂), and cat (♀).[4]

With this kind of criticism what could one not do? It would be very interesting to interpret a page of Bradshaw on these lines, taking all ' up trains ' as (♂) symbols and all ' down trains ' as (♀). This is not, of course, to say that there is no sexual symbolism in literature, nor that elucidation of it is not sometimes valuable for the understanding of some writers as well as painters. But to reduce all literary criticism to this kind of psychological detection, as Mr. Neider at least seems to do, is absurd.

This danger to criticism, has, however, been indicated by many writers in our time,[5] and should be familiar enough. What, I think, has not been so well recognized is the super-session of the naturalistic novel by the psychologist's dossier. Till recently we have been shielded from the realization by the thick screen of psycho-analytical technical language. But now that psychologists are beginning to write books in a civilized tongue we are likely to be increasingly aware of it. As a happy instance I shall quote from one of the cases recorded by Mr. Erik H. Erikson, a doctor who remarkably combines an acute post-Freudian insight with a generously humane culture and a thoroughly readable prose style.

> I had been told that Peter was retaining his bowel movements, first for a few days at a time, but more recently up to a week. I was urged to hurry when, in addition to a week's supply of fecal matter, Peter had incorporated and retained a large enema in his small, four-year-old body. . . .
>
> His pediatrician had come to the conclusion that this feat could not have been accomplished without energetic support from the emotional side.

So Dr. Erikson was called in, and determined to try to understand the conflict and establish communication with the boy as quickly as possible so as to obtain his co-operation.

It has been my custom before deciding to take on a family case problem to have a meal with the family in their home. I was introduced to my prospective little patient as an acquaintance of the parents who wanted to come and meet the whole family. The little boy was one of those children who make me question the wisdom of any effort at disguise. " Aren't dreams wonderful? " he said to me in the tone of a hostess as we sat down to lunch. He then improvised a series of playful statements which, as will be clear presently, gave away his dominant and disturbing fantasy. . . .

" I wish I had a little elephant right here in my house. But then it would grow and grow and burst the house." The boy is eating at the moment. This means his intestinal bulk is growing to the bursting point. . . .

" I had a bad dream. Some monkeys climbed up and down the house and tried to get in to get me." . . . The monkeys want to get at him in his house. Increasing food in his stomach—growing baby elephant in the house— . . . monkeys after him in the house. . . .

They go up to the nursery, and the doctor asks him which pictures in his book he likes best.

Without hesitation he produced an illustration showing a gingerbread man floating in water towards the open mouth of a swimming wolf. Excitedly he said, " The wolf is going to eat the gingerbread man, but it won't hurt the gingerbread man because [loudly] *he's not alive*, and food can't feel it when you eat it! " I thoroughly agreed with him, reflecting in the meantime that the boy's playful sayings converged on the idea that whatever he had accumulated in his stomach was alive and in danger of either " bursting " him or of being hurt. [The next picture the boy showed the doctor was of] a smoke-puffing train going into a tunnel, while on the next page it comes out of it—its funnel *not smoking*.

" You see," he said, " the train went into the tunnel and

in the dark tunnel it *went dead!* " Something alive went into a dark passage and came out dead. I no longer doubted that this little boy had a fantasy that he was filled with something precious and alive; that if he kept it, it would burst him and that if he released it, it might come out hurt or dead. In other words, he was pregnant.

The patient needed immediate help, by interpretation. I want to make it clear that I do not approve of imposing sexual enlightenment on unsuspecting children before a reliable relationship has been established. Here, however, I felt experimental action was called for.

They started drawing elephants together, and after they had become quite good at that the doctor casually asked whether he knew where the elephant babies came from.

Tensely he said he did not, although I had the impression that he merely wanted to lead me on. So I drew as well as I could a cross section of the elephant lady and of her inner compartments, making it quite clear that there were two exits, one for the bowels and one for the babies. " This," I said, " some children do not know. They think that the bowel movements and the babies come out of the same opening in animals and in women." Before I could expand on the dangers which one could infer from such misunderstood conditions, he very excitedly told me that when his mother had carried him she had had to wear a belt which kept him from falling out of her when she sat on the toilet; and that he had proved too big for her opening so she had to have a cut made in her stomach to let him out. I had not known that he had been born by Cæsarean section, but I drew him a diagram of a woman, setting him straight on what he remembered of his mother's explanations. I added that it seemed to me that he thought he was pregnant; that while this was impossible in reality it was important to understand the reason for his fantasy; that, as he might have heard, I made it my business to understand children's thoughts and that, if he wished, I would come back the next day to continue our conversation. He did wish; and he had a superhuman bowel movement after I left.[6]

The history does not end there; there is another emotional entanglement connected with the above to uncover, and further physiological treatment is necessary—" only a combination of dietetic and gymnastic work with many interviews with mother and child could finally overcome a number of milder setbacks." But we have quoted the core of the episode; and have done so because what is striking about this ' case ' is that it could be the germ of a naturalistic novel. It has the structure, the dramatic contours, the build-up to a climax, and the post-climactic quiet which are the marks of any workmanlike piece of imaginative fiction. Translated into the corresponding terms of adult life, and padded out with descriptive accompaniments, it might become any one of the average successful novels that still provide reviewers with a livelihood. As it stands it seems to me something better still, in its own *genre*; and I myself would certainly rather read cases of this kind than most of the novels that form the staple of the circulating libraries. Why, then, should the novelist continue to write, since truth can be found so much stranger and so much more cogent than fiction?

II

This erosion of the imaginative soil has its particular consequences for the man of belief. We saw in the last two chapters that beyond the ' agony of belief' of Dostoevsky there could only be either the advance on the one hand to aggressive unbelief or militant faith, or on the other to eclectic humanism which abandons the belief-unbelief debate as profitless. In Elias Canetti's fecund novel *Auto-da-Fé* (fecund not only in its own proliferation of fancy, but in its crop of imitators) there is a passage which has a wider application than its context suggests. George Kien, brother of the hero, Peter Kien, is a psychologist, and runs a mental home for 800 patients, all of whom love him. He effects many cures; but alas, this is not all to the good.

When George walked along the streets of Paris it sometimes happened that he met one of his cures. He would be embraced and almost knocked down, like the master of some enormous dog coming home after a long absence.

Under his friendly questions he concealed a timid hope.
He . . . waited for just one such little comment as " Then
it was nicer! " or " How empty and stupid my life is now! "
" I wish I were ill again! " " Why did you cure me? " . . .
Instead, compliments and invitations rained on him. His
ex-patients looked plump, well and common. Their
speech was in no way different from that of any passer-by.
. . . When they had still been his friends and guests, they
were troubled by some gigantic guilt, which they carried
for all, or with their littleness which stood in such ridiculous
contrast to the hugeness of ordinary men, or with the idea
of conquering the world, or with death—a thing which
they now felt to be quite ordinary. Their riddles had
flickered out; earlier they lived for riddles; now for
things long ago solved. George was ashamed of himself.
. . . He had been outwitted by his profession.[7]

Faced with the embarrassing success of therapy, which
exorcizes mystery and genius in its triumphal progress, the man
of religion, as much as the artist, may understandably feel
himself threatened—a castaway upon a sand dune with the
waters rising.

He may react by intimidation. The late M. Georges Bernanos, for instance, never argued about the supernatural; he
stated it, more, he hurled it at you. It is hard to duck quickly
enough to dodge the verbal missiles he tosses about. The result
is always powerful and sometimes—as in his best novel, *Sous le
Soleil de Satan*—cogent. It is true that Bernanos is sometimes
accused of lack of charity to his bad characters. As the saintly
Chantal's father, M. de Clergerie, says to his daughter in *La
Joie*, " One feels that you have not sufficient pity for the poor
wretches who wallow like me, in the mud of the world ".[8]

And the villain of the same novel, the Russian, Fiodor, is
admittedly painted in pure black, and with a self-knowledge
that makes him even worse: " Nobody here ", he says to the
cook, " has the courage of good or evil. Satan himself would
appear as nothing but a trail of dust on the wall."[9] But
Fiodor is evidently intended to symbolize the Great Opposer.
And on the other hand there are passages which tell against
this accusation. There are, for instance, few scenes in Bernanos'

novels more moving than that in which, after the old Granny has had a seizure, Chantal gently persuades her to give up the keys—those keys she had clung to till the last, representing her jealousy and greed. There is a tenderness, moreover, about Chantal's purity and sometimes rather absurd precociousness which has, it seems, to have some rocks of brutality to show it off. The real difficulty in assessing Bernanos as a novelist is that the atmosphere he creates is so engulfing that the reader must either take it whole or reject it whole. The action in his novels seems to take place as if it were in a dark tunnel with the voices merging their echoes into each other. If you think the tunnel doesn't exist you can't read the novels. Yet many competent critics, not predisposed to assent, have admitted to their sometimes compelling power. The least we can say is that Bernanos does to unbelief what Chantal, in the above novel, does to Fiodor: " She is too pure," he says of her, " she comes and goes, she breathes and lives with the light, beyond us, beyond our presence. And yet, unknown to herself, she radiates light, she drags our black souls out of the shadows, and the old sins begin to stir, to yawn, to stretch and show their yellow claws."[10]

Paul Claudel's intimidation is of a different kind—though, as the correspondence with André Gide shows clearly enough, intimidation is certainly the right word. His magnificent rhetoric has a hypnotic power which drugs criticism into the silence of stupor. In a different sense he is like the actress in one of his plays who knows that she is only successful because the audience are afraid of the truth and come to the theatre to watch something which will make them forget their own truth:

> And I watch them too, and I know that there is the cashier who knows that tomorrow
> His books will be checked, and the adulterous mother whose child has just fallen ill,
> And the man who has just stolen for the first time, and the man who has done nothing all day,
> And they watch and listen as if they were asleep.[11]

Sometimes we listen to Claudel as if we were asleep. Claudel deals in vast generalities—man's sin and titanism, the decay and recovery of societies, the anticipations of divine revelation in primitive mythology, the elemental conflicts of love and jealousy, etc.—which are matched by the sometimes monotonous sweep of his long lines. His greatest works are his earlier ones; and one cannot but feel that they stand as monuments of a time and of problems which we can no longer see in his way.

There is another way, however, besides the way of intimidation; the way of self-defence. Mr. Graham Greene will do as one sample of this. There is only one hero in every one of Mr. Greene's novels: a vague creature called Grace. The self-defence (for one comes away from his novels with the strong impression that what is meant to be Catholic apologetic is really self-defence) follows faithfully the line of much contemporary theological apologetic which constructs its argument on the foundations of Original Sin, and so exacerbates Original Sin to do it. Mr. Greene's tawdry characters and stale scenery are evidently put there in a deliberately difficult obstacle race which the hero, Grace, is to run—high jumps made specially high to show his paces. The author admits it in one of his novels, *The Heart of the Matter*, which he has situated among the squalors of the West African coast because there " human nature hasn't had time to disguise itself. Nobody here could ever talk about a heaven on earth. Heaven remained rigidly in its proper place on the other side of death, and on this side flourished the injustices, the cruelties, the meannesses that elsewhere people so cleverly hushed up. Here you could love human beings nearly as God loved them, knowing the worst: you didn't love a pose, a pretty dress, a sentiment artfully assumed."[12] But the set purpose is betrayed in the imagery also, and that means in the ugly quality of Mr. Greene's imagination. " His wife was sitting up under the mosquito-net, and for a moment he [Scobie] had the impression of a joint under a meatcover."[13]

Or take the scene in which Wilson, in the same novel, visits the local brothel; gratuitous, because we do not need this addition to persuade us to dislike Wilson—the scales are weighted heavily enough against him already. Or again, there is the odious scene in his best novel, *The Power and the Glory*, when the priest, famished, steals a bone off a dog, and it is noted that the dog has a broken back and drags itself along by its front paws—a quite unnecessary addition. Other examples of the ' cooking ' of the situation, for apologetic purposes, can be seen in the monotony with which Mr. Greene's characters are presented as pursued, heroes in flight, dogged by someone—the police, the communists, the Hound of Heaven. But this frequently results in a slight tilt towards sentimentality; the theme of pursuit has to be carefully handled if it is not to appear a mere fishing for sympathy.

The best test of a writer's sincerity is to imagine his characters on a stage, and then to ask: Are they, really, talking to each other, or are they ostensibly facing each other but in fact talking to the audience? Constantly in Mr. Greene's novels we find that it is the latter that is true. In *The Power and the Glory* there is a scene in the prison in which, while a couple fornicate in a corner (there is, of course, a good deal of gratuitous fornication in his novels) the priest delivers a lecture to a pious woman who is horrified at sex. This is really Mr. Greene, showing us that he knows the answers. Worse still is the scene in which the priest argues with the lieutenant, a grim and humourless communist—he had to be humourless—on the way to his execution; and we know we are listening to Mr. Greene talking to his progressive friends. Again, in *Brighton Rock*, is it really the Boy, Pinkie (the seventeen-year-old gangster and lapsed Catholic), or is it Mr. Greene, who says, " Of course it's [the Catholic Faith] true. What else could there be. Why, it's the only thing that fits. These atheists, they don't know nothing. Of course there's Hell. Flames and damnation."? The diary of the heroine in *The End of the Affair* is one long ' author's intrusion '. And in *The Heart of the Matter* there is a letter which Scobie intercepts, supposed to be written by the Portuguese captain to his daughter, which is quite obviously not what he would say of himself but what Mr. Greene wants to say about him: " I am not a good man, and sometimes I fear that my soul in all this hulk of flesh is no larger than a pea. You do not know how easy it is for a man like me to commit the unforgivable despair. Then I think of my daughter. There was just enough good in me once for you to be fashioned. A wife shares too much of a man's sin for perfect love. But a daughter may save him at the last. Pray for me, little spider. Your father who loves you more than life."[14]

There is a final criticism of Mr. Greene of the same order as

these, and one which interestingly points to a coincidence of
theological weakness with literary failure. Miss Helen Gardiner
long ago in an article in *New Writing*[15] pointed out that Mr.
Greene is almost Calvinist in his predestinating of his characters either to Catholicism or to the invincible ignorance of
Protestantism or Agnosticism (treated, of course, as more or
less identical). Ida Arnold, the blowsy Protestant who only
knows of Right and Wrong, against Pinkie, who knows of
Good and Evil; they are the obvious examples (from *Brighton
Rock*). But so is the heroine of *The End of the Affair*, who 'catches
faith like a disease'. And the result of this conception of his
characters is a narrow Catholic individualism. Stated in
literary terms, Mr. Greene is never really interested in more
than one of his characters, and the rest, in whom he is not
interested, are not even convertible and stand, with their
artificially invented unsupernatural lives, as a very cardboard-
looking back-set for the drama he is trying to put on the stage.
Stated in theological terms, we may ask the question: what
lies before any of his characters? Not the conversion of the
world. Not even, really, Eternal Life. But the 'particular
judgment'—whether merciful, rigorous or (as sometimes)
merely sentimental. Mr. Greene is fond of talking about,
picturing, improbably constructing individual saints; he seems
to be, in his novels, little dominated by a belief in the Com-
munion of Saints.[16]

M. François Mauriac is a more distinguished figure in
European letters than Mr. Graham Greene is ever likely to be—
in spite of the latter's replacement of Mr. Charles Morgan as
'British export novelist number one' for the French literary
journals. Since I have tried at length elsewhere to assess his
total achievement[17] I shall not repeat that attempt here. But
in addition to the serious flaw of 'author's intrusion' (the
frequency of which in M. Mauriac's novels I have pointed out
in the book referred to), there are two other disquieting factors
which suggest that M. Mauriac too has not found the way
out from an eroded land.

The first factor is the extent to which M. Mauriac's serious
work has been distracted by his excursions into journalism.
This is not to say that no creative writer should ever undertake
journalism; not only must writers earn a living today, but

sometimes their excursions into the dailies and weeklies are of considerable value. But it is a dangerous deflection, and when it involves theological (or, indeed, political) controversy it is difficult to dam the backwash and keep it out of a writer's creative work. One comes away from a study of the French Catholic revival in twentieth-century letters with the impression that the noise of the battle is too loud, the expressions on the contestants' faces too deadly serious, the purely personal issues magnified too solemnly and self-consciously for there to be any balance, any proper detachment, in the writing that results from it. Recently M. Jean Cocteau wrote a play in the course of which he satirically referred to the Church as a ' femme-tronc '.[18] M. Mauriac came out at once with a furious article in a paper, anathematizing Cocteau, and (with what would seem to us extreme bad taste) openly reminding him of his earlier ' conversion '.

The priest who one day in that little chapel at Meudon raised his hand over you, pronouncing the word that looses, asked nothing of you in return but a little repentance and a beginning of love. . . . ' The trunk '?—yes, as much as to say, the breast in which beats that heart that was pierced by the lance. You drank at this source, one morning in 1926, and the angels who surrounded you were not called Heurtebise.* However long you may live, the day is near when true angels will surround you anew. . . . God grant that then the ' femme-tronc ' will enter your room for the last time, in the aspect of a consecrated man to whom she will have delegated her power of loosing: " At the hour of the ' Christ Cometh ', at cock-crow." The cock will crow, and against the heart of his Lord, Harle-quin will weep bitterly.[19]

Challenged by this extraordinary parading of his intimate spiritual history in public (" He has struck me in the open street ", M. Cocteau complained), the playwright not unnatur-ally replied with savage vigour.

I ACCUSE YOU, if you are a good Catholic of being a bad Christian, and of cudgelling purity, which is always

---

* *Sc.*, the ghostly Chauffeur of Death in Cocteau's *Orphée*.

difficult to recognize, with the big stick of conventional purity. . . .

I ACCUSE YOU, since you repeatedly tell me that you are an old child, of having preserved nothing of childhood but its sly cruelty.

I ACCUSE YOU of being a judge with a secret soft spot for the defendants. One can't be both judge and defendant. But I accuse you of being one in your articles and the other in your novels.

I ACCUSE YOU of seeing only what is ignoble in our world and of limiting nobility to another world which we can't get at because its code is impenetrable.

At our age we can no longer be beautiful. But we can have beautiful souls. I ACCUSE YOU of not having looked after your soul. . . .[20]

I only mention this episode, so strange to our English ears, because of the self-conscious seriousness with which we see M. Mauriac entering the lists as Catholic champion; and because of the effect that this is bound to have upon his novels.

The second factor is not unrelated to this episode. M. Cocteau, as we have seen, repeats the common charge against Mauriac (it was made by Gide and others) that he professes Catholic orthodoxy in person but abandons it in his novels. I think that this charge arises from ignorance as to what orthodoxy demands in the field of imaginative life; and I think on the contrary that the intrusion into the novels of precisely this orthodoxy and its implications is frequently their ruin. And this applies in particular to that preoccupation of the Catholic apologetic novelist: the final choice at death. We have seen how concerned M. Mauriac is with M. Cocteau's final choice; he is no less concerned with that of the characters in his novels. Several of them have—like, indeed, many other Catholic novels such as M. Roger Martin du Gard's *Jean Barois*, Mr. Evelyn Waugh's *Brideshead Revisited*, M. Roger Bésus' *Le Refus*, and no doubt countless others—dramatic death-bed scenes: the last confession or the conversion *in extremis*. The situation provides, of course, a ready, an easily accessible, tension. But that is precisely its weakness or rather its temptation to the novelist: it may become a cliché, it may

score its successes with too little effort. And at the level of
sheer technique why should the effective presentation of a
death-bed conversion be any better, as literature, than the
effective presentation of a death-bed rejection? I am thinking
of a neat and in its way a moving little novel called *Lève-toi et
Marche*, by M. Hervé Bazin. Up till the writing of this novel
no one would have thought of mentioning M. Bazin's name in
any sort of proximity to that of M. Mauriac; but this latest
work does show a strength which makes it not unworthy to be
referred to in this discussion. And the central theme in the
novel is the heroine, Constance's, remarkable stoicism in the
face of a gradually but certainly approaching death from
paralysis, and her refusal to allow that to become merely a
gambit for her conversion. She occasionally utters cynical
blasphemies, directed against her friend Pascal, the Protestant
pastor who is so anxious to save her soul. For instance, when
she has to have a peculiarly repulsive operation owing to her
increasing inability to perform certain bodily functions, she
comments, with a giggle:

> My dear Pascal, do you see how your Providence
> recompenses a clean, well-behaved little girl? You're
> becoming so pressing, and you said the other day " God
> is prowling round your suffering. Offer it to Him. . . ."
> Well, can you find a pretty formula to prove to me that He
> likes this business, that He sniffs it up like incense. . . ?
> The Lord has a liking for curious merits! And if I
> honestly am working to His glory in this posture . . . [she
> laughs nervously, and the doctor has to readjust the
> tube].[21]

She describes herself as a ' test case ' for Pascal, and she even
toys with the idea of feigning a ' conversion ' for his sake, out
of pity. He is just packing his bags, ready to go as a missionary
to the Cameroons, and he comes to see her.

> Crossing my room he cried out gaily to me:
> " My packing will soon be done! "
> And then he dared to lean over me, dared to smooth my
> hair and murmur with extraordinary sharpness:
> " Constance, Constance, do think of doing yours too! "

He went out with these words, and I wondered what he meant. There where I am going no one takes anything with them. . . . But no doubt it was all apostolic zeal: the missionary would love to convert, *in extremis*, his first heatheness. Perhaps after all I'll give him the gift of this illusion. Doctors say to those who nurse the dying: " You can give him anything he wants. Nothing can do him any harm now. . . ." The dying too can give the right change.[22]

Their last meeting is graphic and tense.   Constance thinks disgustedly that he is counselling resignation.

" No [he replies], acceptance. It isn't only heroes who are capable of sacrificing their lives. As you've done up till now, act through a third person. Give God power of attorney."

" But I don't believe in Him," groaned Constance, holding back her feeble breath, visibly torn between sincerity and the desire to give her 'client' satisfaction. . . .

" He believes in you, since you exist. . . . You think you don't believe in God. Your pride masks Him from you, because you have lived this virtue like a vice, because you have centred it upon yourself. . . . Ah, Constance, faith has such a power, it can make the whole action, in one last act, so easy . . . that's the miracle! "

" But the initiative isn't mine," said a little obstinate voice.

" Oh, what pride," Pascal burst out, losing patience. . . .

" I think it must be ", said Constance at last, " that God's exchequer is economizing on miracles in my case. . . . But let's talk about you instead, Pascal. Where are you going exactly? What I'd like to know is whether you're going to make a success of your life."

And suddenly Pascal stood up, higher than his shadow, his head in the middle of the cone of light from the lamp. He lifted one of his hands to the level of his forehead and, brightly lit from behind, cast a shadow on the wall like a sort of crab, a shrivelled head. Spectacular the repartee which sprang to his lips:

" How could I succeed, if you are my first failure? "

And he leans over her, urges her to make one gesture, and then suddenly seizes her swollen, paralysed hand and forces it to make the sign of the Cross. She summons up enough strength to dismiss him—" Go, go on, go to the Cameroons, to the Cameroons! " Pascal meets Constance's friend, old Roquault, on the landing: Roquault witnessed the scene (and recounts it afterwards in the first person):

> " She's not entirely responsible for her actions," I said to him, very low.
>
> " No doubt! " he replied, drily.
>
> He gripped the banisters, and moved forward a pace. But at once he stopped.
>
> " Look," he said, in an expressionless voice, " I've no illusions any more. She is dying as she lived: without God. Yet one could say of her what Claudel said of some Brazilian hero or other: ' Religion apart, he was an evangelic figure '."
>
> He seemed so put out that I hadn't the courage to reply " Exactly! That's just the worst scandal for you: those sort of people do you out of your job." Instead I mumbled a conventional formula, to console him:
>
> " I know there are thunderbolts of grace which can unseal, at the very moment they are closing, eyes which have deserved the light."
>
> But that didn't satisfy him. . . . He breathed right in my face:
>
> " I'll get my own back in the Cameroons. You just see how I get my own back! "

And when Roquault goes back into Constance's bedroom, she merely whispers feebly: " I couldn't ". She dies a few days later.[23]

I have quoted this scene at length, because though a trifle melodramatic, it seems to me effective. No doubt it depends for its effectiveness upon the belief whose rejection is precisely its theme. But set beside the death-bed scenes of the Catholic novelists, as one drama beside another, can the literary critic, within his own province, say that one is better than the other? If it is supposed to be here that the superior illumination of faith reveals itself, then one must conclude the demonstration

not proven. We must give M. Mauriac his due, and concede
that he is theoretically well aware of this; that in some of his
novels* he is scrupulously careful, and successfully so, not to
tilt the scales in an apologetic direction; and that much of his
insight into and depiction of motive and character could only
belong to a novelist of some stature. But in the last resort we
are too aware of his preoccupation with results, too conscious
of his conclusions already wrapped up in his premises, to see
in him the major artist that he has so often been presented.

III

What I have called the erosion of the imaginative soil has
affected the self-consciously Catholic writers we have been
considering in a further sense; they are incapable of full-
blooded doubt. What, in fact, one is most conscious of in
them is a deficiency of that creative scepticism which was
described by Donne (leaning on St. Augustine): " Would you
know of a truth? Doubt, and then you will inquire. . . . As no
man resolves of any thing wisely, firmly, safely, of which he
never doubted, never debated, so neither doth God withdraw a
resolution from any man, that doubts with an humble purpose
to settle his owne faith, and not with a wrangling purpose to
shake another man's."[24]

Of course there can be a parallel deficiency in those who have
rejected belief. The petulance with which, for instance, Joyce
once dismissed the suggestion that his daughter might return
to the faith he had abandoned[25] has left its marks on much of
the *Portrait of the Artist as a Young Man* and on some of *Ulysses*—
perhaps one of the few ways in which *Finnegan's Wake* can be
regarded as an advance on the earlier works is its nearer
approach to serenity. On both sides, the rejectors and the
enthusiastic acceptors, one feels that the genuine agony of
belief (or disbelief) has passed them by. The terrible suspense
of the following conversation seems to occur at a level to
which they have not penetrated:

" What is faith? "

---

* E.g. in *Destins*, where the author refuses to present, what must have been
very tempting, a ' conversion ' of Elizabeth Gornac, and instead gives us her
quiet, unspectacular return to a gentle if rather wistful faith.

(Kafka): " Whoever has faith cannot define it, and whoever has none can only give a definition which lies under the shadow of grace withheld. The man of faith cannot speak and the man of no faith ought not to speak. And in fact the prophets always talk of the levers of faith and never of faith alone. . . ."

" And Christ? "

Kafka bowed his head.

" He is an abyss filled with light. One must close one's eyes if one is not to fall in it. . . . I try to be a true attendant upon grace. Perhaps it will come—perhaps it will not come. Perhaps this quiet yet unquiet waiting is the harbinger of grace, or perhaps it is grace itself. I do not know. But that does not disturb me. In the meantime I—have made friends with ignorance."[26]

(It is, I suppose, fairly certain that another member of the Jewish race, the late Simone Weil, who came a generation after him, cannot have known of these words of Kafka's— since they have only come to the light recently, that is, since her death; and that makes it all the more remarkable that she should have so exactly echoed his phraseology in her *Attente de Dieu*.[27])

This sort of scepticism, which in itself is, as I have called it, creative, since it proceeds from a centre of such absolute spiritual and intellectual integrity, is no doubt partly a product of the shrinkage of the imaginative field—of the sense that there is so little left that it is possible wholly to believe in. Now, one popular way out from this shrinking area is into the expansive field of comparative mythology. This has had a great attraction for critics, especially those who can respond to Jung's evocation of ' archetypes '. Mr. W. H. Auden as a practitioner is clearly influenced by the mythological detective work whose results appear in such books as Mr. Joseph Campbell's *The Hero with a Thousand Faces* or Miss Maud Bodkin's *Archetypal Patterns in Poetry* and *Studies of Type Images in Poetry, Religion and Philosophy*.[28]

As an example of what is meant we might recall some of the themes Miss Bodkin discusses in her earlier book. She takes (i) the ' Rebirth ' Archetype, and studies it especially in

The Ancient Mariner, with its guilt-laden fall into the deathly stillness of the doldrums—and here she compares the story of Jonah, and notes well that the ' Jonah atmosphere ' is so well conveyed in the Bible that we do not observe the incongruity of the psalm which Jonah is made to quote. Then, through Mary's prayer and the moon's name and image (the moon standing for the Queen of Heaven, the Earth-Mother) there comes sleep to the protagonists, and a relaxing of tension which leads at the end of the poem to new life. (ii) The ' Paradise-Hades ' or ' Heaven-Hell ' Archetype, studied in *Kubla Khan*, Virgil, Dante and Milton. In Dante " the whole Heaven-Hell pattern, as communicated experience, has become poetry "[29]; and she notes that " the horror of Dante's Hell is made bearable for the reader by the fact that its interest is concentrated upon a forward movement ".[30] (iii) The ' Image of Woman ' Archetype—studied in the traditional figure of the Muse inspiring the poet, in Dante's Beatrice, in St. Augustine's weeping for the sorrow of Dido (into which he projects his own grief at giving up his mistress), and in the closing scene of Goethe's *Faust*. (iv) The ' Images of the Devil, the Hero and the God '—studied in *Paradise Lost*, in Æschylus' *Seven Against Thebes*, in Faust's yielding to Mephistopheles, and in Shelley's *Prometheus Unbound*. Finally (v) various Archetypes of Eternity which can still find currency in modern days—studied in *The Waste Land*, *Wuthering Heights*, Virginia Woolf's *Orlando*, etc. She adds that music may do the same: " A symphony may . . . be felt to carry us through Hell and Heaven, to plunge us in an underworld of despair, and raise us again from the dead. . . . Even for those who do not interpret music thus dramatically, there may be something in the texture of musical experience, with its recurring factors of pain or tension, of discord followed by relief in its resolution, and delight in harmony, that corresponds to the continual interplay of opposites, glimpses of heaven's joy amidst earthly frustration and pain, by which poetry renders the sense of our mortal state."[31]

Now many of these connections are illuminating; and there is no doubt that the poet, novelist or dramatist who reveals these basic and therefore very ancient patterns, especially if he is quite *un*conscious of doing so, or at any rate only half-conscious of echoes and scarcely remembered themes, adds thereby an extra depth to his writings. But there are two difficulties which suggest that this alone is not the way of escape from the threatened sandbank. First, that the ' racial unconscious ' (if for the sake of argument we allow Jung's hypothesis) is highly indiscriminate; it can betray itself in the appeal of an advertisement for tooth-paste as much as in that of a great epic poem. And it is significant that Miss Bodkin, both in the book we have cited and in her later book which continues the theme-chase, shows just such indiscrimination. (In the earlier book she analyses not only *The Waste Land* but also with equal care Mr. Charles Morgan's *The Fountain.*) And, in the realm of creative poetry, we sometimes sense that Mr. Auden mars his verse by being just a bit too know-all about the mythological origins of some of his allusions. And, secondly, it is doubtful whether this appeal to universal archetypes does in fact so decidedly re-establish the possibility of affirmation in a world of imaginative erosion. It is true that there are certain experiences and relationships that are basic to man, and that can never be eroded out of existence so long as man remains man. And these the ' archetypes ' expound. But among them there is one, a privileged one, the pull and interplay between fact and fiction, which evaporates if it is itself treated as fiction—if, that is, one side of the balance is eliminated. " We are concerned ", says Mr. Campbell, describing the purpose of his book, " with problems of symbolism, not of historicity. We do not particularly care whether Rip van Winkle, Kamar al-Zaman or Jesus Christ ever actually lived. Their stories are what concern us. . . ."[32] And Miss Bodkin is no less explicit. There is no distinction, she says, for her between poetic and religious faith; for her " The image of cavern or abyss, with the accompanying horror of fall or descent, does constitute a satisfying symbol for a certain phase of experience [Hell]. . . . A recurring phase and permanent element of lived experience is symbolized by the image of the high garden land, sunlit . . . of the earthly Paradise. . . . So far as Plato or Virgil, Milton or Dante, by the power and magic of speech, lights up for me these symbols, so that I, with the poet, exult in fuller possession and mastery of my life's experience, so far I respond to the poem with full poetic faith. It has for me all the truth that poetry can claim." Poetic faith, she holds, is not a " momentary suspension of unbelief ", but " A quickening of belief in a truth more comprehensive, more philosophic, than either the abstract schematism of physical science, or the limited and partial glimpses that make up [one's] practical personal outlook." And the poetry that demands that sort of faith " in which we relive . . . the tidal ebb towards death, followed by liferenewal, affords us a means of increased awareness, and of fuller expression and control, of our own lives in their secret and momentous obedience to universal rhythms."[33]

But is it not just such language which reminds us of Mr. Eliot's warning against finding a substitute for religion " in poetry, or even in religion "? And it is quite clear that any historical religion which allowed itself to be satisfied with this merely ' poetic ' or ' imaginative ' acceptance would be on the way to its own abolition. The Greek religion did not long survive the stage of being presented as useful and necessary mythology. In the case of these historical religions, the truth or falsity of the ' myth ' by which they meet our ' patterned ' emotions becomes precisely a vital question to those emotions themselves.

Thus, to take Christianity as another example, when St. Paul said to the Corinthian Christians that if Christ did not rise from the dead then all Christians have not ' risen ' either and are yet dead in their sins, he is indeed making his meaning clear by appealing to an archetypal pattern. But it is a pattern which depends here for its life upon the truth of a specific historic event; if the event is true, the pattern comes alive—if not, the pattern is dead, like a figure traced out in flowers but now undecipherable since the flowers have withered and decayed into the soil. And the difficulty for the artist is this: If he confines himself to myths that have never been believed to be historically true, he is on safe ground; but the imaginative erosion has washed away so many of such myths from the region of responsiveness. If, on the other hand, he tries to supplement them by borrowing from myths that have been believed (and are still by many believed) to be true, his very use of them as ' merely ' myths has in fact the effect of dissolving them, so that they do not even do their work as myths.

The man of belief, therefore, the artist who wants to be able to make affirmations in an age of relativism, is in a peculiarly embarrassing position. The easiest way out of the shrinking area where assertions are possible is into the field of myth; but here he finds himself forced to make a decision which, as artist, he would prefer not to have to make—a decision about historical fact. In concluding that he must find his way out of the dilemma as best he can, we are at least implicitly recognizing his difficulties, and thereby we are also nearer to an understanding why our age is one, relatively speaking, of creative paucity.

IV

I have used the phrase that the artist's desire is to make affirmations in an age of relativism. And this function, so long as he is an artist, he will perform, however eroded the soil. For however many collective archetypes he is expressing, the actual expression of them is his and his alone.

> The modern hero [says Mr. Joseph Campbell in the book already referred to], the modern individual who dares to heed the call to and seek the mansion of that presence with whom it is our whole destiny to be atoned, cannot, indeed must not, wait for his community to cast off its slough of pride, fear, rationalized avarice, and sanctified misunderstanding. " Live ", Nietzsche says, " as though the day were here." It is not society that is to guide and save the creative hero, but precisely the reverse. And so every one of us shares the supreme ordeal —carries the cross of the redeemer—not in the bright moments of his tribe's great victories, but in the silences of his personal despair.[34]

Rhetoric apart, that is a good statement of one side of the writer's vocation. The other side is that he is the world's seismologist, the delicate recording instrument that first registers the shock of the distant earthquake. Or if you wish a gloomier analogy, he is the ' white rabbit in the submarine '.

> " I once went a cruise in a submarine [said the novelist]. I stayed under water for about forty-five days. In

submarines there is a special apparatus for indicating the
exact moment when the air has to be renewed. But a
long time ago there was no such apparatus, and the
sailors took white rabbits on board instead. The
moment the atmosphere became poisonous the rabbits
died, and the sailors knew then that they had only five or
six hours more to live. . . . It is a gift which we have—the
rabbits and I—to feel six hours before the rest of human
beings the moment when the atmosphere becomes un-
breathable. . . ."

" What atmosphere? " asked Nora.

" The atmosphere in which contemporary society lives.
Human beings can no longer endure it. The bureaucracy,
the army, the government, the State machine, the administration, all combine to stifle man. Modern society is
at the service of machines and of enslaved technicians. It
is created for them. But men are condemned to
asphyxiation. . . ."[35]

The particular phenomena which this writer expects the
artist to record are perhaps a little obvious; but the principle
is sound. And this recording activity of the artist is in itself a
product of faith. The greatest living (the only great living)
novelist has said:

> Were I to determine what I, personally, mean by reli-
> giousness, I should say it is *attentiveness* and *obedience*—
> attentiveness to the inner changes of the world, the
> mutations in the aspects of truth and right; obedience
> which loses no time in adjusting life and reality to these
> changes, this mutation, and thus in doing justice to the
> spirit. To live in sin is to live against the spirit, to cling
> to the antiquated, obsolete, and to continue to live in it
> because of inattentiveness and disobedience. . . . Peace
> . . . signifies a gift of intelligence before God.[36]

There is a sense in which any work of real integrity, a work
arising from true disinterestedness, is the product of ' intelligence before God '. And to however small an area the field of
creative imagination may seem to have shrunk, so long as man
is man there will still be this intelligence.

The sense in which this activity of the artist is a product of faith is worth examining. For all that we have said in this book leads to the clear conclusion that even Christian faith is not a univocal concept at every moment in history. Dr. Leavis, speaking from outside that faith, has stated the matter in classic terms. Having discussed ' humanism ' as a creed (he is thinking of the humanism of Irving Babbitt) he says of himself: " My own aim is to deal in doctrine, theory and general terms as little as possible. The main concern of these pages is with methods and tactics." Some assumptions, of course, the literary critic must have: e.g. that it is worth trying to establish a real liberal education in England; which means trying to create in students an awareness of the continuity and concrete tradition of English culture. " It is the preoccupation with cultural values as human and separable from any particular religious frame or basis, the offer of a cultural regeneration that is not to proceed by way of a religious revival, that prompts the description ' humanist '. Literary criticism must, in this sense, always be humanist; whatever it may end in, it must be humanist in approach, so far as it is literary criticism and not something else." It may well lead the student beyond literary criticism to religious and philosophical issues, even to Christian conclusions there; but that will not excuse us from the task of starting where we are, without doctrinal frame and without aiming at inculcating one. For

> This is the age, not of Dante or of Herbert, but of T. S. Eliot; and Eliot's genius, which is of the kind that makes a poet profoundly representative, runs to that marvellous creative originality in the use of language because he cannot, for the ordering of his experience in poetry of directly religious preoccupation, make anything like that direct use of a received doctrinal frame or conceptual apparatus which for Dante or Herbert was natural or inevitable. . . .
>
> In such an age the business of quickening and concentrating into strong conscious life the cultural sensibility in which tradition has its effective continuance . . . will not be forwarded by any proposal that implies conditions at all analogous to those of the age of Dante. . . . The pre-

vailing spirit must be tentative. . . . To make it a matter
of trying to impose in advance the order that can only be
expected to emerge in course of time, if things go well with
civilization, would be vain.[37]

These are fine words, which we must respect for the concealed
faith that they (perhaps unconsciously?) imply; for who would
work so utterly in the dark for so long a period if there were no
hope of light beyond?

At this point it is important to note that the gap between
this kind of 'humanism' and that which is specifically
grounded in Christian belief is or can be today much less wide
than it is usually made out to be. And the point can best be
made by glancing at a characteristic example of the opposite
contention. Some years ago there appeared two pamphlets by
that intelligent critic, Mr. R. C. Churchill, which are worth
examining not so much for their intrinsic value (they are
deliberately polemical, and so occasional works) as for their
representative nature: *English Literature and the Agnostic*, and
Art and Christianity.[38] We shall discuss the first only, but a
quotation from the second sums up the theme of the first well
enough to be worth quoting: " The religious mind, being a
mind ' made up ', usually by someone or something outside
itself, by ' authority ', tends to be inflexible; flexibility is of the
essence of the artist mind." This thesis is then defended in
literature by referring to leading English poets and novelists,
showing their ' agnostic mentality ', and then comparing them
favourably with others who have had ' faith '. It is not difficult
to do, and dissent may be brushed aside by such a simple
generalization as " I don't need to show in detail [amid over-
whelming proof] that Coleridge, Wordsworth, Burns, Peacock,
Lamb, Byron, Hunt, de Quincey, Hazlitt, Keats and Shelley
were all in their different ways of an agnostic turn of mind."

Nobody would wish today to bid heavily for the loyalties of
Hunt, Lamb, de Quincey and Hazlitt; and taking ' agnostic
turn of mind ' in its broadest and least-defined sense, there is
no doubt that the phrase is applicable even to Coleridge and
Wordsworth, as also to Shakespeare or any great imaginative
writer. But it is precisely the employment of the term in this
broad and undefined sense, so as to establish ' agnosticism ' as

an ultimate philosophy, which I should challenge. Of that, more in a moment. Meanwhile, let us look at some more of Mr. Churchill's examples.

It is significant, he goes on, that " a writer of great intelligence and genius like George Eliot should have been an agnostic, while a writer of more prolixity than literary talent, like Charlotte Yonge, should have been an admirer of Keble."

This cries for qualification. George Eliot's wistful agnosticism in fact leads her, as Mr. S. L. Bethell has well pointed out, [39] to create most roundly and warmly when dependent upon the old traditions she can admittedly no longer believe in. Coming to modern times, Mr. Churchill produces D. H. Lawrence, T. F. Powys and L. H. Myers as examples of fine writers who have " not merely accepted a more or less agnostic view of life, as [E. M.] Forster has, but tried to justify it ". But here again we find an ambiguity in the word ' agnostic ' which begs large questions. L. H. Myers comes nearest, perhaps, to the official agnostic point of view by expressing, in his best writing (for we must exclude the bad earlier novels), an Indian philosophy. But it seems to me precisely not the ' agnostic ' elements in Buddhism which come out in the crucial parts of Myers' work *The Root and the Flower*: the contrast, for instance, between Rajah Amar and the sensualist, Prince Danyal, with his lascivious Camp: " The Camp was withdrawn because it had to be: . . . moreover the idea that they [Danyal and his followers] were sufficient unto themselves was very necessary to them; but it was nothing else than the truth, that they depended basically upon a solid, shockable world of decorum and common sense. They had to believe that a great ox-like eye was fixed upon them in horror. Without this their lives lost their point."

The main theme of this book is the twin influence upon young Prince Jali of his father's (Amar) Buddhism and his mother's (Sita) Syrian Christianity. Moreover, the profoundest part of the last book, *The Pool of Vishnu*, is the conversation with and direction by the ' Guru ', who is to provide the contemplative check upon the aggressiveness and ruthlessness of local administration, and also to dispense spiritual advice to a couple whose marriage had become disharmonized. But here again, it is not the ' agnosticism ' of Eastern thought which is brought out, so much as the essentially (and, it would seem, inconsistently, for the Indian) creative element in mysticism— that element which brings it closest to the mysticism of the Christian West; and it is brought out, we must note, *by contrast with* the rootless atheism of the English Smith (earlier in the book), the power-principle of the Muslim Abul Fezl or Sheik Mobarek, and the suffocating conservatism of the caste system. Mr. Churchill quotes the Guru's statement of faith: " What is this body of authority of which you speak? It is a mound of corpses. . . . Your priests will pretend to enclose the Spirit in churches. But those churches will be empty. Spirit is waiting in the market-place—waiting for the re-awakened and re-awakening man." This will sound, to those who have not read Myers' novel, like an effective attack upon the dogma- and institution-ridden Christian Church; actually it is directed against the static Indian caste society which Christianity has, in historic fact, been one of the main agents in demolishing! So much for Myers. Lawrence and Powys are, of course, even more equivocal exemplars of ' agnosticism '—with their imaginative dependence upon, if not belief in, myth and magic.

Mr. Churchill's thesis has been expressed in better terms by another critic, Mr. D. W. Harding. In a review of Mr. T. S. Eliot's *The Idea of a Christian Society*, Mr. Harding complained that for the Christian the goal of all movement is predetermined, so that he can only be a ' pilgrim ' now, never an ' explorer '. The Christian's " peace of mind depends on the conviction that he knows what he is ultimately aiming at; all his activity must be directed towards a goal which he has already postulated. By this means he escapes the insecurity of being in a strict sense an explorer and becomes instead a pilgrim."[40]

This again sounds cogent. But when one makes a distinction between ' agnostic mentality ' and ' agnosticism ' as a positive creed, the case falls, it seems to me, to the ground. For the former is found in a degree in any artist, and is not incompatible with faith, even Christian faith. Montaigne, said Mr. T. S. Eliot in a well-known phrase, expresses the scepticism of *every* human being. " For every man who thinks and lives by thought must have his own scepticism, that which stops at the question, that which ends in denial, or that which leads to faith and which is somehow integrated into the faith which transcends it." [41]

It is a common misconception to think of the Christian belief as a cosy society enclosed safely within strong castle walls, very pleasant if you can sell up your mental property and climb in, but once in there is nothing to do but walk round and round the yard. And if we are to play Mr. R. C. Churchill's game of citing one personality against another, we could refer to Mr. Eliot's own later poems, where it is clear that the pilgrim *is* still somehow the explorer. Though for faith victory may be certain, yet here man is still in the battle; and that is why Mr. Eliot can explore the meaning of time and history, the place of tradition, the reality of the past enfolded with the future into the present—tentative, hesitating (that is the effect, as Dr. Leavis notes, of his honesty), yet with one secure point of leverage, the still point of the turning world, " the moment of time but time was made through that moment ". It is no centrifugal Pilgrim who says,

> We shall not cease from exploration
> And the end of all our exploring
> Will be to arrive where we started
> And know the place for the first time.

If ' the agnostic mentality ' can thus find its valid place in the work of the believer, in a corresponding sense it is not ' agnosticism ' as a positive philosophy that, say, pleads for humanity in *The Pool of Vishnu*; that pleads for integrity in the novels of Virginia Woolf (who strove so hard to achieve a ' negative capability ' yet could not help asserting her own values); that cries out at religious persecution in Breughel's art (another of Mr. Churchill's examples); that inveighs with D. H. Lawrence against the complacent certainties of scientists and cocksure Christians. It is natural human sympathy, a thing given by God and (the Christians say) vindicated on the Cross. A true agnosticism would have to question that too—why should it be exempt? And taking, as we should do, not individual decisions about belief or unbelief, so much as the general moral, philosophical, religious beliefs that lie at the back of a whole culture, can it be confidently affirmed that natural human sympathy has always and best been preserved where divine faith has been lost? We do not need to press the issue any closer than in the very general words of the late P. E. More. Replying to a criticism by Mr. Lewis Mumford, he said: "Mr. Mumford . . . is right in feeling that the truth and fineness of art at any time depend largely on the philosophy behind it, and that no relief from the present confusion is possible until society re-establishes for itself some body of ideas in which the artist can live and breathe and expand. . . ."[42]

Faith is, we believe, a preservative, even an illumination, but never (if it is genuine faith and not some *ersatz* soporific) an excuse for inaction; it is an incentive to exploration, not a predestined itinerary for a Karma-pilgrimage. We have seen some of the difficulties that lie in the way of creative writing today; and we have concluded that those difficulties have ultimately a religious origin. Mr. Edwin Muir, writing on " The Decline of the Novel ", put it thus:

> The contemporary novel is a story of time against a background of time. The traditional novel is a story of time against a permanent pattern. This does not mean that Fielding or Jane Austen were religious in any sense, or that when describing Tom Jones or Elizabeth Bennet they were concerned with eternal truths. But they lived in an order in which everybody possessed without thinking about it much the feeling for a permanence above the permanence of one human existence, and believed that the ceaseless flux of life passed against an unchangeable background. Men still felt this whether they were Christians or not. . . .
>
> It may be advanced that without this permanent background there can be no whole picture of life. Seen against eternity the life of man is a complete story. Seen against time it is an unfinished one, a part of endless change, a fleeting picture on an unstable substance. The traditional recognition of a permanence beyond the duration of the happenings told in one story belongs to a certain mode of thinking and feeling which has prevailed during the known past of European civilization; it now prevails effectively no longer. That mode was auspicious to imaginative literature; and originally it was the creation

of religion. So that in a sense imaginative literature is, if not the child, at least the grandchild or great-grandchild of religion. . . .

The norm of human existence remains. There are certain beliefs which are natural to man, for they satisfy his mind and heart better than any alternative ones. . . . In a state of irremediable imperfection such as man's, the circle can be closed only by calling on something beyond man; by postulating a transcendent reality. So the belief in eternity is natural to man; and all the arts, all the forms of imaginative literature, since they depend on that belief, are equally natural to him. When that belief partially fails, imagination suffers an eclipse, and art becomes a problem instead of a function. If that belief were to fail completely and for good, there would be no imaginative art with a significance beyond its own time. But it is inconceivable that it should fail, for it is native to man.[43]

If this contention is sound, and I think it is difficult to deny its essential soundness, then the survival of the imagination, as well as of man, will be seen to depend upon hope; and it is not irrelevant that hope is one of the ' theological virtues '. We have praised Kafka for his intellectual integrity. But we cannot deny that a prolonged reading of his work leaves us gasping for breath (the same symptoms that the theologian feels after a thorough Barthian pummelling); and is not the reason for this precisely that Kafka's basic conviction was that outside the world there is " plenty of hope—for God—no end of hope— only not for us "?[44] (What sort of a God is this who keeps His hope to Himself?) After Kafka it is certainly a relief to turn to other fantasists, such as Jules Supervielle, who though without Kafka's greatness do have the effect of opening ventilators. It is, for instance, instructive to contrast a little *jeu d'esprit* of Supervielle's, *Les Suites d'une Course*, with Kafka's *Metamorphosis*. In the latter Gregor Samsa suddenly finds himself—characteristically—transformed into a nasty kind of little vermin. In the former Sir Rufus Flox, ' gentleman-rider ', loses his horse in the Seine and gradually becomes a horse himself. He is engaged to be married, but as he can't do much about that now, the

best he can do is to take his fiancée out for rides in a light trap
to which he is harnessed. But now she insists on taking a new
young man out with her in the trap; and when Sir Rufus, the
horse, overhears in their talk that they are making plans to
have him gelded, he viciously crashes them both against a tree
and becomes a man again.

But best of all is Supervielle's exquisite story *L'Enfant de la
Haute Mer* (the title story of a volume of tales). There is a
sailor who suddenly thinks " longuement, avec une force
terrible " of his dead child, drowned at sea. She is happy in a
submarine village; but her father's longing brings her up
towards the ship. But the humanlike wave which sweeps her
towards the ship cannot quite reach the sailor; and while he
thinks better of it, and of the child's suffering should she
succeed in returning, " la vague ramena l'enfant chez elle dans
un immense murmure de larmes et d'excuses."[45] As M. Denis
Saurat says of this tale, " It goes beyond Kafka—or soars
higher—as you like. And how perfect and comforting the
tragedy is—Kafka could not see tragedy as comforting, as the
great solution, because he did not know of the world to come
after the dread passage."[46]

Supervielle may be a slight figure to set beside Kafka; but he
is significant beyond his stature if only as a sign that hope is a
word that can still be found in the dictionary of imagination.
This book has been concerned with the varying relationships
between literature and faith. A famous hymn by St. Thomas
Aquinas, the *Tantum Ergo*, will perhaps make the relationship
I have been working towards clearer:

> Faith, our outward sense befriending,
> Makes the inward vision clear.*

But if it is faith that ' befriends the outward sense,' then the
recovery of hope is scarcely less important : for hope propels
it, while charity transforms it. And what the talented painter,
Mr. David Jones, said of the visual arts applies no less to the
works of creative writers: " The ability to paint a good picture
does not come through philosophy or religion in any direct
manner at all. *They* could only have, indeed, a damaging effect
on the making of things if thought of as providing some theory

* E. Caswall's translation of *Præstet fides supplementum/Sensuum defectui.*

to work by—a substitute for imagination or direct creativeness, and would so sadly defeat their own object—which is to protect the imagination from the slavery of false theory and to give the perfect law of liberty to our creativeness. To protect, in fact, what is natural to man.''[47]

That is the negative function of ' belief ', in art, as in poetry; the clearing of a space where things can be seen as the things they are, where creatures can be appreciated in their dependence and yet their bright individuality. And the positive function?—Not, at any rate, a mere Guide to Holy Places, a Brochure issued free to Pilgrims. For in a land where we are told, on the best authority, that the wind blows where it lists, the one thing certain about the adventure of belief is its unpredictability. With it we can find ourselves standing—

> Derrière moi la plaine, comme jadis en Chine quand je montais
> l'été vers Kouliang,
> Le pays aplati par la distance et cette carte où l'on ne voit rien
> tant que l'on marche dedans;
> Tant de kilomètres et d'années que l'on couvrirait maintenant
> avec le main!
> Le soleil d'un brusque rayon ça et là fait revivre et luire
> Un fleuve dont on ne sait plus le nom, telle ville comme une vieille
> blessure qui fait encore souffrir!
> Là-bas la fumée d'un paquebot qui part et la clarté spéciale que
> fait la mer—
> L'exil à plein cœur accepté dont nous ne sortirons qu'en avant et
> ne pas en arrière!
> Le soir tombe, considère ce site nouveau, explorateur!
> Ce silence à d'autres étonnant, qu'il est familier à ton cœur!
> Les montagnes l'une sur l'autre se dressent dans une attention
> immense
> Il faut beaucoup d'espace pour que la vie commence . . .[48]

NOTES

PREFACE

[1] Auden and Pearson, *Poets of the English Language* (Eyre and Spottiswoode, 1952), vol. II, p. xv.

[2] F. R. Leavis, article, " The State of Criticism: Representations to Father Martin Jarrett-Kerr ", in *Essays in Criticism*, vol. III, no. 2 (April, 1953).

CHAPTER I

[1] E. Batho: *The Later Wordsworth* (C.U.P., 1933), p. 312.

[2] E. Pound, *Guide to Kultur* (Faber, 1938), p. 155. Since the book is not easily obtainable, I give the whole passage:

" Repeating from a forgotten article: after working in the Vatican library and comparing the civility, in the high fine sense of the word, of that ambience, I said to Wm. Yeats: Anti-clericalism is no good (it being known between us fairly well what we did and did not believe). I said: I can see a time when we may all of us have to join together, that is everyone possessed of any degree of civilization. We will have to join the Monsignori against Babbitt.

" ' But CONfound it! ' said the propagator of the Celtic Twilight, ' In my country the Church IS Babbitt.'

" For the duration of this essay Babbitt is Sinclair Lewis as well as Sinc's affable and superficial caricature of American nullity. . . ."

[3] G. Santayana, *Three Philosophical Poets* (Cambridge, Harvard, 1935), p. 134.

[4] T. S. Eliot, *Selected Essays* (Faber, 1932), p. 243.

[5] T. S. Eliot, *Use of Poetry and Use of Criticism* (Faber, 1933), p. 130.

[6] T. S. Eliot, *Selected Essays*, p. 257.

[7] *Ibid.*, p. 138.

[8] *E.g.*, Theodore Spencer, Kenneth Muir, S. L. Bethell, G. Wilson Knight, etc.

[9] G. Ryle, " Knowing How and Knowing That ", in *Proceedings of the Aristotelian Society*, N.S., XLVI, 1945.

[10] Calderón, *Vida es Sueño* (the *Comedia*, not the *Auto*), I, vi.

[11] Ramón Silva in *Liverpool Hispanic Studies* (University of Liverpool, 1946), vol. I, p. 133.

[12] *Vide* S. L. Bethell, *The Cultural Revolution of the Seventeenth Century* (Dobson, 1951), *passim.*

[13] *Selected Essays*, p. 96.

[14] G. Santayana, *Tragic Philosophy.* (Works, Triton ed., Charles Scribner's Sons, 1936). II. *Poetry and Religion*, p. 132.

[15] Auden and Pearson, *Poets of the English Language* (Eyre & Spottiswoode, 1952), vol. II, p. xxiv.

[16] *The Bookman*, lxx, no. 6, February, 1930 (quoted by M. D. Zabel, *Literary Opinion in America*, p. 25).

[17] Reference may also be made to G. R. Elliott, *Humanism and Imagination* (University of N. Carolina, 1938), esp. p. 15; and D. G. James, *Scepticism and Poetry* (Allen & Unwin, 1947), esp. p. 117.

[18] M. Turnell, *Poetry and Crisis* (Sands, 1938), p. 43.

[19] *Scrutiny*, vol. XII, no. 2 (Spring, 1944), p. 158.

[20] H. Vaughan, Preface to *Silex Scintillans* (1654). Miss M. M. Mahood, however, has put up a spirited defence of the minor devotional poets of the seventeenth century in *Poetry and Humanism* (Cape, 1950).

[21] See my essay " The Literary Criticism of F. R. Leavis " in *Essays in Criticism*, vol. II, no. 4 (October, 1952), pp. 357, 366.

[22] H. Read, in a review of D. Saurat, *The End of Fear*, published in *The New English Weekly*, 22 December, 1938.

[23] Max Müller, *Hibbert Lectures*, 1878, p. 131.

[24] H. M. and N. K. Chadwick, *The Growth of Literature* (C.U.P., 1933-40), vol. II, p. 629.

[25] *Ibid.*, p. 460.

[26] T. S. Eliot, review of Wyndham Lewis' *Tarr*, in *The Egoist*, September, 1913 (quoted by E. Drews, *T. S. Eliot, The Design of his Poetry* (Eyre & Spottiswoode, 1950), p. 55).

CHAPTER 2

[1] Wladimir Weidlé, *The Baptism of Art* (Dacre Press, 1951).

[2] No doubt apologists for the contemporary poverty—shall we call it austerity? —of Russian art and literature will appeal to just such a necessary historical process in their case as well. We must await the verdict of time to decide whether the appeal is fair. Though we must note that the parallel with the art of the Catacombs is inexact; it is not the crudity but the commonplace ' bourgeoiserie ' of contemporary Marxist art that most strikes competent observers.

[3] *Vide* M. L. W. Laistner, *Christianity and Pagan Culture in the Later Roman Empire* (Cornell U.P. and O.U.P., 1951.)

[4] *Vide* article by R. E. Woolf, " The Devil in Old English Poetry ", in *Review of English Studies* (vol. IV, no. 13, January, 1953).

[5] U. Ellis-Fermor, *The Frontiers of Drama* (Allen & Unwin, 1945).

[6] This applies especially to Serbian and Danish ballads, but also to the society of the Scottish Borders and of Aberdeenshire. *Vide* M. J. C. Hodgart, *The Ballads* (Hutchinson, 1950), p. 132 f.

[7] L. C. Wimberly, *Minstrelsy, Music and the Dance, etc.* (University of Nebraska, *Studies in Language, Literature and Criticism*, no. 4, 1921), p. 46.

[8] L. C. Wimberly, *Death and Burial Lore in English and Scottish Ballads* (Nebraska *Studies*, no. 8, 1927), p. 9.

[9] Wimberly, *op. cit.*, p. 84.

[10] Cited by Wimberly from Greig, *Last Leaves of Traditional Ballads*, p. 16.

[11] 79C.; 39, D.17; G.32: in Wimberly, *op. cit.*, p. 85 n.

[12] Hodgart, p. 20, quoting F. Sidgwick, *Notes and Queries*, 29 July, 1905.

[13] Hodgart, *op. cit.*, p. 19.

[14] T. S. Eliot, *Selected Essays*, p. 133.

[15] Mon. Germ. *Epist.*, Carol. II, 124 (quoted by Chadwick, *The Growth of Literature*, I, p. 556).

[16] Rebecca West, *Black Lamb and Grey Falcon* (Macmillan, 1942) II, p. 97.

[17] Hodgart, *op. cit.*, p. 112.

[18] *Ibid.*, p. 153.

[19] *Ibid.*

[20] Introduction to his collection of ballads.

[21] Hodgart, p. 158.

[22] *Ibid.*

[23] Gerould, *The Ballad of Tradition* (O.U.P., 1932).

[24] Mr. Hodgart disputes whether the ballad-monger has had such a universally deteriorating influence, vide op. cit., p. 143.

[25] Gerould, op. cit., p. 264.

[26] F. B. Gummere, The Beginnings of Poetry (Macmillan, 1908); of course, Gummere was an extreme champion of ' communal origins'; we should need to qualify his description somewhat today.

[27] Child, Ballads, I, 180 (quoted, Wimberly, op. cit., p. 126 n.)

[28] But this ballad was probably by Sir Walter Scott!

[29] For Scott's work, see Hodgart, pp. 43-4, 110-12, 133-4, etc.

[30] D. H. Lawrence, Foreword to Fantasia of the Unconscious.

CHAPTER 3

(For the whole of this chapter my largest debt, obviously, is to Mr. R. Pring-Mill, of the Spanish Department, Oxford University, who has saved me from numerous blunders and spared no pains to comment and elucidate. He is not, of course, to be committed to my conclusions.)

[1] His court plays are no less secular than before. Mr. R. Pring-Mill supplies the following details: He wrote, or collaborated in, some seventy-seven plays between 1623 and his ordination in 1651, and some forty more (including libretti for ' zarzuelas ') between 1651 and 1680; and about twenty autos between 1632 (i.e. beginning nine years after he began to write plays) and his ordination, to about fifty-three afterwards. But the apparent stress on autos after his ordination is largely due to the balance of his work after 1669; four plays to thirty-one autos; whereas he only wrote about twenty-two autos to thirty-six plays in the years from 1651 to 1669.

[2] I take these extracts, and much of the information about Calderón's life, from the Introduction to the two-volume French translation, Œuvres Dramatiques de Calderón, by Antoine de Latour (Didier et Cie, 1871).

[3] The late Professor W. J. Entwistle has defended these theatrical devices, with reference to the convention in which Calderón was working, in an interesting article on the play in Bulletin Hispanique (T.L., nos. 3-4, 1948), Bordeaux.

[4] Mr. R. Pring-Mill, in a review-article in The Month (March, 1952), observes, with regard to the ' baroque marvels ', that " Calderón, a casuist, always takes an extreme case so that his ruling shall embrace all eventualities; it is this choice which produces that bewildering complexity of action, but the basic situation remains simple even in La Devoción de la Cruz ".

[5] Gerald Brenan, The Literature of the Spanish People (C.U.P., 1951), p. 284. The whole chapter on Calderón is excellent, however.

[6] Mr. Pring-Mill points out to me that the king's ratification of Crespo's de facto jurisdiction is required by the convention; and that all Calderón's 'casuistical' plays end with some formal approbation, the verdict, as it were, of some impartial jury. But though this would make the stroke more acceptable to his audience, who lived within such a convention, it still seems to me dramatically an anti-climax.

[7] " The Constant Prince ", trans. D. F. MacCarthy, in B. H. Clark, World Drama (Appleton Co., New York, 1933).

[8] Though I think Mr. Brenan is a little over-sanguine when he says of the second of these " It is a play so well known in England that I will spare the reader a description of its plot " (op. cit., p. 288).

[9] Ramón Silva, " The Religious Dramas of Calderón ", in Spanish Golden Age Poetry and Drama (Liverpool Institute of Hispanic Studies, 1946, Liverpool University Press), p. 168.

[10] FitzGerald translated six of the important plays, freely and with many omissions, in 1853.

[11] It seems to me that Shelley has here missed something of Calderón's skill. He translates

> CYPRIAN   So bitter is the life I live,
>   That hear me Hell! I now would give
>   To thy most detested spirit
>   My soul, for ever to inherit,
>   To suffer punishment and pine,
>   So this woman may be mine.
>   Hear'st thou Hell! Dost thou reject it?
>   My soul is offered!
> DEMON (*unseen*)   I accept it.

But this is to miss the unexpectedness, to Cipriano, of the Devil's response. Cipriano is clearly saying more than he means, and is taken aback when Hell accepts him at his word. Of course, he has to stand by it then.

[12] Mr. Pring-Mill has kindly supplied me with the following extract from the *loa* (preface) spoken by the Demon to the audience, which is in the MS. of the play but not in most editions : " This is where I come to use the licence which I have from God (for though I recognize neither obedience nor law to Him, I cannot attempt anything without His licence). . . . There are two who seek by their lives to astonish Hell and sadden all that obstinate host—the Court of pride and impatience: a Woman and a Man; she by her virtue, he by his knowledge. This lovely woman (human deity!) is secretly a Christian; this learned man (a rare individual) is noble in effect. She by penitence travels to become as saintly as she is fair; he makes a pilgrimage through knowledge, travelling until he attain the truth of a single God. Hence it behoves me (if this volcano do but vomit up sufficient fire) to change the present state of both—hers, so that she may lose what she has gained, and his, that he may not gain it by his subtle intellect. . . . It is to this end that I have come with this appearance, in this dress, and it shall not be in vain. Today shall Justina and Cipriano perish! . . ."

And, as Mr. Pring-Mill points out, it is actually by the Devil's introduction of Justina to Cipriano, which is meant to bring the latter's downfall, that he (the Devil) causes his own ruin, since by Justina's resistance to temptation Cipriano is brought back to a true subordination of passion to reason.

[13] I forbear to discuss the, otherwise interesting, relation between this passage (and others in Calderón) and the contemporary controversy between Jesuits (Calderón's teachers) and Molinists on free will and ir-Resistible grace.

[14] The title of the play is not, as Mr. Pring-Mill has pointed out (*loc. cit.*), intended to cast any doubt on the reality of sense-experience. Segismundo is awakened to a true sense of values by ' dreaming ' (i.e. by learning that earthly glory is illusory compared with heavenly); but the audience knows it is not a dream, and Segismundo ultimately learns this too.

[15] *Atrevido*, lit. ' audacious, brazen '; Mr. Pring-Mill points out that there is a constant play on the words ' atrevido ' and ' advertido ', the latter meaning ' aware, taking notice of warnings '.

[16] Here, for a sample, I give R. C. Trench's translation, which attempts to reproduce something like, not only the metre, but the vowel assonances of the Spanish—with, I fear, somewhat jingling results. See Richard Chevenix Trench, " *Life's a Dream and The Great Theatre of the World*, from the Spanish of Calderón, with an essay on his Life and Genius " (Parker, 1856). However, Mr. Pring-Mill points out that Trench's translation is misleading in some details. A more correct prose version would be: " Since life so quickly closes, let us, in case this may prove true, dream once more: but always mindful of, and counselled by, the fact that we must wake from this [brief] joy into the better time [of eternity]. For, this once

known, the undeception will not prove so sad or costly: for to take counsel against a foreseen evil is to cancel it. And, bearing in mind that, if all this is true, the power is all a loan which must be repaid to its owner, let us venture upon all."

¹⁷ They have one: the admirable book by A. A. Parker, *The Allegorical Drama of Calderón* (Dolphin Book Co., Oxford, 1943). There is also a useful, if rather pedestrian, study and analysis of a large number of these plays in Lucy Elizabeth Weir, *The Ideas Embodied in the Religious Drama of Calderón* (University of Nebraska, *Studies in Language, Literature and Criticism*, no. 18, 1940).

¹⁸ Mr. Pring-Mill tells me that six contiguous carts were involved, two carrying the stage, two for the wings, and two across the back; these four were of two storeys high—each storey being divisible into two ' rooms ', giving sixteen compartments (on two levels) off the actual stage, which could be opened or closed at will, or carry devices such as globes which open to disclose an actor, etc., or contain machinery to enable actors to ' fly ' on to, off, or to right and left, and such effects as the movement of a ship across the stage.

¹⁹ I take this account, and the translation, of the *auto* from Norman MacColl's *Select Plays of Calderón* (Macmillan, 1888), p. 127 ff.

²⁰ There is a translation of " The Feast of Belshazzar " in W. Knapp Jones' *Spanish One-Act Plays in English* (Tardy Publishing Co., Dallas, Texas, 1934).

²¹ Trans. R. C. Trench.

²² Calderón's view of Beauty is no doubt much subtler than the simple summary we have given in the text, and, backed as it is by Catholic dogma, avoids the one-sidedness of platonism, strongly platonic though it is. Mr. Pring-Mill comments: " I am sure that the true distinction in this passage is between the soul of the *player* cast as ' Hermosura ' (Beauty), and the ' cuerpo ' (body) of Hermosura which the soul has donned to play the part—Hermosura being solely ' cuerpo ' and ' mortal flor ', whereas the soul which existed before it donned beauty is eternal and can outlive its doffing."

²³ R. C. Trench, *op. cit.*, pp. 70-1.

²⁴ See Chapter I, note 11 *supra*.

²⁵ G. Brenan, *op. cit.*

²⁶ Ramón Silva is quite clear that this interpretation of Segismundo is an after-thought of Calderón's, when he came to write the *auto* many years later, *op. cit.*, p. 148.

²⁷ In *Four Plays by Lope de Vega*, trans. J. G. Underhill, with a critical essay on " Some Characteristics of the Spanish Theatre of the Golden Age ", by Jacinto Benavente (New York, (Charles Scribner's Sons), 1936), p. 292 f.

²⁸ This is the burden of two recent books: Karl Jaspers, *Tragedy is Not Enough* (tr. Reiche, Harry T. Moore and K. W. Deutsch), Gollancz, 1953; and H. Weisinger, *Tragedy and the Paradox of the Fortunate Fall* (Kegan Paul, 1953).

²⁹ Mr. Pring-Mill comments on this: " Calderón wasn't trying to write true ' tragedies ' or dramas but merely to produce dramatic illustrations of certainties. Within those illustrations, his whole bias is surely in favour of the Freedom of the Will, and the importance of the right use of that freedom, and the importance of the individual and of the problems which confront individual—not abstract—men; surely the ' genuine independence and validity of creaturehood ' must, in the last resort, be based upon a theocentric attitude? For the apparent ' independence and validity ' of Man in an anthropocentric universe leads, as Maritain and Berdyaev have shown so graphically, to an ultimate dependence upon nature, and so to the most pessimistic depths of materialistic determinism. . . ." While agreeing with the conclusion in general, I would maintain my point that, at least compared with some of the other writers studied in this book, Calderón's dramatic practice, whatever his theoretical correctness, leaves us with a sense of overwhelm-

ing heteronomy—and that is an atmosphere in which the *greatest* works of the creative imagination cannot be easily produced.

NOTE ON SOURCES For those who, like the present writer, have little or no Spanish, there is a very great paucity of translations of Calderón, and those that do exist are difficult to come by. Apart from the French translation mentioned in note 2, and Trench's renderings mentioned in note 16 above, there are: Edward FitzGerald's translations of certain plays (Everyman ed.); also *Works*, Vol. II (Houghton Mifflin, 1887); and, of course, Shelley's. D. F. MacCarthy's *Dramas of Calderón translated from the Spanish* (1835), and his *Mysteries of Corpus Christi* (Dublin, 1867), I have not seen. Norman MacColl's *Select Plays of Calderón* gives a useful account of some of the *Comedias*, but no translations except of incidental passages.

Trench mentions articles in English periodicals which showed a live interest in Calderón in the nineteenth century: fragmentary translations in *Blackwood's Magazine*; " Life's a Dream " in *The Monthly Magazine*, 1842 (nos. 549-51); *Fraser's Magazine*, August, 1849; *Justina*, by ' J. H.', 1848. Also articles on Calderón in *The Atheneum*, 19 and 26 November, 1853; *The Quarterly Review*, April, 1821; *Blackwood's*, December, 1839; *Westminster and Foreign Quarterly*, January, 1851.

For comparison of translations with the original, and for Act- and Scene-divisions I have referred to the standard four-volume edition of the *Comedias*, ed. D. Juan Hartzenbusch.

Mr. Pring-Mill suggests the following additions, some of which I have not been able to consult: W. J. Entwistle, " Justina's Temptation: an Approach to the Understanding of Calderón " (*Mod. Lang. Rev.*, 1945).

W. J. Entwistle, " Calderón's *La Devoción de la Cruz* " (in *Bulletin Hispanique*, 1948). *Id.*, " Calderón et le théâtre symbolique " (*ibid.*, 1950).

E. M. Wilson, " The Four Elements in the Imagery of Calderón " (*M.L.R.*, 1936), and, in conjunction with Entwistle, " Calderón's *Principe Constante*: two appreciations " (*M.L.R.*, 1939).

A. E. Sloman, *The Sources of Calderón's ' El Principe Constante '* (Blackwell's ' Modern Lang. Stud. ', 1950) and " The Structure of Calderón's *La Vida es Sueño* " (*M.L.R.*, July, 1953).

E. R. Curtius, Excursus XXII and XXIII in *European Literature and the Latin Middle Ages* (Routledge & Kegan Paul, 1953).

CHAPTER 4

[1] *The Betrothed*, by Alessandro Manzoni, newly translated by Archibald Colquhoun (Dent, 1951).

[2] C. M. Yonge, *Musings Over the Christian Year*: Gleanings, p. ix.

[3] G. Battiscombe, *Charlotte M. Yonge*, p. 61.

[4] Morley, *Gladstone*, I, 173.

[5] *Ibid.*, III, 549.

[6] Ward, *Newman*, I, 142.

[7] Omond, *The Romantic Triumph*, p. 359.

[8] Goethe, *Conversations with Eckermann* (Bohme ed.), pp. 270-3.

[9] Cross, *Life of George Eliot*, III, 77.

[10] D. H. Lawrence, Preface to translation of Verga, *Maestro Don-Gesualao*.

[11] Trevelyan, *Macaulay*, p. 636.

[12] I have summarized his life from G. T. Bettany's Biographical Introduction to an edition of the novel in 1889, using a translation which appeared in 1844. A more extended, and more racy, biographical sketch is given by Mr. Colquhoun in the edition mentioned in note 1 *supra*. A brief account of Manzoni, as man and

writer. may be found in Giovanni Papini, *Labourers in the Vineyard* (Sheed & Ward, 1930). Mr. Bernard Wall's admirable *Manzoni* (in ' Studies in Modern European Literature and Thought '—Bowes & Bowes) appeared too late for me to make use of it.

¹³ In these extracts I have used an anonymous translation which was issued by George Bell & Sons, *Standard Works*, 1876. This has long been out of print. Mr. Colquhoun, in his usually admirable translation mentioned above, occasionally overdoes the ' slanginess ' of his expression, perhaps, in his desire to reproduce something corresponding to the original dialect. There is a most valuable article on Manzoni's prose style by Mr. D. A. Traversi in *Scrutiny* (Cambridge), September, 1940, to which I am much indebted in numerous ways.

¹⁴ D. H. Lawrence, *Letters* (Ed. Huxley), p. 773 (to Lady Ottoline Morell, 1928).

CHAPTER 5

¹ N. Zernov, in *Three Russian Prophets* (S.C.M. Press, 1944).

² Paul Evdokimov, *Dostoevski et le problème du mal* (Editions du livre français, Lyons, 1952).

³ L. Zander, *Dostoevsky* (S.C.M. Press, 1947).

⁴ J. Middleton Murry, *Dostoevsky* (Secker, 1927).

⁵ N. Berdyaev, *Dostoevsky* (Sheed & Ward, 1934, Eng. tr.).

⁶ R. Curle, *Characters of Dostoevsky* (Heinemann, 1947).

⁷ Freud, *Dostoevsky and Parricide*, in *Stavrogin's Confession* (Lear Publications, N.Y., 1947). It is only fair to add that Freud, in this essay, says that " Before the problem of the creative artist, analysis must lay down its arms." *Cf.* also A. Adler, *Individual Psychology*, p. 290.

⁸ V. Ivanov, *Freedom and the Tragic Life* (Harvill Press, 1952), p. 119.

⁹ *Ibid.*, pp. 115-16.

¹⁰ Curle, *op. cit.*, p. 166.

¹¹ *Ibid.*, p. 176.

¹² *Ibid.*, p. 177.

¹³ *The Gambler*, p. 18.

¹⁴ *The Eternal Husband*, p. 76 f.

¹⁵ *Crime and Punishment*, p. 269 f.

¹⁶ *The Possessed*, p. 362 f.

¹⁷ *Crime and Punishment*, p. 342 f.

¹⁸ *Nyetochka Nyezvanov*, pp. 281-6.

¹⁹ *Ibid*, p. 289 f.

²⁰ *The Possessed*, pp. 184-6.

²¹ *The Idiot*, p. 65 f.

²² *Crime and Punishment*, p. 291.

²³ *The Idiot*, p. 318.

²⁴ *The Possessed*, p. 442.

²⁵ *Crime and Punishment*, p. 168 f.

²⁶ *The Criterion*, vol. xvi, no. LXV (July, 1937). I am indebted to Mr. Raymond Preston (Brother Michael Preston Nov. C.R.) for referring me to this article.

²⁷ *Cf.* Dostoevsky's letter to his niece on the subject of *The Idiot*: " The chief idea of the novel is to portray the positively good man. There is nothing in the world more difficult to do, and especially now. All writers, and not only ours, but even all Europeans who have tried to portray the *positively* good man have always failed. Because this is an enormous problem. The good is an ideal, but this ideal, both ours and that of civilized Europe, is still far from having been worked out. There is only one positively good man in the world—Christ. . . . I recall that of the good figures in Christian literature the most perfect is Don Quixote. But he is

good only because at the same time he is ridiculous. Dickens' Pickwick (an infinitely weaker conception than Don Quixote, but nevertheless immense) is also ridiculous and succeeds by virtue of this fact. One feels compassion for the ridiculous man who does not know his own worth as a good man, and consequently sympathy is evoked in the reader. This awakening of compassion is the secret of humour. Jean Valjean is also a powerful attempt, but he arouses sympathy by his horrible misfortune and society's injustice to him. In my novel there is nothing of this sort, positively nothing, and hence I am terribly afraid that I shall be entirely unsuccessful." (Quoted by E. J. Simmons, *Dostoevsky, the Making of a Novelist* (Lehmann, 1950), p. 166 f.

[28] E.g. E. H. Carr, *Dostoevsky, A New Biography* (1931); E. J. Simmons, *op. cit.*, etc.

[29] *Cf.* notes 8 and 9 above.

[30] *A Raw Youth*, p. 1 f.

[31] *Ibid.*, p. 550.

[32] *The Eternal Husband*, p. 135.

[33] *Ibid.*, p. 137.

[34] *Criterion*, *loc. cit.*, p. 595.

[35] *Crime and Punishment*, p. 287 f.

[36] Quoted by N. Berdyaev, *op. cit.*, p. 40.

[37] *Diary of a Writer*, February, 1876 (English ed., trans. B. Brasol, Charles Scribner's Sons and Cassell, 1951). I, 207.

[38] The view here taken of Dostoevsky's attitude to nature is confirmed also by an interesting, if enigmatic, passage which has never, to my knowledge, appeared in English before. It is taken from an appendix to his *Diary of a Writer* (1873), [' Little pictures—Travelling ', in Russian edition, *Ladyshnikoff*, published in Berlin, 1922, p. 578]. It runs thus: " The steamer comes up at length to the pier, and everyone rushes to the exit, as out of the close air of a prison. What a hot day, what a clear, beautiful sky! But we do not look at the sky, there is no time. We hurry, hurry; the sky will not go away. The sky is a domestic affair; but to live one's life through—that is not just a matter of crossing a field." (I am indebted to the Russian priest, Father Antony Bloom, for this passage, and to Father M. Tweedy, C.R., for translating it.)

[39] *The House of the Dead*, p. 216.

[40] *The Eternal Husband*, p. 75.

[41] *Letters from the Underworld* (trans. C. J. Hogarth, Everyman ed.), p. 13.

[42] *The Idiot*, p. 381 ff.

[43] *The Possessed*, p. 158 f.

[44] *The Idiot*, p. 65 f.

[45] *The Possessed*, p. 215.

[46] *Crime and Punishment*, p. 230.

[47] *Ibid.*, p. 479 f.

[48] *The Idiot*, p. 404.

[49] *Ibid.*, p. 414 f.

[50] *Ibid.*, p. 596.

[51] *Cf.* the similar rôle played by flies in General Epanchin's ' confession ' earlier in the same novel. He tells how as a young officer he had abused an old woman— only to find later that she was dying as he cursed her. " I poured out a stream of abuse. . . . Only there seemed something strange as I looked at her: she sat, her eyes round and staring. . . . I stood hesitating: flies were buzzing, the sun was setting, there was stillness. Completely disconcerted, I walked away " (p. 145).

[52] This Russian custom is well brought out in L. A. Zander, *op. cit.*

[53] *Crime and Punishment*, p. 285.

[54] *The Brothers Karamazov*, p. 73.
[55] *Ibid.*, p. 300.
[56] *Crime and Punishment*, p. 463.
[57] *The Brothers Karamazov*, p. 343.
[58] *Ibid.*, p. 345.
[59] *The Possessed*, p. 129 f.
[60] *The Brothers Karamazov*, p. 305.
[61] *A Raw Youth*, p. 354 f.
[62] Works, tome 6, pp. 170, 161, *On Thanksgiving*. (Cited, N. Gorodetsky, *St. Tikhon Zadonsky*, S.P.C.K., 1951, pp. 162 ff.)
[63] Mr. C. M. Wodehouse, in his excellent little book on our author, has also noted—as who could fail to do?—this fascination for 'insect' imagery; he suggests that it can be accounted for by "preoccupation with the power-instinct", since the bugs, etc., are so often introduced only in order "metaphorically to be crushed" (*Dostoevsky* (Andrew Barker, 1951), p. 95.) This is only a part of the explanation.
[64] *The Brothers Karamazov*, p. 317.
[65] *Ibid.*, p. 256 f.
[66] *The Idiot*, p. 213 f.
[67] *Diary of a Writer*, English translation, *loc. cit.*, II, 672 ff. There is also a version of this story in *Three Tales* (Russian Literature Library, no. 3, Lindsay Drummond, 1945), trans. by Beatrice Scott; the translation is excellent, except that in this last quotation the final words are rendered: "I have sought out that little girl . . . and I will go on!" Dr. Zernov informs me that Brasol's rendering is the more exact. See also in the Constance Garnett ed. the vol. *An Honest Thief and Other Stories*; and in *A Gentle Creature and Other Stories* (John Lehmann, 1950), trans. D. Magarshack.

CHAPTER 6

[1] Translated by Allan Ross Macdougall and Alex Comfort (Routledge, 1946): revised translation; an earlier translation, entitled "The End of All Men", was published in America, 1945.
[2] *Journal 1896-1942* (Grasset, 1945), p. 14.
[3] *Ibid.*, p. 147.
[4] *Ibid.*, p. 186 f.
[5] *Ibid.*, p. 15.
[6] *Ibid.*, p. 269.
[7] *Ibid.*, p. 107.
[8] *Ibid.*, p. 133.
[9] *Salutation Paysanne*, p. 59.
[10] *Journal*, p. 373.
[11] I quote from the English translation by Mervyn Savill (Hutchinson, 1951), p. 253 f.
[12] *Garçon Savoyard*, p. 202.
[13] *Ibid.*, p. 213 f.
[14] *La Guerre dans le Haut-Pays*, p. 345 f.
[15] There is a translation of this in English, entitled "When the Mountain Fell", (Eyre & Spottiswoode, 1950), which I have not seen.
[16] These quotations are taken from *Salutation Paysanne* (first published 1921; 2nd ed. 1929), especially the section "Le Chemineau Couché".
[17] *La Beauté sur la Terre*, p. 97.
[18] *Joie dans le Ciel*, p. 134.
[19] *Le Règne de l'Esprit Malin*, p. 73.
[20] *Journal*, p. 314 f.

[21] *Salutation Paysanne*, p. 107.

[22] *Le Règne*, p. 212 f.

[23] I have used throughout the excellent translation entitled " The Triumph of Death ", mentioned in note 1 *supra*.

[24] *Joie*, pp. 47, 53.

[25] *Ibid.*, p. 97.

[26] *Ibid.*, p. 113 f.

[27] *Ibid.*, p. 118.

[28] *Ibid.*, p. 123.

[29] *Ibid.*, p. 173 f.

[30] *Ibid.*, p. 177 f.

[31] *La Guérison des Maladies*, p. 8 f.

[32] *Ibid.*, p. 69.

[33] *Ibid.*, p. 197 f.

[34] *Ibid.*, p. 207 f.

[35] *Ibid.*, p. 122.

[36] *Questions* (Grasset, 1936), pp. 71, 73 f.

[37] *La Guérison*, p. 126. (" They wanted to come and see, because man's nature is mistrustful, because he needs to touch and prove—and long ago it was just such a one who would not believe until he had put his finger into the holes in the Hands and the Feet.")

CHAPTER 7

[1] Stuart Hampshire, in symposium " Are all philosophical questions questions of language? " in Aristotelian Society Suppl., vol. xxii, pp. 45-6 (1948).

[2] Charles Neider, *Kafka: His Mind and his Art* (Routledge & Kegan Paul, 1949).

[3] *Ibid.*, p. 124.

[4] *Ibid.*, p. 126.

[5] E.g. Lionel Trilling, *The Liberal Imagination, passim*. An admirable essay on Kafka by the philosopher, Dr. F. Waismann, using medical and psychological insights with real sanity and balance, may be found in *Essays in Criticism*, vol. III, no. 2 (April, 1953).

[6] Erik Erikson, *Childhood and Society* (Imago, New York, 1950), pp. 49-54.

[7] Elias Canetti, *Auto-da-Fé* (trans. V. Wedgwood, Cape, 1946), p. 404 f.

[8] *La Joie*, trans. ' *Joy* ', by Louise Varese (John Lane, 1947), p. 84.

[9] *Ibid.*, p. 123.

[10] *Ibid.*, p. 125.

[11] Claudel, *L'Échange* (*Théâtre*, III, p. 196).

[12] *The Heart of the Matter*, p. 30.

[13] *Ibid.*, p. 15.

[14] *Ibid.*, p. 53.

[15] Article on " François Mauriac: A Woman of the Pharisees ", in *New Writing*, no. 31, 1947.

[16] There have also been published two useful studies of Graham Greene: by F. N. Lees in *Scrutiny*, vol. XIX, no. 1 (October, 1952); and an admirably careful and critical one by Mr. D. A. Traversi in *The Twentieth Century*, March and April, 1950. My own criticism of Mr. Greene, as set out in this chapter, is condensed from two articles written for *The Student Movement* in March, 1946, and March, 1949.

[17] *François Mauriac* in ' Studies in Modern European Literature and Thought ', ed. E. Heller (Bowes & Bowes, 1954).

[18] *Bacchus*, played 20 December, 1951, in the Marigny Theatre.

[19] *Figaro Littéraire*, 23 December, 1951.

[20] *France Soir* (Paris ed.), 30 December, 1951. (I take the whole correspondence as quoted in *Réforme*, 12 January, 1952.)

[21] Hervé Bazin, *Lève-toi et Marche* (Grasset, 1952), p. 220.

[22] *Ibid.*, p. 246.

[23] *Ibid.*, pp. 264-9.

[24] Quoted, E. M. Simpson, *Prose Works of Donne*, p. 58.

[25] See an article, "My Friend James Joyce", by Eugene Jolas, in *Partisan Review*, Mar.-Apr., 1941.

[26] Gustav Janouch, *Conversations with Kafka* (Lehmann, 1953; I take the quotation from excerpts published in *Partisan Review*, Mar.-Apr., 1953, p. 178).

[27] Simone Weil, *Attente de Dieu* (Gallimard, 1951): English translation, *Waiting on God* (Kegan Paul, 1952).

[28] Joseph Campbell, *The Hero with a Thousand Faces* (Pantheon Books, New York, Bollingen Series, no. xvii, 1949); M. Bodkin, *Archetypal Patterns in Poetry* (O.U.P., 1934), and *Studies of Type-Images* (etc.) (O.U.P., 1951).

[29] Bodkin, *Archetypal Patterns in Poetry*, p. 151.

[30] *Ibid.*, p. 136.

[31] *Ibid.*, p. 322 f.

[32] Campbell, *op. cit.*, p. 230.

[33] Bodkin, *op. cit.*, pp. 152, 83, 89.

[34] Campbell, *op. cit.*, p. 391.

[35] The words are those of the hero, a novelist, Traian Koruga, in C. Virgil Gheorghiu, *La Vingt-cinquième Heure* (trans. from the Rumanian), (Plon, 1949), p. 117 f.

[36] Thomas Mann, in a speech at the Library of Congress, quoted in *The Stature of Thomas Mann* (Ed. C. Neider, New Directions & Peter Owen, London, 1951), p. 229 f.

[37] F. R. Leavis, "Education and the University", *Scrutiny*, Spring, 1943 (also published in his book of the same name).

[38] 'Thinkers' Forum' (Rationalist Press Association), no. 32, 1944, and no. 35, 1945.

[39] S. L. Bethell, article, "George Eliot", in *The Criterion*, October, 1938, where he contrasts the early, but warm and rich, *Adam Bede*, or the central and magnificent *Middlemarch*, with the later *Daniel Deronda*, weakened by its too explicit philosophy of evolutionary radicalism.

[40] D. W. Harding, article in *Scrutiny*, December, 1939.

[41] T. S. Eliot, Introduction to Pascal's *Pensées* (Everyman ed.).

[42] P. E. More, *The Demon of the Absolute* (New Shelborne Essays, O.U.P., vol. I, 1928), p. x f.

[43] E. Muir, "The Decline of the Novel", in *Essays on Literature and Society* (Hogarth Press, 1949), p. 148 ff.

[44] Quoted in Max Brod, *Biography of Franz Kafka*, p. 61.

[45] J. Supervielle, *L'Enfant de la Haute Mer* (Gallimard, 1931); there is an English translation of this story, but not of the *Suites d'une Course*, in D. Saurat's collection, *Angels and Beasts*.

[46] From D. Saurat's introduction to the above collection.

[47] This saying of Mr. David Jones is quoted by H. S. Ede in an article in *Horizon*, August, 1943.

[48] Paul Claudel, Preface to *Morceaux choisis* (Gallimard, 1921), quoted by Jacques Madaule, *Le Drame de P. Claudel* (Gallimard, 1936), p. 343 f.

(Behind me the plain, as once in China when in summer I travelled up to Kouliang,

The country flattened by the distance, and this map on which you can see nothing so long as you walk in it;

So many miles and years that you can cover now with your hand!

The sun with a sudden flash here and there lights up once more into life
Some river whose name you no longer remember, some town like an old wound
    that still gives pain.
Down there the smoke of a steamer that's sailing out, and the special clarity
    cast by the sea—
Exile fully accepted from which there is no way out by the back but only in
    front.
The evening is falling: look at this new site, explorer!
This silence, amazing to others, is so familiar in your heart.
The mountains one above the other line up in a colossal attention.
We need plenty of room for life to begin. . . .)

INDEX